TSUNAMI:
Our Shock, Pain,
and Resilience

The coast of the City of Rikuzentakata, is being swept away by a massive tsunami (photo provided by Futoshi Toba).

Rikuzentakata City Hall completely destroyed (photo provided by Futoshi Toba).

Authors spending a relaxing Halloween in October 2015.
(photo by Amya Miller).

Amya Miller reads a picture book to children in a preschool in the affected area in May 2016 (photo by Amya Miller).

TSUNAMI: Our Shock, Pain, and Resilience

Amya Miller and Futoshi Toba

TSUNAMI: Our Shock, Pain, and Resilience
Copyright © 2024 Amya Miller
Published by
Trans Pacific Press Co., Ltd.
PO Box 8547, #19682, Boston, MA, 02114, United States
Web: http://www.transpacificpress.com

Distributors
(USA, Canada and India)
Independent Publishers Group (IPG)
814 N. Franklin Street, Chicago, IL 60610, USA
Web: http://www.ipgbook.com

(Europe, Oceania, Middle East and Africa)
EUROSPAN
1 Bedford Row, London, WC1R 4BU, United Kingdom
Web: https://www.eurospangroup.com

(Japan)
MHM Limited
3-2-3F, Kanda-Ogawamachi, Chiyoda-ku, Tokyo 101-0052
Web: http://www.mhmlimited.co.jp

(China)
China Publishers Services Ltd.
718, 7/F., Fortune Commercial Building, 362 Sha Tsui Road, Tsuen Wan,
N.T. Hong Kong
Email: edwin@cps-hk.com

(Southeast Asia)
Alkem Company Pte Ltd.
1, Sunview Road #01-27, Eco-Tech@Sunview, Singapore 627615
Email: enquiry@alkem.com.sg

Library of Congress Control Number: 2023922669

ISBN 978-1-920850-26-5 (paperback)
ISBN 978-1-920850-27-2 (eBook)

Contents

About the Authors

Amya Miller was a U.S.-Japan business consultant and interpreter with over 35 years experience specializing in U.S.-Japan relations. Born and raised in Japan, she attended both Japanese public schools as well as international boarding schools. She flew to Rikuzentakata and Ōfunato in Iwate Prefecture after the triple disaster of 2011 and returned to the U.S. in 2020.

Miller co-authored a bilingual children's book, *The Extraordinary Voyage of Kamome: A Tsunami Boat Comes Home* (Humboldt State University Press, 2021).

She currently lives in Seattle, Washington with her husband. Miller and her husband are parents to one child.

Futoshi Toba was born in Kanagawa Prefecture in 1965 and spent his youth in the City of Machida, a suburb of Tokyo. A graduate of Machida High School, he studied in the U.S. for several years in his youth, moving to his father's hometown of Rikuzentakata in his twenties. From April 1995 – March 2007 he was a city council member in Rikuzentakata. In March 2007 he became deputy mayor, running for and winning the seat of mayor in

February 2011. Toba served three terms as mayor. He has written two books in Japanese about the Great East Japan Disaster of March 2011.

Toba has two adult sons and lives in Rikuzentakata with his wife.

Map of Japan

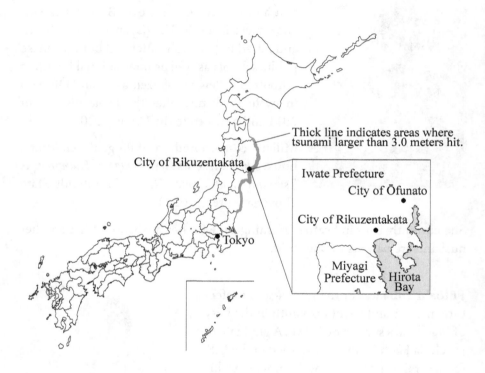

Thick line indicates areas where tsunami larger than 3.0 meters hit.

City of Rikuzentakata

Tokyo

Iwate Prefecture

City of Ōfunato

City of Rikuzentakata

Miyagi Prefecture

Hirota Bay

Prologue

Amya Miller

As children, many of us played this same game. Visits to the ocean inevitably included us daring the waves—running in and out in time with the surf, trying to stay just out of the water's reach.

On April 1st, 2021, a newspaper in the rural Tōhoku region of Japan called *Tōkai Shimpō* published a photo of a boy playing chicken with a wave on the beach of Hirota Bay. His stance is firm and his feet are planted wide. A sheen of water, capped with foam flows toward him along the sand. Perhaps he plans to move before the water can soak through his shoes. Perhaps he doesn't think the water will rise high enough to reach him at all.

I can remember my own attempts to outsmart the ocean. My brother and I would run up to a gentle wave, getting as close as we dared before squealing in delight and running away as it crashed behind us. Sometimes we were quick enough, escaping to shore to watch the white foam linger and the bubbles pop on the wet sand. Other times the wave overtook us with a last-second burst of energy, covering our toes in salt water and sucking the sand from beneath our feet.

Growing up in Japan, I was familiar with the power of the ocean even as a young child. In school the teachers ran us through earthquake drills and made it clear that if we felt the ground shake, there was a chance that a wave might come ashore not long after. As a nation built on a series of islands, especially along active fault lines, there came a certain level of awareness of the sea's power to tear us down. And alongside it, the defiance to plant our feet and dare the water to touch us.

Hirota Bay is a crescent-shaped inlet along the coast of Rikuzentakata. Just over ten years prior to the photo of that boy playing on the beach, the water rose much higher. That body of water was the source of one of the most devastating tsunamis in history.

Just offshore from the northeastern Tōhoku region of Japan, a Magnitude 9.0 earthquake caused a massive tsunami. Numerous giant waves struck one of Japan's most vulnerable areas, destroying coastlines, cities, towns, and villages along the way. The scale of the earthquake and the tsunami it caused are hard to imagine. We have data that describe the event, but these numbers will never allow us to comprehend what was lost when these villages, time capsules of rural Japanese life, were destroyed.

We can start with what we do know. On March 11, 2011 at 2:46 PM an earthquake occurred off the coast of Miyagi Prefecture, just southeast of the city of Rikuzentakata, the southernmost city in Iwate Prefecture.

The fault along the eastern coast of Japan is made up of two tectonic plates with a total length of nearly 400 kilometers.[1] Most of our information is guesswork, but seismologists have determined that one of these plates slipped against the other, rising up sharply and displacing the water around it, creating a tsunami.

There's a famous painting, *The Great Wave off Kanagawa*, painted by Katsushika Hokusai in the early 19th century. It depicts the ocean rising into a graceful wave topped with white foam. It's beautiful and striking, and it's considered an iconic piece of Japanese art. Is the wave meant to be a tsunami? The question matters as, it's not at all how a tsunami appears in reality. But it's not at all how a tsunami appears in reality. Real tsunamis are massive onslaughts of water. They contain fish and boats and sand and boulders churned up from the seabed. Real tsunamis shear off buildings at their foundations, toss cars around like toys, snap telephone poles with a whipping crack, and collect all of them into a mass of debris that pounds the coastline and destroys everything in its path.

This massive wall of water hit from northeastern Japan all the way down to Chiba Prefecture, just north of the Tokyo Metropolitan area. Typically, Japanese coastal communities and fishing ports construct seawalls to protect them from these kinds of waves. But after this one tsunami struck, no known seawall was left standing. The seawalls along the city of Rikuzentakata in Iwate Prefecture were no exception.

Rikuzentakata comprises eight smaller towns, five of which surround Hirota Bay on the Pacific Ocean. Historically, Rikuzentakata was a rich city with gold mines that have long since closed, and now the region relies on fishing and farming. The city also boasted a small tourism industry centered around the Takata Matsubara, a 70,000-pine tree forest grove planted intentionally by the city's ancestors as a tsunami barrier along a white sand beach on Hirota Bay.

For a city with a pre-disaster population of around 24,000 people, Rikuzen-takata takes up a lot of land for relatively few people. It takes over an hour to go from one end to the other. Downtown is located centrally in the village known as Takata. Before the disaster, the area was complete with many buildings recognizable to any city center—a city hall, the fire department headquarters, the main hospital, a civic center, a large gymnasium, a public library, and multiple schools, shops, homes, and museums. Every one of these buildings was damaged and many were destroyed when the tsunami struck at around 3:30 pm. Within four minutes, all of Takata was completely swallowed under 15 meters of water.

The oceans are our source of food and energy. They embody immense beauty and are the base of passage for boats and ships. But every so often, an event like the tsunami of March 11, 2011 reminds us that the oceans have a capacity to be cruel and destructive. They can be violent and uncaring, and rise up with impossible force to sweep away everything we love.

As the world mourned, Japan was left shell-shocked by the magnitude and scope of the destruction. Twenty years after leaving the land of my birth, the news of this disaster left me outraged, heartbroken, livid. I was enraged at the cruelty of nature; I wanted to cry and scream and call the ocean a murderer and a coward. I knew I shared that grief with hundreds of thousands of people all across the north-eastern coast of Japan—and I knew the devastation and grief those communities must be feeling was surely incalculable compared to mine. I had to do something, even though I had no idea what.

Originally, it wasn't my goal to approach these communities with a specific offer. This whole situation was unclear, even to me. Surely I could do something. Some sort of liaison role? Fundraising? I could help connect recipients with donors, perhaps. Or, I could share stories; help them express through words what they had gone through, and what they were still going through. Experience with Japanese social norms—values of quiet stoicism and the suppression of emotion—told me that the survivors of this disaster were unlikely to be loudly spreading their stories. In the weeks following the disaster, the media shared a very specific portrayal of these Japanese survivors. They reported polite and quiet survivors queueing to make telephone calls, and highlighted that there had been little to no looting in the aftermath. But what the international media called resilience, the Japanese knew as a widespread social norm, the expectation to bury trauma.

I couldn't have known the role that long-term reconstruction would play in exacerbating these people's pained silence. Particularly, the hurdles these communities faced were staggering. Governmental obstinance, recovery efforts stymied by red tape, fatigue and favoritism from the donors funding the reconstruction, and the media slowly dropping their story and letting the world quietly forget these disaster victims existed. For everything that went well, just as many things went wrong, but few outside of the affected communities know of this reality.

Despite growing up in Japan and making a career out of communication in Japanese, it still took me years in Tōhoku to fully understand the true sources of their silence. In the communities I worked with, I encouraged many people to share their experiences. There were many who just wanted to feel heard, no matter how small their audience. There were others who wanted to make sure the world hadn't forgotten about them. But the roots of *gaman*—the Japanese ethic of repressing your pain lest it infect others—ran deep. I met few people in Tōhoku who were willing to shout their stories from the rooftops, to speak up and make a fuss and get in the face of the whole world in order to agitate for progress and secure the assistance that these people desperately needed.

In the ten years I spent there, I only ever met one man who never stopped fighting that fight. Futoshi Toba, Mayor of the City of Rikuzentakata, spoke up loudly and repeatedly to denounce the slow pace at which recovery and reconstruction was progressing. Though he drew much attention and sympathy, especially at an international level, Mayor Toba's outspokenness flew in the face of Japanese social norms. I understood why he refused to remain silent—he had witnessed an unthinkable disaster and his people were anguished and demoralized, yet they were not receiving the assistance they needed. Where *gaman*, patience and quiet stoicism was required of him, he pushed back and cried foul. A reluctant politician, he had only taken office with the intention to advocate for people whose voices were often overlooked within the rigidly hierarchical structure of Japanese society. By speaking up and criticizing a system that inherently did not prioritize the Tōhoku region, Mayor Toba was also challenging a core tenet of Japanese culture.

There is so much to say about the long journey to recovery that this community faced. But there is only one place to start, and it is undeniably with his words.

Part 1
Our Shock

Chapter 1

Futoshi Toba

Twenty-six days. That's how long I had been mayor before the tsunami hit.

In those twenty-six days, I'd seen very little of my two sons and my wife, Kumi, as I attended an endless series of meetings. With April 1st right around the corner—a new fiscal year—last-minute details needed addressing and resolving. Retirement parties, personnel changes, budget meetings, the quarterly city council session, and general end-of-the-year issues all converged. My desk overflowed and my calendar was booked. At night I called my supporters and election volunteers, and would end up going out drinking with others, partly social and partly business. I was tired but invigorated.

At 2:40 pm on March 11, 2011, I called Kumi and suggested we go out for dinner that night. I wanted to make it up to her and the boys, to take them all out somewhere nice. I thought Korean barbecue would go over well, and she agreed. She said she would look around for the right place and let me know when she had a reservation. We hung up.

Kumi had been happy with me as Deputy Mayor but wasn't thrilled with my running for Mayor. The job of Deputy Mayor already kept me away from home more than she would have liked. The new title naturally meant more responsibility, more business trips within the region and beyond, and even more nights out. As the mayor's wife, people would watch her more now in the supermarkets, downtown, at restaurants, everywhere she went. She would always have to be on her best behavior; her actions reflected on me, and vice versa. This additional pressure that came with being the mayor's wife was a lifestyle she neither invited nor enjoyed. I promised I wouldn't let the new job change anything. Her bobbed hair framed her round face as she smiled, her eyes crinkling; she accepted my promise.

Our boys, aged twelve and ten, were used to being home with Kumi while I was out at night meeting constituents and political peers. To them, this was what dad did. My new title meant they might see me a little less than before, but I didn't think they would mind. With the recent focus on my work and then the election, I'd been so busy that the boys had grown even more attached to Kumi. She would stand outside in the driveway with them for hours watching them play basketball, laughing, chiding. They adored her and she loved them back. Basketball was followed by dinner with mama. The boys were fine with that; having three at the dinner table instead of four didn't seem to bother them.

Dinner tonight was meant to be special. Family night out, just the four of us. I had missed them during the past month and felt guilty I had not seen more of them.

I could still hear Kumi's voice after I hung up and returned to my duties. Aides swarmed me with documents and scheduling questions, and for a moment my routine returned to normal.

Six minutes later the shaking began. The force of the earthquake was immense, violently toppling bookshelves and sending the television crashing to the floor of my office, shattering the screen. Books and keepsakes thudded all around me, my metal desk screeched, and tables scraped the floor as they slid from side to side. A cacophony of deadly sounds assaulted me from all directions. I felt my stomach churn.

Everyone in Japan practices routine earthquake drills. Children grow up with regular rehearsals, and every business or organization I'd been part of had an earthquake evacuation plan. Our city, Rikuzentakata, had been through a fairly large earthquake just two days prior that had made me uncomfortable. But this earthquake today was different. I knew no one in the building had felt an earthquake this powerful before.

There was commotion and shouts of confusion and fear outside my door, as City Hall employees rushed to grab doorways or hug walls to keep themselves from falling. Why wasn't the shaking over yet? I had to act now. Barely able to stay on my feet, I started to make my way toward the door, picking my way through the landslide of books and fallen furniture. The floor pitched and rolled under my feet, and I struggled to stay upright. I had almost reached the door to my office when in came my chief of staff, Kenta. He shouted, "Let's go! Get out!"

A tall, good-natured man known in town as a star baseball player back in his youth, Kenta occupied the coveted position as my secretary and right-hand man. He sat right outside my door with several of his assistants in a pod. We emerged into a scene of utter chaos. Shelves had fallen and the floor was strewn with the fallen contents of desks—files and pens and cups and photos from the walls, broken glass. Desks screeched as they slid back and forth, and aides grabbed anything they could reach for support, their faces blanched with fear. This earthquake was unlike anything any of us had experienced.

Get out of the building. Get to safety. That much I knew. But how? It had taken me longer than I'd have liked just to get out of my office. People were screaming. I called out to my panicked staff, rallying everyone who could hear me. "We're evacuating! Everyone get downstairs to the parking lot, now!"

I yelled for my staff to get out as Kenta led the way toward the stairs. Nearby a few people shrieked as a young man jumped out of a nearby room, followed by a crumble and roar and crash, the sound of shredding masonry. "The floor collapsed in there!" he screamed. "Go the other way!"

The building hadn't stopped shaking yet. My staff supported each other and tried to grab the walls as they headed toward the stairs. Every room we passed was in shambles, their contents picked up and hurled by the unnaturally long and intense tremors. Some of the walls seemed to be warped or uneven, though we did not stop to check. We filed down the stairs quickly. Lights flickered as we clutched the handrail, the building pitching around us.

None of it felt real. We'd all lived our lives hearing about "the Big One,"[2] how one day Japan would experience an earthquake larger than anything that had hit us before. Was this it? What could be bigger than this? It all felt like a dream. Just minutes ago I had been on the phone to Kumi. We were supposed to go out to dinner tonight. I checked my cell phone for a signal. Nothing. Then the shaking stopped.

We burst out the doors into the parking lot where a large crowd had gathered. Others throughout the building had evacuated on their own. My staff rushed away to join them, and many stumbled or gripped nearby cars for support as an aftershock knocked us off our feet. Even standing was difficult as the uneven ground rolled and jolted. My mind raced and I struggled to keep my footing. I counted each second as the whole world shook, praying for time to speed up and let this be over.

The aftershock finally stopped, and many of my staff had grouped together to talk in low whispers. Some waved off the warning as another false alarm, declaring wishfully that we'd all be fine. As they laughed, I heard the strain in their voices. Some had even stepped around the corner out of sight for a cigarette, no doubt necessary after the stress.

Suddenly the sound of voices nearby brought me out of my trance. Someone had turned on a car radio, and I heard an even-toned female voice repeating a brief emergency broadcast. A major tsunami warning was in effect. I checked my cell phone again but the service was still gone, no doubt knocked out by the earthquake. The only source of information was the repeating broadcast on the car radio.

"...this is a tsunami warning. Please avoid coasts and rivers. This is a tsunami warning. The coastal areas of Fukushima, Miyagi, Iwate, and Aomori, please be aware..."

The broadcast continued on a loop. A tsunami? Really? Just a year ago we had received a major tsunami warning after an earthquake in Chile, but nothing happened. There was even a tsunami alert for the earthquake two days ago, and nothing happened then either. Maybe this was just another false alarm? Looking at the faces around me, I could see that my staff were having the same thoughts.

From the open car door, the emergency broadcast repeated. I looked around at the faces of my staff, confused and scared. And the realization slowly dawned on me: We are at sea level. We are in danger. Before me loomed our four-story Rikuzentakata City Hall, its interior still torn up and contents scattered on every floor. I had no idea whether the building was structurally sound, but it was the only place high enough to offer us any amount of safety. I had to get people up as high as I could. Now.

"Everyone listen!" I called out to the staff in the parking lot. "If a tsunami is coming, we can't stay here. We have to get to the roof as quickly as possible. Get moving!"

At once there were murmurs and nods, and we filed back into the building we had just escaped. The younger staff worked together wordlessly helping the elderly and those in walkers, pushing and pulling, sometimes carrying them. All around me, my staff whom I'd gotten to know for barely a month rushed up the stairs of City Hall. We hoped the height of the building would protect us, that it wouldn't crumble under us. I couldn't stop to reassure them. All I could do was keep running up the stairs.

~~~

We didn't have much time to outrun the tsunami. I burst onto the roof of City Hall alongside a crowd of others. More and more of the staff piled past the heavy steel door, fanning out across the dingy concrete to make room for others. As the last of them arrived and they closed the door behind them, I did a head count. A total of 127 people altogether. It was windy on the roof and many huddled together to stay warm, too scared even to mutter or gossip. A few clustered by the building's water tower, a squat basin on metal struts that rose a few meters above us.

Some people had made their way to the edge, gripping the fence that ran the perimeter of the roof as they anxiously watched the ocean. All at once they started to call out to the rest of us. I moved to join them, and what I saw was like something out of a horror movie.

The coastline of Rikuzentakata had disappeared. The waters were rising, swallowing up the streets and first floors of downtown buildings less than a kilometer away. The city below us became an extension of the ocean, a deep and dirty wave containing rooftops, cars, trees, everything that once made up the downtown area. The speed of the churning wave was unreal.

I heard the voice of Kenta from somewhere next to me. "There's a group of elderly folks down there on the sidewalk!" I looked at where he was pointing and saw a cluster of older citizens in the shadow of our building. But they were moving too slowly, and from where they stood, I could see they wouldn't make it before the waters reached us. Before I could say anything, Kenta turned to me. "Mayor, I'm going down."

"No! Don't you dare," I yelled. "You won't make it in time!"

But Kenta had already flung open the metal roof door and was sprinting down the stairs. I stood there stunned, looking around at the others. When the Mayor's chief of staff deliberately and openly disobeys his superior, there's an unspoken expectation that others would follow suit. I saw a group of four young men sprint down the stairs after him. I yelled for them to stop as well, but I knew they wouldn't.

With Kenta gone, all we could do was watch the water rise. Down below, the wave impacted the side of City Hall. It surged past the cars in the parking lot, and the vehicles quickly disappeared under the murky seawater. As the windows on the ground floor groaned and then shattered under the pressure, I noticed that the group of elderly folks were gone. Had Kenta and the other young men made it to them in time? I had been so focused on watching the water rise that I hadn't noticed. But the group had not returned.

The pavement in all directions had disappeared. Together, all of us on the roof watched in stunned silence as the water continued to rise. It rolled over the tops of the buildings all around us, drawing them under. Street lights bent and toppled, telephone poles snapped as wires cracked like a whip and were dragged below the surface from the force of the wave. The water carried muck and shards of wood and pieces of buildings too small to stand up to the impact. Some remained partially intact—whole walls and storefronts that had been ripped from their foundations were dragged along by the current.

As buildings around us were ripped apart by the grip of the tsunami, I began to worry about the structural integrity of City Hall. Although a structure four stories tall, some of the floors of our own building had given out in the earthquake, leaving massive cracks in the walls and shaking the building to its bones. Beaten as it was, the structure now had to withstand a constant attack from the battering waves. If the building gave out, there was no way we would survive. How much more of a beating could these walls take? And what if another wave came? How many more waves would there be?

The water surged upward toward the roof. We could feel the spray, cold and briny. From our height we could see that the wave had risen to the third or fourth story of the buildings at the seafront. Water coursed around them like water does around boulders in a river, funneled into the streets of downtown. But water also poured from the broken windows at the rear of the buildings, flowing completely through each floor with astonishing force.

I heard scattered cries among my staff who worried that the wave would overflow onto our roof. Some began to climb onto any raised bit of the roof they could reach. Railings, the tops of the emergency doorways, even the water tower. But all any of us could do was watch the water rise, slowly obliterating the landscape around us until Rikuzentakata became an ocean. I knew in a second this is how I would die, swallowed by a wave and drowned.

Then, miraculously, the wave slowed and finally stopped. For a minute, everything stood still. Around us we could see the tops of a tree or two in the distance, or the scattered rooftops of occasional tall buildings emerging from the water like islands. I could have reached down and touched the surface of the dark and murky water, no more than 50 centimeters from the edge of our roof.

I heard the metal storm door of the roof swinging shut. Kenta had finally returned. He was soaking wet and shivering. And alone. We shared a long look, but neither of us said a word.

Our lives were spared, but that didn't save us from having to watch what happened next. The tsunami, now at its full height of 15 meters, started to recede. Just as quickly as it had risen, the waters started to rush back out to sea with inconceivable force and speed. We watched as the tsunami sucked back into the ocean everything it had destroyed. A slurry of broken timbers and crumpled metal surged past us, battering the rear of the building and turning the entire downtown area into a swift-moving mass of water.

We saw people in the water hanging onto debris or pieces of cars, anything that would float. They screamed up at us for help as the water carried them past. But all of them were too far out of our reach. We could only shout desperate encouragement as they were swept away toward the sea. "Don't let go! Don't you let go! Hang on!"

~~~

A gentle snow had begun to fall. We stood on the roof together all night, huddled against the cold. All through the night, wave after wave crashed through the city—or what was left of it. The water rose and receded five more times, and each time the water smashed and tore away what little remained of our town. I felt as though I was taking every one of those blows personally. As the sea struck our city again and again, taking more and more from us, I felt like I was taking that beating as well.

We felt the pressure of the water crash against City Hall, over and over, and I wasn't sure how much more damage this building could handle. None of us knew if the building's stairs would be sturdy enough to support our weight. So we just stood dumbly, gathered on the roof and hollow-eyed, staring out through the darkness. No one could believe what had happened. This couldn't be real. We all wanted to wake up from this nightmare.

At some point during the night, I realized that during the commotion I had happened to grab a wireless emergency telephone from its cradle. It had sat forgotten in my coat pocket for a long time, but it still had some charge left. With thin hope I dialed the number for the fire department, and miraculously it connected. Whatever damage had knocked out our cell service seemed to have spared the land lines.

I heard a click as someone from the fire department picked up on the other end. Frantically, I shouted into the receiver. "There are 127 of us on the roof of City Hall. Please send someone as soon as you can!" I got out those words before the phone died in my hand. At least the fire department knew we were here, but how long would they take to rescue us? It was hard to imagine how much they must be dealing with right now, and no doubt their resources had been heavily damaged by the tsunami as well. All we could do was wait.

Perhaps it was around 5 am that the sky began gradually lightening. With the increase in visibility came another shock. We stood at the fenced edges of the roof looking down in utter disbelief. There was no city. No roads. No homes. No shops. Nothing resembling the Rikuzentakata we knew was left. All we saw was a wet mess of debris. Trees torn up by their roots. Heaps of mud-covered timber scraps and shattered remains of buildings. Masonry and plaster torn into unrecognizable chunks, cars flipped and piled among the city's remains. Anything that could have served as a landmark had been destroyed, and many of us couldn't even tell where exactly our houses had stood.

We started to hear and see helicopters circling in the distance. Perhaps they belonged to the press or the Japanese Self Defense Forces, but we had no way of knowing. We tried to signal them by shouting and waving our jackets. Did they see us? We didn't know. Even if they did, they could not have communicated that to us, and there was no room for them to land. They all flew away, and things fell silent again.

I'd had enough of waiting. I knew the dangers of going down to sea level—if one could call it that—but I knew I had to find help. Between the earthquake shaking the building to its foundation and the tsunami gutting its interior, this building might as well have been built on sand. It could come crashing down at any moment. I had to get these people to safety. It was my responsibility. I didn't know what to expect once I got down to the ground, nor did I know what I would see when I walked through the city up into the hills. I hoped the areas with higher elevation had survived with less damage, but I couldn't be sure.

I found myself running through the city's disaster preparedness plan in my head. What building had we designated as our backup command center if City Hall was ever flooded? Mentally, I thumbed through the handbook. It was the city's school lunch center, I remembered. The building had a massive industrial kitchen that made all of the food for the school lunches citywide. In meetings over the years, we had designated this building to be used as a temporary City Hall and base of operations in case of a disaster. In case of something like this.

I looked around at the staff and civilians standing on the roof around me, all shivering in the cold. I could see that many were uncertain. Should they stay up here? Should they leave and try to find higher ground? Was the building still safe? I didn't know, nor did they. But I knew I had to get our backup command center established. Our city needed leadership. That meant me. I had to step up. All of these people around me and everyone else throughout the city who had fled to a rooftop or climbed a hill and watched their city disappear underwater only to reappear a skeleton of its former self were counting on me to come up with a plan. I felt eyes on me and I needed to lead.

I told everyone on the roof I was headed to the school lunch center to set up a command post, and that's where I would be for the foreseeable future. Though they were cold and scared, many of them nodded. They knew what needed to be done, and with help on the way they could either wait for a Self Defense Force helicopter to rescue them, or could also come down when they felt safe.

I took four or five men with me, very slowly climbing down the stairs, making sure each step would hold our weight. It was tedious and took a long time for all of us to get down, perhaps half an hour to traverse just a few floors. But safety had a new meaning for me now. I had to be smart about every move I made. I was responsible for this city's safety and whether people know it or not right at this moment, eventually they would come to me for answers. I had to be sure I stayed free of injuries.

As we passed each floor, I could see what the tsunami had left in its wake. Heavy metal doors were torn askew in their frames or missing altogether. There was no trace of our offices. Desks, chairs, even entire sections of walls that had separated rooms had been torn away, and in places the ceilings had fallen in.

The scenery on the ground was worse than what we saw from above. Each step we took was a different kind of wet. We alternated between walking on sand, mud, and sodden dirt, avoiding pools of leftover tsunami water. The air smelled of an intense sharpness, perhaps a metallic or ozone tinge that I couldn't quite place. I don't think many people will smell this particular odor in their lifetimes.

Once our group had gained some distance, I turned and looked back at City Hall. I would never have recognized it as the building I worked in. A car had been jammed into the front entrance, probably one of the cars from the parking lot. Another car was resting sideways on the landing of one of the staircases. Parts of the outer wall had been punctured, giving a clear view of the inside or even all the way through. The building's iron support structure was visible in places. It felt like looking at a skeleton.

We pressed ahead toward the hills, hoping the land at a higher elevation had been spared. As we passed through what was left of town, we saw a new vision of horror with every building left standing. It was a quiet hell. There was no sound except our squishy footsteps. With the roads gone and everything covered in wetness, the terrain was unrecognizable. The ruined remains of buildings were indistinguishable from one another, and we had no way of knowing what part of town this used to be. All we could do was head toward the higher ground rising in the distance.

My house stood on the long road leading up the hill. Although I hadn't planned it, muscle memory must have taken me back here. While walking toward the hill, I suddenly found myself standing in front of what was left of my home. The others stood a little way off, down the road, giving me a respectful distance.

The building's exterior still remained, but I could see the warping and swelling where the water had damaged the structure. Dents and gouge marked the outer walls where bits of debris had chewed at the building as they were swept back out to sea. The roof was partially caved in on one side, crushed under the weight of a massive chunk of another roof from someone else's house. My home must have been totally underwater at some point. Completely submerged.

Was Kumi inside when the house was swallowed by the wave? Did she get out? I felt a stabbing pain in my gut. I should go in. I should check to see if Kumi made it out. I considered climbing over the broken walls and the windows to see if perhaps Kumi was still inside. Maybe I could reach her. But I just stood there in silence. My feet felt heavy, stuck to the ground. At that moment my home might as well have been a thousand kilometers away. I couldn't have raised my feet if I wanted to.

I'd never known actual despair in my life until that moment. I'd watched scenes of horror and evil on television and in movies, but never before had my own emotions experienced this degree of damage and terror. When I proposed to Kumi I swore to protect her. Here, now, I was walking away from that promise and choosing my civic duties as Mayor over my personal commitment to my wife. Horrified and feeling torn to shreds, I let those feelings burn inside of me as I kept walking. At that moment, right then, I needed to be Mayor Toba. Not Kumi's husband. I had to lead. I felt I had no choice.

We reached the hill, and as we walked up the road to high ground, we started seeing the first buildings and homes untouched by the tsunami. Surely people here were safe. With purpose, I made for the school lunch center. I was in full Mayor-mode, crowding out every other painful thought from my mind. What else had we discussed in our disaster planning? What else was set in stone? I wanted to rely on something certain and clear, and official precedent felt a good place to start.

Assuming the school lunch building was structurally sound and functional, this would be the new temporary headquarters for all things related to recovery. It featured an office area as well as a large warehouse that would make it an ideal gathering place for the food that would hopefully arrive soon. In addition, one of the fire brigades was next to the school lunch center, and I knew they would be instrumental in the weeks to come.

The walk there was slow, but when we arrived, I exhaled with relief. The building was undamaged. We pushed open the double doors to find a crowd of people inside, rattled but otherwise unharmed. As I surveyed the crowd, the crew chief of the fire brigade emerged and pulled me aside. He said he was missing dozens of firefighters, both the full-timers as well as the volunteer force. I felt sick. Surely it meant we just hadn't found them yet. Perhaps they were somewhere in the hills, having taken initiative and were already out looking for survivors in one of the fire trucks. Maybe, they just hadn't reached us yet. Maybe with the communications systems down, they couldn't report in.

I asked the crew chief about the police force. He said he knew some were unaccounted for, including the police chief.

"What about City Hall?" he asked me. "How many staff members did you lose?"

My chest tightened. I shook my head but didn't answer him. I didn't know.

~~~

The next several days were a blur. With the electricity out and cell towers non-functional, nobody had any way to communicate. News of the makeshift City Hall up at the school lunch center had to travel by word of mouth. We had formed a temporary command center, but what could we do next?

All of our lifelines were nonfunctional. We had no water or electricity. Our only source of fuel was the gasoline in the surviving cars and the kerosene and emergency gas canisters in the houses and buildings that had not been destroyed. I had no idea when we would have power, water, and telephone access again. Now what?

Chapter 2

Politicians and people all over Japan said a disaster of this magnitude hit only once every 1,000 years. It was unlike anything we've seen for centuries and I hope it's another 1,000 years before anyone else goes through this again. Calling it a fluke disaster did nothing to appease me. Frustrated by the fact that there is no manual anywhere that tells me what to do and in what order–not for anything of this scale–at first, I made split-second decisions based on what I knew at the time and hoped for the best. Not since World War II has there been a massive flattening of a region that comes even close to this magnitude, and that was over sixty years ago. I have to work this out as I go.

Figuring out what to do immediately after the disaster wasn't hard. I had to prioritize human life. That meant gathering the fire fighters together and taking inventory of what vehicles were available and sending them out to find survivors. Quickly. I did the same with the police force. The Self Defense Forces assisted us in this as well, though I didn't have the authority to give orders to them. The three organizations divided themselves into smaller groups of five or six to find and rescue the injured and those trapped under rubble.

The Town of Sumita and the City of Ichinoseki, both just west of Rikuzen-takata, were far enough inland that there was no tsunami damage. At around 5:30 pm on the 11th, the first group of firefighters from Ichinoseki arrived into town to help with the search and rescue missions already underway. I would find out about this later, as I was still on the roof of City Hall at the time, unable to get down.

The day I reached the school lunch center, I would also find out a harrowing story of survival. There were nine firefighters and one city hall employee who had survived by climbing up the antenna of the fire department headquarters, a two-story building that had already been submerged in water. They were rescued by a Self Defense Force rescue helicopter from the antenna and taken to high ground. From there, they came to the school lunch center and immediately lined up to offer their help along with the others. They had just escaped death, but it was already time to get back to work.

We had all done what we could and what we had to in the initial moments after the earthquake and tsunami. I would hear of more stories about survival in the days and weeks to come, but I put those aside in the moment to process at a later date. I had to concentrate on what was going on in front of me right here, right now.

On the morning of the 12th after I arrived at the school lunch center, I found out the firefighters were already out searching for survivors, having started at 5 am. At 9 am, we received our first out-of-prefecture (state/province) deployment of firefighters, this one from Yamagata Prefecture. They would be followed by more firefighters from Saitama, Chiba, Fukui, and Miyazaki Prefectures, with their workloads coordinated by the Tokyo Metropolitan Firefighters who were also in town. In total, over 4,000 firefighters came to help from throughout Japan. They gathered information, helped transport the injured to hospitals in other cities, searched for survivors, and recovered the bodies of the deceased. I owe them a debt of gratitude I don't know how to repay.

The fire department had already made headway by the time I arrived at the school lunch center. I realized immediately that the amount of work ahead of us was unlike anything any of us had encountered before. I vowed to lead by example, head down and pushing on. When I had a moment to myself, when clarity hit out of nowhere, I found myself stuck in a state of disbelief. This simply could not be happening. This is a lie, a dream. I'll wake up soon next to Kumi and sigh deeply.

It was, of course, real. Back at the school lunch center, people started to show up in droves; City Hall staff as well as residents of the city. I gathered my staff together and delegated. Word came in that one of the cell phone company giants had placed a temporary cell tower up on a hill. Someone found some bicycles and I sent several of the younger staff up the hill with a list of people to call for help. This was our only way to contact the outside world on our cell phones. I needed to reach someone at the Self Defense Force. I knew they would be here soon and I wanted to talk before they arrived. Indeed on March 12th we welcomed our first troop.

The Self Defense Forces I couldn't dictate to, but we worked well together. Some of the Self Defense Force crews cleared roads or built new ones, and others searched for survivors. Once the period of search and rescue had concluded and there was a general agreement that we weren't going to find survivors, they switched to search and recovery. When we needed water, they procured water trucks. When we needed fuel for our stoves, they got us kerosene. They provided bathing facilities, hauled relief goods, transported the sick and injured to hospitals and brought in medical equipment and supplies. They disinfected contaminated sanitation facilities and helped with sewage disposal.

They also ran the strategy meetings, coordinating all first responders who were operating in the area. I simply could not be everywhere I needed to be. Delegating became key, and I relied upon the competence, will, and knowledge of others to help move recovery along.

~~~

Also up on the hill was a convenience store. Although a lot of their merchandise had fallen off the shelves, breaking bottles and damaging boxes of food, we found items we could eat. The electricity was out so the frozen food would soon go bad. This convenience store was our source for food and water for the first several days. We didn't eat until we were full, making sure the food lasted as long as it could. We were constantly hungry but that was the least of our concerns. Random trucks carrying food came and although we didn't know who these people were, food was accepted gladly. City Hall staff had access to food from the convenience store. The rest of the citizens relied on the goodwill of those whose homes weren't damaged. Soon, food items were brought in from these homeowners and with this, we survived until a steady stream of food was delivered.

Life was a constant ebb and flow of the right people showing up at the right time and the wrong people coming in, trampling our self-worth and everything we valued. I sorely wished we had a skilled foreign correspondent at City Hall when the first group of foreigners—the U.S. Military—showed up five days after the disaster.

Operation Tomodachi[3] was a joint U.S. Military and Japanese Self Defense Force operation. I was constantly in awe of the speed at which foreigners, Americans in particular, got things done. Maybe they just bulldozed their way through or maybe they were hard to say no to, or maybe they were just right. I didn't particularly care.

Because I didn't have an interpreter to liaise and coordinate with the aid Operation Tomodachi was offering, it fell to the General Administration Department within City Hall to deal with them. Men from this department who had spent their professional careers filling out paperwork and attending meetings, men who had never seen a foreign soldier, were now face-to-face with foreigners. None of us knew what we were doing.

Many of my staff commented on how large the military men seemed, both large in stature and persona. They seemed larger than life. Though most of them were probably soldiers—we could infer that by their fatigues and physique—they had arrived on our shores to assist us, wearing expressions that were a mixture of sternness and kindness. It was surreal, but strangely comforting. My people needed all the comfort they could get. We were all in varying stages and degrees of shock, operating on gut instinct and the sheer will to survive.

Unexpected needs and visitors became our norm. Every day we had something or someone new to address and deal with. Some issues were immediate and others more long-term, not meant to be solved now. Many in town had crises needed dealing with immediately. We didn't have the luxury of choice.

Starting the day after the disaster and to this day, departments within City Hall had tasks to complete that they had never signed up for. None of the staff who joined City Hall as a civil servant, myself included, ever expected we would someday have to rebuild our city. None of us had that expertise or knowledge. How was a group of 300 people supposed to come up with the ideas and plans to recreate an entire city? From scratch? Some had barely survived. Others were lost, although we still weren't sure how many or who from City Hall had died. Whatever trauma we were going through, we tried to either ignore it or deal with it on our own privately.

As we soon learned, the tasks we faced contained those answers. Between prioritizing and delegating, it was explicitly clear that our lives and work were all rooted in survival. Ours, and the city's. We did what needed to be done. We did what we knew how to do. If we didn't know how to do something, we went forward with it anyway. Whatever felt right, whatever we knew how to do, whatever we could, we did.

We found places to sleep, whether it was on the floor of the school lunch center or in an evacuation shelter that took us in. If our homes survived, we went home and lit candles for light and huddled with family. If we were alone, we cried.

At night, those of us who were spending the night at the school lunch center would light a bonfire behind the building and sit around it. Some would chat. Others would try to wipe away their tears hoping to avoid detection. I stared into the fire a lot. What happened was real. We knew that. What we didn't know was why. Why us? Why now? We also didn't know how. How were we going to get through this?

We dug ditches for our latrines as we tried to maintain our dignity as we relieved ourselves in the dirt. We wore the same clothes for weeks. We missed our families, those who were alive and those whom we had lost. I asked the impossible of my staff. I asked them to put on a brave face, to make sure the needs of those who came to see us were taken care of. We had to be professional bureaucrats. We had to be kind, understanding, and patient all while we were grieving. It was an unfair ask and yet one that was necessary. I had to personify this and show through my behavior that I was willing to do what it took. Evidently, and the realization came much too late, shock makes sound decision-making nearly impossible. I see that now. I didn't see that then. My staff, all grieving, did what they could.

When the U.S. Military showed up, our people stepped up even though they had never dealt with foreigners before. When celebrities and politicians, people whose names we knew because we saw them on television, showed up with food or cash or a camera crew, the General Administration Department sent staff to accommodate their needs. If they wanted a tour, they got a tour. If they wanted a photo op, we gave them a photo op.

Staff from this department called the prefectural headquarters in Morioka, riding their bicycles up to the hill with the satellite WiFi connection, asking for specific kinds of aid: medication, first-aid kits and supplies, enough food for 10,000 people for three meals a day indefinitely, access to cash, fuel, and water.

They created a database about which buildings were damaged and to what extent. They created a list of the missing and the confirmed dead, including their colleagues. Massive quantities of food and water were donated and distributed to the evacuation shelters. They monitored the health of other City Hall staff on what could be done to care for the mental and emotional needs of the staff and people in the city. This was the department that worked on getting prefabricated building materials and contractors to start construction on the temporary housing and buildings necessary. This department filed paperwork for compensation against TEPCO (Tokyo Electric Power Company, the parent company of the Fukushima Nuclear Power Plant) claiming damages.

In truth our list of tasks was never-ending, as was our work load. Maybe, many years from now before we die, someone can sit all 300 or so of us down and ask us what each person did. I don't remember anymore, as much of it was a blur and my memory has become selective. There was so much to do and I've had to shed a lot of the memories of what I did because it was too painful or because my brain was so full. Some say that human potential is unlimited, but I have learned there are limits to emotional capacity. Everything was a priority all at once, and it left me overwhelmed. I knew we had to triage, but the list of items we had to choose from—what to prioritize when—was all too much.

Some lists did survive. From these, we can extrapolate some of the specific tasks each department worked on in the aftermath. Partial at best, these lists serve as a foundation for future manuals that could prevent a repeat of what many of us went through in Rikuzentakata.

We needed electricity. Until it could be fully restored, we had to rely on generators. We called neighboring municipalities. We called the prefectural headquarters. We called donors. We called anyone who we thought could help, and we were uncharacteristically not shy in asking. In addition, we needed to replace many essential devices that relied on electricity—telephones (cell, satellite, and landline), televisions, laptops and desktops, fax machines and printers, and devices for internet connectivity all had to be purchased and/or restored.

Water needed to be reconnected. We daily needed running water for our meals, and for washing and bathing. Until it could be restored city-wide, we had to arrange for water trucks and had to notify the communities throughout town over the loudspeaker when trucks arrived. The public announcement system echoed throughout the hills with times and locations of when and where to pick up water.

People found items in the rubble, some of monetary value and some sentimental value only, and brought them in for owners to reclaim. We needed a centralized location where people could drop off and search, and we needed a list of these items, where they were found by whom and when.

A list of functioning crematoriums was created, starting nearby and reaching further out. Phones were made available for those who needed to call and make arrangements to have the bodies of their loved ones transported to a crematorium.

City Hall coordinated with the fire department and Self Defense Force on what to do if a large aftershock caused another tsunami. A better plan for public safety was paramount and the need was immediate. With the constant aftershocks we were experiencing, it was a distinct possibility that we might be hit by another tsunami, and we had to be ready.

People in evacuation shelters needed to be interviewed so that allergies could be taken into account in preparation of food. The right food items consumable by those who had special dietary needs had to be delivered to the right locations.

With medical records lost, there was general confusion over which children had received what immunizations and who needed more, especially the babies and toddlers. City Hall staff worked with parents to recreate medical records of each child and continued with immunizations.

Several schools were completely destroyed. How would these children return to school? Schools needed combining and relocating. Those that could be repaired needed help from construction crews right away, as giving children a semblance of normalcy—a routine, something to do—became a key component of their mental health as well as their education.

A comprehensive list of cars damaged and lost in the tsunami was necessary for insurance purposes. With the police department gone and many police officers missing, this fell on City Hall to provide documentation identifying who owned what kind of car.

Agricultural land that had been covered in salt water had to be desalinated. New soil needed to be brought in and decisions needed to be made on how long the land had to remain idle before planting could begin again.

The piles of debris that were being made needed sorting and removing. Industrial waste, environmental waste, contaminated soil, damaged cars, and saturated clothing and bedding all had to be disposed of in different ways.

A key part of my work became delegating. I did so with the knowledge I was asking the impossible. Most people in City Hall had no idea how to do what was being asked of them. Everyone was in crisis mode. Everyone was traumatized. Only in hindsight do we realize we were all in a state of shock. We didn't know what we were doing. I certainly didn't. We did what we could because we had to. It was messy. We made mistakes. It was thankless work, and many days we wanted to give up. We spent too much time asking ourselves why this was happening, only to have a new task assigned to us, quickly removing the luxury of misery. It was hard not to be bitter.

~~~

The city's vast footprint and topography meant there were makeshift evacuation shelters that became operational purely because they were on high ground. The wave that struck Rikuzentakata was much higher than anyone could have predicted, larger than the city's disaster plan accounted for. Many people had to seek out structures on higher ground, from warehouses to community centers to shrines. When people ran to the shelters after the earthquake, they came with what they had. That could mean anything from a bottle of water to a bag of groceries. A diaper bag or a handful of cash. Many came with nothing.

Men and women divided up tasks, and once there were enough people confident to leave the premises to go find food, water, bedding, and fuel, people did go out looking. Soon rice, vegetables, soy sauce, and *miso* were brought from nearby homes in the hills that hadn't been damaged. People took turns getting water from nearby wells. They located plastic containers of kerosene and brought them to the shelter for fuel for the stove. People found candles in homes and temples and brought in bedding and clothing.

Overall, the city had an immediate count of 63 evacuation shelters, many of which were never meant to be used as such. In total, the city managed to identify 84 locations where people had taken shelter. In these places there were almost 9,000 people in the immediate aftermath, and the number steadily rose to over 10,000 as other evacuees found these impromptu in the ensuing weeks. Until City Hall staff could determine who was where and who needed what, these residents were on their own.

A benefit of living in Japan, perched on the Pacific Ring of Fire, is that the country is accustomed to earthquakes. The actions many took were based on what we knew from the past: to search for our families, always move in pairs and never go out alone, take turns leaving the shelter, set up signage in their homes (if still standing) notifying people who came by of where they had evacuated to, help clear roads, share cars available at the shelter. Above all, keep safe.

Many shelters held meetings every morning and evening dividing out tasks and sharing information. In the days following, food and more bedding, clothes, and supplies were brought from residents who lived further inland who still had their homes and who had items to share or donate. The bedding and clothing were given to the elderly first, and the rest were distributed by drawing straws.

If water wasn't running in the shelters, toilets couldn't be flushed and that meant until portable units could be brought in, people had to use newspapers to gather their waste and dispose of it later. If the shelter was a larger facility like a school gymnasium, useful items like white boards and chairs were brought in from classrooms. On the white board, the gymnasium was divided into sections so everyone knew where other people were. Initially, everyone slept on the floor without cardboard partitions to create barriers for privacy. All shelters created a list of who had arrived, and the list was made available to people from throughout the region who had come to search for loved ones.

In a time of catastrophic trauma and grief, many of the residents, including myself, functioned on autopilot. We were operating on pure survival instinct. Our goal was to live. Every decision we made was critical and pressing, serious and agonizing. Sometimes I knew I was on the right track. Other days I was purely guessing. With every new day, priorities became clearer until we would hit an unexpected roadblock. We would find ourselves on a roll only to stop dead in our tracks because something had gone wrong. So we regrouped and tackled the problem, determined to come out on the other side. Every day felt the same and every day felt different. Many nights I fell asleep on the floor of the school lunch center wondering if tomorrow was going to be the same as today. Or better. Or worse.

~~~

The death toll continued to climb. Every day the police, fire department, and Self Defense Force personnel recovered more bodies. We had one functioning crematorium in the city, up on a hill, safe and undamaged. I had it running nonstop. Unfortunately, we had to use the other half of the building as a shelter. The building had rooms of all sizes, where, under normal circumstances, families could gather to put the bones of the deceased into an urn. We had to use every bit of space available for shelters, even if that space was in a building where bodies of friends and neighbors were being cremated just a few rooms away. I knew it was cruel to ask them to sleep next to this constant reminder of our loss. Of death. But I didn't have a choice.

With the city's main hospital nearly demolished, we also had no morgue. I tasked City Hall staff with creating makeshift morgues, but the only large spaces we had were school gymnasiums. Tarps and makeshift coffins were lined up on the gymnasium floors and bodies were brought in, one after the next. These gymnasiums themselves were large boxes meant to be filled with cheering children and sports events, but instead they filled up with the dead, over and over, one gymnasium after another. So many had died. One gymnasium would fill up and I would have to task my staff to find another. This went on and on. I was numb. We were all numb.

I tried not to think about the children whose gyms were being used to house the dead. "When this is over," I thought to myself, "They will run and play during recess and gym class on the exact spot where bodies were laid out side-by-side. The kids might not know this, but the parents will surely know. The teachers will know." Again, I didn't have a choice.

I did, very briefly, consider burying the dead in a mass grave. The idea was that we would exhume the bodies at a later date for DNA identification so that they could be handed over to the families. But I realized very quickly how unrealistic this was, and the idea never took hold. That I even considered this as an option is difficult to accept. It's infuriating, humbling, and frustrating to have so few options.

In the immediate aftermath of the disaster, all my focus was on work. It was three days after the disaster when my uncle brought my sons to the school lunch center. They walked toward me, each holding my uncle's hand. My younger son waved at me as if nothing was wrong. I didn't talk about their mother and they didn't ask.

I saw my boys every now and then when I went to my uncle's house, but for the most part I fell into a rhythm of eating, working, and sleeping at our makeshift City Hall. Most of the rest of my staff did the same. We were overworked, tired, sad, and running on fumes.

Every day more and more press arrived, mostly from elsewhere in Japan. Word had gotten out throughout Japan as to just how badly we'd been hit, and everyone wanted updates. The fact that I was a young mayor with two small kids held appeal as well. It humanized me, I'm told. It was an open secret that my wife was missing. I was a man in shock that took questions from the press, my hair a mess, my face gray. My exhaustion was obvious. I repeated the same line at every interview. "We need help."

By now we had a count of how many at City Hall had died. Before the disaster, we had 443 full-, and part-time staff. We lost 111 people out of the 443. Many, like the men who ran down the stairs after Kenta, trying to bring the group of elderly up to safety, died in the act of saving others. Though we were proud of their heroism, we were equally gutted by their deaths, and our guilt ate away at us for surviving when they didn't.

Politicians arrived with the press as well. They would find me and ask for a tour of the school lunch center where we'd made our temporary headquarters. They wanted to see the city or what was left of it. They nodded and appeared earnest while I told them about the difficult times we were having, hoping to garner some sympathy and perhaps move them to support our reconstruction. But then they asked me to stand with them on the steps of the former City Hall, a skeleton of its former self, flashing the peace sign as they posed for a photo-op.

My restraint was tested at times like this. I wanted to shout at these men, "How dare you?! This is the building where over 100 of my staff and colleagues died. And you come here for a publicity stunt? You flash a peace sign and smile like a tourist? How can any human being demonstrate such a lack of sensitivity? Do you not get it, or do you just not care?"

I didn't shout at the politicians, but I made myself scarce when they continued to show up. I had work to do.

~~~

One day while eating lunch brought in by a group of residents, I sat and read the newspaper. I happened to glance at the missing persons listing and saw Kumi's name. I looked again. Kumi Toba. Missing.

I hadn't reported her as missing. I didn't have the time to file the paperwork. So who did? I scoured the listing, looking for the name of the person who made the report. At the bottom, I saw it. My 12-year-old son. He must have come into City Hall without telling me to report his mother missing. I practically lived here, and I hadn't even noticed.

I sat with this information for a while, just staring at the listing. Work had consumed all of my time and attention. I was in charge of leading the recovery and reconstruction efforts, and the people of this city looked to me for leadership. They needed someone to help them find shelter, to organize rescue efforts, to pick up the pieces, and help them rebuild their former lives. They needed to be told we would get through this. But while I slept at my desk and stretched myself thin trying to find solutions to impossible problems, my sons were living with my uncle and his family up in the hills. They had shelter and food. They had an extended family surrounding them. I was barely there and their mother's absence was hard to ignore. I hadn't wanted to think about any of this. About Kumi. About how distant I'd become from my boys. There was so much work that needed to be done, and so many people counting on me. I'd pushed thoughts about family away.

But now, staring down at this paper, they all came flooding back. My Kumi, the love of my life, still hadn't been found. I didn't know if she was safe. Just thinking about it hurt. Was I an absolute failure as a father? As a husband? Was I wrong in focusing my energy on reconstruction? I couldn't imagine a worse feeling than this guilt.

I set the paper down and abandoned my lunch. Maybe I was a disappointment to my sons, but I was still able to do some good by rebuilding the town they lived in. I would help these people put their lives back together. Maybe one day I would even get around to mine, too.

~~~

For every politician I dealt with who was self-serving and insensitive, there were also those who seemed worse unbelievably emotionless. Many times I had to deal with bureaucrats who insisted on following protocols that could easily have been waived for the sake of saving lives. It seemed at every turn that there was more paperwork to fill out just to get permission to do the simplest of tasks.

The first major ordeal came when a truck full of barrels of gasoline arrived in the city. We desperately needed fuel in order to move emergency vehicles full of workers and supplies, but all of our gas stations were destroyed in the disaster. Whatever gas we had was salvaged from the tanks of the few cars that had survived. So many people, myself included, had lost their cars and had to rely on the generosity of others in order to get anywhere, and with every trip our finite supply of fuel dwindled.

Obviously, emergency vehicles needed gasoline. Ambulances were required to transport the injured to the hospital in Ōfunato—the closest location, since the hospitals in Rikuzentakata had been leveled or made inoperable. As well, the few fire trucks that had survived the disaster were deployed to search for the dead. Meanwhile, citizens who had lost loved ones needed to drive from one morgue to the next, constantly hoping to learn if the body they were trying to find had been recovered. But with every trip, we grew closer to exhausting our limited fuel supply, which left people walking for hours to reach the morgues every day or else staying put in anxious uncertainty, waiting for word to reach them.

This truck full of gasoline was a godsend.

The Self Defense Force personnel were about to start portioning out the gasoline into canisters and fuel tanks, but they were stopped by a phone call from a ministry official in Tokyo. His ministry had sent us the gasoline, so it belonged to them, he said. The Self Defense Forces didn't have proper jurisdiction to handle the gasoline that belonged to his ministry.

"In order for fuel to be disseminated from a tanker into any kind of container or vehicle, you need a license to handle hazardous materials. Go find some-one who has this license. Otherwise, the gasoline stays in the tanker."

Violent rage and utter disbelief churned in me. You idiot. Tell me this is a joke in bad taste. What heartless, soulless monster says this? We needed this gasoline. We had such an important task ahead of us, and this man was stop-ping the process over a license? Jurisdiction? What kind of person had the audacity to hold up the lives of disaster victims over a bit of protocol?

Where was I going to find this person with this special license? I had no idea. Surely there was a list of them somewhere in City Hall. Except all of our records were destroyed. And how was I supposed to communicate with this person? Many places were still running on emergency power, which was frequently disrupted by aftershocks. The only other reliable power came from our generators—gas generators, which we couldn't refuel if we couldn't empty this tanker. Communication just among ourselves took time, let alone talking with other prefectures. How far was I supposed to go to look for someone with this obscure license?

News of this politician's actions spread through the community. Now everywhere I looked, a quiet rage showed on the faces of people around me. We don't—we can't—yell at this man. He was too important, and that kind of thing was not done. But do not mistake our silence for complicity.

Word traveled faster than I expected, and someone said they knew a guy. Was he alive? Who knew. Did someone have his number? No, but they knew someone who knew someone who did. We sat through delay after delay while we tried to track this person down. The politician didn't care. Rules are rules. Finally, we were able to locate a man with the proper certification and ask him to pour our gas for us.

I was livid. And I couldn't let these types of delays continue. I needed to start going around problems like this. Luckily, politics is a two-way street. It was a politician who stopped us due to rules, but I'm a politician, too. It was time to call in favors. During my campaign, I became acquainted with a Diet member who represented Iwate. Maybe she could help me go around the red tape in order to get us what we needed. We still needed so much, and I couldn't let bureaucracy hold us up one more second. I wouldn't let that happen again. I dialed her number.

While the phone rang, I went over my mental checklist. We needed another tanker of gasoline, certainly. We also needed water. Due to our short supply, we'd been stuck using baby wipes to clean ourselves. We needed to start bathing. I was being told some people were losing white patches of skin almost like dandruff. We desperately needed to bathe. As well, we were low on kerosene to power our heaters. Although it was April and soon enough it would be summer, right now it was still very much winter. We needed portable stoves. All of this passed through my head in a few seconds.

One more ring. I didn't owe the Tokyo politicians anything. It was time to draw a line in the mud still covering much of downtown. We're on this side of the line. We're the ones who need help. I couldn't keep the politicians from showing up, but when they did, if they wanted to step on our mud, they needed to be willing to help. Otherwise, I was unavailable. I was done coddling them.

There was a click, and I heard a voice. "Hello?"

"Hi Takahashi-*san*,[4] it's Toba calling from Rikuentakata. Can I ask you for a favor?"

Chapter 3

"I think it's her." The phone rang and it was my cousin, a police officer. "I think I found Kumi." I needed to sit down. Yesterday had been Kumi's birthday, the first time in our marriage we hadn't celebrated together. I put my head in my hands and leaned my elbows onto my knees. Breathe. This is real. Of course, it's real. There was no way she could be alive. I'd known that almost immediately, from the moment I'd seen the state of my house that day I walked up the hill. But I'd never said it out loud.

I was told where my cousin had taken her body. I borrowed a car and started to drive. Even now, years later, the whole trip is still a blur to me. I don't remember how I got there.

The image that greeted me as I arrived at the morgue made my blood boil. The press were there waiting for me. Bastards. Camera shutters clicking, they shoved cameras and miniature recorders in my face. They all wanted a statement. I took a step back and spoke.

"If this is my wife, I would like a minute to grieve. This is a personal moment. I'll give a statement when I come back out, but no television cameras. My boys don't know and I don't want them to see this on television before I get a chance to tell them."

Journalists started shouting complaints. Something about having a duty to inform the public. I ignored whoever was speaking and went inside.

One of the attendants came up to me. "Come this way please," and I followed them. There were rows of bodies, all covered by sheets. The windows were open and incense hung in the air, but there was still an unmistakable odor of death. The person guiding me stopped walking. No one said anything. I looked down and saw a body lying on a blue plastic tarp, covered with a sheet and a blanket. The sheet covered her face, but somehow I knew it was her.

All at once, it was as if she and I were alone in this giant room full of the dead. Sounds faded away except for my heart pounding in my ears. Everyone else seemed to disappear. I felt my body slide down onto my knees, and I gently lifted the sheet off her face. Her skin was completely black, her features barely recognizable. If you didn't know it was her, it could be just any other dead body. But I knew. In my mind I could see her face smiling up at me, but the reality of the empty eye sockets staring at nothing broke what was left of my heart. I heard myself starting to sob. I apologized to her over and over. I begged for forgiveness. I had promised her I would protect her, but I didn't. I could have gone home to help her get to safety but I hadn't. I am a terrible husband, a terrible man. I failed her and now she's dead.

I don't know how long I was kneeling next to her sobbing. Eventually, I grew too exhausted to keep crying. My heaving chest calmed and slowly my breathing returned to normal. Someone, I don't know who, passed me a packet of tissues. I took one out, wiped my nose, then took another and wiped my tears. Now what? The love of my life is gone. She's really dead. I had known it before, of course I knew, but now it was real. I couldn't push the thought away anymore. She was here in front of me, a shell of what she had been. The tears started flowing again, and I sat down on the floor. I had no strength in my legs. Kumi is gone. I will never hear her laugh, and I will never wake up next to her again. This is my reality. It feels like a nightmare. First, the tsunami and the city wiped out. Now my wife, my beloved, is gone forever. Why was this now my life?

I realized I had to go. I couldn't stay there forever. I had to move my legs. I had to stand. I was filled with dread at what I had to face next. The press were outside, then back to my staff where everyone would want to look at me but would try to avoid eye contact. Then my boys. What was I going to tell them? After that, I had to get on with my life without Kumi. From the immediate to the rest of my life, I was starting over right here, right now, without Kumi. I had to deal with everything that comes my way alone, starting with the vultures outside.

I stood up and straightened my pants. How many days had I worn these pants now? I took another tissue and moved it over my face, knowing it did nothing to soften my eyes which were surely red and swollen. The journalists outside would all know I'd been crying. I took a deep breath, trying to release the tension in my shoulders, and walked toward the swarm of individuals I knew I was going to hate in the next three minutes.

The questions hit me as I stepped outside into the light. I didn't think it was that dark inside, but I blinked in the glare anyway. My eyes stung from the tears and the sudden brightness. I heard several people yelling out questions but I didn't really hear the words and instead raised my hand.

"I ask that you turn off the television cameras. I'll answer your questions, but not on camera please. My sons deserve to hear what I have to say from me and not from television."

Several cameramen pointed their lenses toward the ground.

"But, Mayor!" One man called. "As journalists, we have an obligation to inform the public. We need to record you on camera."

I'd never felt fury like this before. My face burned.

"Put the cameras away," I told them. Despite my rage, I kept my voice under control. I was shocked at my calm. "Put them away," I said again. "If you don't, I'll leave without giving you anything."

Slowly the rest of the cameramen put their cameras down, and I saw tablets and pens and recorders in everyone's hands, all eyes on me. I heard myself say, "I have just confirmed the death of my wife, Kumi Toba, as I have identified the corpse I was shown as her body."

Then I saw it. A square camera lens, just like the hundreds I've seen over the past several weeks, perched near my feet where the handrail on the stairs met the concrete ledge. It was pointed up at me. Some asshole was recording this. After I made it clear I didn't want to be on camera, some asshole was recording me speak.

"Whose camera is this?" I demanded, pointing at the square, black lens. No one answered.
"Whose is it?" I roared. A hand goes up in the back.
"What television station are you from?" I demanded. The reporter replied, giving me the name of one of the major Japanese news outlets.
"Didn't I tell you not to record me?" I demanded, my voice rising.
He nodded, "But, Mayor, we have to come back with something to air."
"You have to have something to air?" I repeated back at him, yelling now.
"That's more important than my two sons finding out about this from me, their father? They should hear of their mother's death for the first time on television? That's what you're telling me?" I spat my words. The reporter

stuttered and started to answer, but I was already walking away. I crossed the parking lot, shouldering my way through the crowd until I reached the car. Furious, I climbed inside and just sat there. My body was shaking and my hands were burning from gripping the steering wheel so tight. I forced myself to exhale several times and drove off, knowing full well I was being watched. I cried all the way back to City Hall.

We face events in our lives that seem impossible to deal with, and we just muddle through. The death of a loved one is one such event. I had already lived without Kumi for some time, knowing but not openly acknowledging her death. Now that I had seen her, I had to move onto the next phase: She needed to be laid to rest. I arranged for her cremation and scheduled her funeral for a month hence.

Then I faced the problem of telling my sons. I had to, I knew I had to. But I couldn't. Once I returned to the school lunch center and my life of cleaning up after this disaster, it became easier to fall back into work. If I buried the pain under my work, I didn't have to confront it. I could pretend it wasn't real, and I could spare my sons having to know the hard truth. Of course, I know now how wrong this was. But back then I couldn't have articulated what I was doing or why. Grief-stricken, heartbroken, I wasn't thinking straight. Somewhere deep inside I knew my choices didn't make sense, and yet I didn't know what else to do. When it came down to it, I didn't tell my boys about Kumi because I couldn't handle hearing myself say it. I couldn't bring myself to sit them down in front of me and say that their mother was gone. Forever.

I threw myself into work with more energy than before. I chain-smoked. I filled my time with meetings and appointments. The press were all over me wanting a statement, wanting to see tears. I granted some interview requests and ignored others, staunchly denying them the emotional breakdown they wanted to see. I kept my words level. All that was necessary was for one or two of the big news outlets to report Kumi's death, and then the rest would poach that article. Have at it. After what happened the day I found her, my relationship with the media had definitely soured. It would be a long time before I would warm to them.

Finally, the morning of the funeral arrived. I knew if I was going to say something to the boys, it had to be now. I pulled my elder son aside and told him, stating it as a matter of fact.

"I know, dad," he said, flatly. "I read it in the paper." I didn't know what to say.

Not only was I a terrible husband, I was also a terrible father. First, he reported his mother missing and didn't tell me. Next, he read in the paper that she'd been found dead, and he still didn't tell me. All because I wasn't honest with him. I was disgusted with myself. A feeble excuse for a father.

The three of us got in the car, the boys in the back seat. Kumi's absence was palpable. She usually sat in the front passenger seat. It was empty, and would forever be empty. I still hadn't told my younger son where we were going. Did he read the paper, too? What was happening to me? Why was I like this?

We arrived at the funeral home in the city just north of us, Ōfunato. We walked inside, and my younger son saw the photo of his mother on the altar, framed in black with a black ribbon bound across the two top corners. He burst into tears. He wailed and sobbed. He cried for three days straight.

I was a failure as a human being.

Chapter 4

Prioritization was key. I was determined not to make the same mistakes I had made with Kumi and our boys. I would put sadness aside and deal with the situation. I would focus. I would ignore my exhaustion. I would be a mayor Kumi would be proud of.

School needed to start again. The academic year was meant to start in early April but this was impossible. Some schools were damaged and entirely unusable. Those schools had to be consolidated into another existing school or I had to find a new campus somewhere else completely. The kids were restless. Temper tantrums and outbursts were commonplace and I saw plenty of examples of quivering lips that tried to hold in sobs and tears. The disaster was not their fault. It wasn't anyone's fault. Whereas we adults had the words to describe what we were going through, the kids didn't have that. I had alcohol. I had nicotine. I had an escape when I wanted one. The kids didn't. I thought of my boys. What did they do all day at my uncle's house while I was at work? Did they complain? Whine? Were they a burden on my uncle and his family? I was now a single father to two young boys. How was I going to create a home life on my own with them? One that included laughter?

We all needed a routine. The children all needed to get back to school to feel like their lives weren't in shambles. The view outside proved life in general was in shambles, but their inner lives could be filled with purpose again if they could fall back into something comfortable. Even if that meant school and homework.

I worked with the board of education, tasking the chairman to create a time-line that was as quick as possible and yet realistic. Not knowing what my boys were doing at my uncle's house made me realize that I was one of thousands of families in a similar situation. I had to get these kids back in school.

It worked. Perhaps not perfect, but the board of education had a plan and they got children back in school again. New schools still needed rebuilding. Kids who had lost homes and family needed care. This was just the beginning of a new sense of normal, but it was a step in the right direction.

With school in session, we needed to move out of the school lunch center to let the kitchens be used for the school children again. That meant we needed a new Rikuzentakata City Hall. Quickly. The location needed to guarantee safety and be up in the hills. In theory, I understood nothing and nowhere offered any kind of guarantee of safety–the tsunami took away any sense of complacency–life needed to move on. A location high up a hill was selected as the temporary spot where we would put up our headquarters. There wasn't a lot of room to build, but there was enough to expand several additional buildings if necessary. It simply had to work.

The construction began in earnest and the new but temporary Rikuzentakata City Hall was done by mid-May. New desks and chairs, bookshelves, printers and desk tops, boxes of paper and office supplies, telephones and toiletries were delivered to the new building. Gray and thin steel walls held us in place as we began what would be home, not our personal homes but work home. We were tense, tired, lacking in joy, but alive. We had to get back to normal, whatever form that would now take. We had to create a feeling of lightness and cheer or this despair would swallow us. We needed joy, but I didn't know how to offer it or where I would find it.

A new building was the beginning of a new chapter. I had new faces to get used to, names to learn. We all trotted on, trying to find a routine that fit, that might work. The intensity of the collective sadness was palpable. Few people laughed and faces were intense. I would walk into a room and find everyone facing down, a row of black and dark brown hair where faces should be, their eyes glued to their paperwork. How long would we, could we last like this?

Next on my biggest and immediate priorities was getting temporary housing complexes built. Having people living in evacuation shelters wasn't a solution and with the summer months approaching, I had to get them out soon. None of the shelters had air conditioning, and while our summers weren't as hot and humid as areas south of us, it was hot enough that stagnant air in a gymnasium wasn't a healthy, sustainable solution. I had to figure out how many units we needed as well as where they would go. I delegated again. Decisions were made and we made the request to the powers that be at another ministry.

The units themselves weren't hard to assemble. Japan had been through enough natural disasters in the past twenty years or so that there were plenty left over that could be brought to town and put together. It was a matter of contacting the right ministry, and giving them our information: how many of what kinds needed where.

Since they were prefabricated housing, each unit looked roughly identical. A small entryway led straight into a hallway that doubled as a kitchen, with a toilet and bath on the other side. It opened into an all-purpose room that served as a living room and bedroom.

These were temporary measures, just enough to get people through the next year or two as they worked on rebuilding their homes or until we get post-disaster public housing complexes constructed. Asking people to live in such cramped quarters was neither fair nor kind. Then again, I didn't have a lot of other options.

The size of each unit depended on how many family members there were, and I had to consider that some families would need larger units with more rooms. All temporary housing spaces would be offered free of charge while people lived there, including all utilities.

People who lost their homes were for now living either in evacuation shelters or with relatives. Some had moved away from the city and likely would not return. Most of the shelters were communal facilities with one very large shared room for all. They were community centers or gymnasiums that weren't used for morgues—all of these that had not been damaged in the earthquake or tsunami were put to use as shelters.

Life in these places meant that people must live, eat, and sleep right next to each other with very little privacy. Many had nowhere else to go. If they were caring for aging parents or young children prior to the disaster, then they were likely in the shelter all day doing the same thing as before, only without the aid of any furniture, toys, books, cooking utensils, televisions, computers, or their familiar items. Crying or fussy children were to be shushed to not annoy the neighbor who was only a cardboard wall away. Donations of bedding and clothing were distributed to give as many people as possible the comfort of a *futon* to sleep on instead of a sleeping bag or the floor. Most people slept on *futons* on the floor, a family here was next to another family there. Snoring, and stirring, privacy always a concern, the arrangement was far from ideal.

Meals were provided. Those who were lucky enough not to lose their homes often volunteered to prepare and serve food. Ingredients, appliances, utensils, and other things related to food preparation were donated along with all other daily consumables necessary for regaining a semblance of normalcy.

The large rooms in these shelters had poor circulation and no air conditioning. Installing any kind of climate control was not an option. I wanted to get these people into their new temporary homes as quickly as possible. Give them privacy. Give them four walls. Give space for babies to cry and mothers to nurse, to watch television and laugh again, to change their clothes with some privacy, to make their own food and eat together as a family. These people needed hope that life can return to normal, to anything that resembled the lives they remembered. I wanted this for my people and I wanted it done as quickly as possible.

Once we identified the locations where the temporary housing compounds would be built, they were constructed at incredible speed using government money. Construction crews arrived and set up row after row of temporary interlocking walls made of sheet metal and thick plastic and plywood. Within days of the disaster the prefectural disaster relief command center had told us they would begin building temporary homes. My goal was to get everyone out of the evacuation shelters by summer. By the end of June, everyone that needed to have access to a temporary housing unit in Rikuzentakata had it.

Now we needed to move the families in. I started to form plans for creating neighborhood wellness and ensuring that communities were as closely knit as possible. People had gone through so much, and living next to strangers was one more element causing unrest. As I was trying to figure out how to do this, I started hearing from shelter leaders that people who lived in the same neighborhoods prior to the disaster wanted to keep their neighborhoods intact. On the surface, this was a wonderful idea. There would be some semblance of life from before the disaster, familiar faces next door and nearby. An ideal situation for all.

But how would I choose which neighborhood got to pick their housing first? They all wanted to dictate the arrangements of their new living situation, but not all of the compounds were the right size or arrangement for every neighborhood to return to the way it was. Someone would have to live next to a stranger. No matter what I decided, this couldn't be done without the appearance of favoritism.

That killed the idea. Once there was any hint of favoritism, I couldn't quelch that assumption. Nothing I said would change that person's mind. We were all traumatized, and many of us weren't thinking straight. People wanted continuity and familiarity, and when they couldn't have that, they felt like their old lives had been uprooted and destroyed all over again. Although it broke my heart, I had to turn down the request to move entire neighborhoods together.

Instead, we proposed a lottery system. Each family would pick a number corresponding with a unit. This was the closest I could come up to a random selection with no possible way of being accused of favoritism. I had no control over which number they pulled. With this system it was highly likely that everyone would have new neighbors, and although we wouldn't be able to maintain neighborhood cohesion, at least we were getting people a home. Even though it was only a home for now, it was still a home.

Moving out of shelters into their new homes was met with resistance by some, as this also meant they would now need to buy their own food. Many people had lost their homes and livelihoods, and had come to rely on the free food in the shelters. However, we couldn't return to normal without people being willing to take up some responsibility for their family's own meals.

Oppositions aside, people had to move out. Staying in a shelter was not a long-term solution. They had to move on with their lives, and that required them to make the first of many moves. Shelters were to be returned to their original functions; gymnasiums and community centers, as well as the space in the crematorium where civilians had stayed.

It was becoming clear to me that this wouldn't be the only time I'd have to choose the lesser of several bad options.

~~~

"If you could go back in time and prevent the disaster from occurring, would you?" I was asked this question when people felt they could be open with me, or by the press who just wanted a sensational story or comment. After all I've been through, would I want to go back to being a Mayor of a sleepy little city on the coast of Iwate? Have my life back? Or would I embrace the changes in my life, accept this as my new reality and try to grow?

It's an unfair question, and I refused to answer it every time I was asked.

Instead, when people posed this question to me, I told them about all the incredible people I've met, all of whom I never would have met had it not been for the disaster. In the course of my recovery work, I've been intro- duced to Prime Ministers, actors, athletes, and all kinds of celebrities. I've even met the Emperor and Empress of Japan. Each meeting meant some- thing to me and for most of the visits and meetings I can say I am genuinely grateful. But one meeting stands out from the others.

My office started receiving calls that the United States Ambassador to Japan, John Roos, was coming to town. We had received Japanese politicians and actors before, but here was a representative of a foreign government. In the history of Rikuzentakata, we'd never been visited by a foreign dignitary. My staff didn't have any experience in diplomacy or international etiquette. None of us knew the protocol for this.

By now we had moved out of the school lunch center and had a temporary prefabricated facility built as our new City Hall. We were perched high on a hill next to one of the main roads leading into the city. Here we were safe. On the morning Ambassador Roos was supposed to arrive, I was in my office making preparations when my chief of staff Kenta suddenly burst in and said, "Ambassador Roos is here!"

"What do you mean, 'Ambassador Roos is here'?" I said, just as the Ambas- sador from the United States of America walked into my office. How had we missed his arrival? No one had been downstairs at the front entrance to greet him properly, and he just walked in like every other guest with no pomp and circumstance to honor his title and position. I should have been ready at the front door of our makeshift City Hall to greet him properly. This was a gross oversight on our part.

I bowed and shook his hand, hiding my embarrassment. I motioned to Kenta, who quickly left to get some food and tea. Ambassador Roos sat down with his interpreter and several other staff at his side. They sat in a row before me, their attitudes intense and collected. I suddenly felt very aware of the fact that I was mayor of a disaster area in a rural town. An international diplomat was sitting across from me, and my town barely had running water.

At once, all I could see was the cluttered state of my office. Stacks of papers, requisition forms and boxes of office supplies, a hundred small mountains of disorder that made this place feel too untidy and too unprofessional for an ambassador and his aides to be here. What must they think of me? I didn't even know what Ambassador Roos wanted. Why was he here? I kept my demeanor calm and mustered up as much poise as I could.

Kenta returned with a few other aides, bringing small mugs of green tea. The ambassador and his staff waited patiently as the tea was distributed. I didn't touch mine, mortified by what little I was offering.

Ambassador Roos leaned forward, his expression earnest. "Mister Mayor, I came here to see how you are. How is the city holding up? Tell me, please." I was taken aback by his question. This was something people asked me in front of the cameras, not in a quiet meeting in my office. The Japanese politicians I'd dealt with up to this point were only interested in being seen asking these questions. They'd ask how we were, and put on a solemn look when I told them how bad the disaster had hit us. They'd praise us for our bravery and tell us to hang in there. Smile, photo-op, gone by noon.

But as I looked across my desk at this foreigner—an ambassador of all things—I could find no trace of pretense in his eyes. Even though I only understood his words through his interpreter, I could hear the compassion in his voice. He was actually, genuinely, asking me this. I had been to the U.S. in my youth, and even lived there for several years. I thought I was used to Americans and their mannerisms. Here was someone entirely different.

Ambassador Roos kindly let me process the question. He must have known how bewildered I would be, and even though I'd gone almost a minute without answering, my reaction was probably reply enough. Before I could say anything, the ambassador spoke again.

"What can my country do for you? What do you need?"

I almost started to cry. Who says this? No Japanese politician would ever put a question like this in front of another. It's too dangerous. How honest do I dare be in my reply? I decided instinctively to go with my gut. He means it. Whatever I ask for, he'll try to make it happen. I'll match his directness with my own.

"The disaster took everything from us. Our elderly lost their way of life, our young people lost their future. A lot of people in Rikuzentakata have lost hope. Our young people need a reason to have hope. They need to have something in life to look forward to. We need hope."

Ambassador Roos considered my words for a moment, then nodded. Secretly, I felt ecstatic, touched by the fact he asked this of me. I exhaled. This man got it.

Looking back, I can't believe that was all I said. I asked for nothing specific. How is he going to give us hope? What did I even mean? But when I said that, I knew it was the right thing to ask for. The ambassador's honesty brought me to a realization I never could have reached without that prompt. We did need hope. I could rebuild a hundred fire stations and City Halls, and fight through all the red tape in the world to make it happen. But my people needed something to be happy about, a reason to look forward to the future. I didn't know what that thing was—how could I? I needed it, too.

When Ambassador Roos left, I felt emboldened by this strange yet sincere interaction. What would come of this? I had no idea. But Americans got things done in ways I couldn't quite understand.

~~~

When I first heard Ambassador Roos had launched the TOMODACHI Initiative[5] through the U.S. Embassy in Tokyo, and that it was backed by the U.S.-Japan Council based in Washington, D.C., and the Government of Japan, I didn't fully understand the implications. Though it was surely named after Operation Tomodachi—the assistance project offered by the joint operation between the U.S. military and the Self Defense Force of Japan in the days following the disaster—I knew that this new project must be the result of my conversation with Ambassador Roos. But I wasn't prepared for what it would become.

From what I could understand, he had reached out to raise money from many of Japan's well-known brand name companies, and the funds were pouring in. It's as if these CEOs were just waiting for the call. Next thing I knew the program was up and running, and Japanese youth were on their way to the United States. As the program grew, thousands of Japanese youth, including my oldest son, got to travel to the U.S. and experience a homestay with American families. Others went for study missions to learn at some of the best universities in the country.. The TOMODACHI Initiative gave these children every possible opportunity—music camps, sports camps, jazz and symphony exchanges, youth baseball programs—so much more than they could have had otherwise.

They were able to learn about entrepreneurship and leadership, ways to promote tourism in the disaster region, and best practices of new healthcare advances. Adult women mentored Japanese high school girls on how to assert themselves in universities and the Japanese workforce, to find their voice. Youth athletes learned from the best Major League Baseball and professional basketball players.

It was an impressive list. The TOMODACHI Initiative gave young people from this rural devastated area some incredible opportunities and access to otherwise unattainable resources. The region's infrastructure had been destroyed, making it unlikely for them to be able to learn these skills on their own. Give these kids a chance to become leaders, get a broader education and expose them to many fields. This is the best case scenario of what diplomacy offers. I felt truly humbled to be part of the reason that it began.

On a class trip, a group of students from Rikuzentakata got to meet Ambassador Roos at the U.S. Embassy in Tokyo. My oldest son was among them, and I heard about that remarkable visit from him. The group of children, none of them older than sixteen or seventeen, met with the Ambassador in his office. With the same warm and genuine tone he'd expressed to me, Ambassador Roos asked how everyone was doing. There were a few vague murmurs from the teenagers, all hesitant to open up to a strange man—a foreigner, and a man of such significance.

But as he asked them more questions, some of the girls opened up and began to share personal stories about their experiences. Girls at this age are generally more open than boys, and many of the stories became emotional and led to tears. As more and more of the girls began to cry, the Ambassador noticed that the boys were collectively silent. He gave them a comforting smile and told them that it was also okay for boys to cry too.

"It was as if something lifted in us," my son told me. "All the boys just burst into tears, one after the other. It was embarrassing, but it felt good to be able to cry."

I also had several opportunities to meet with Ambassador Roos in his office at the U.S. Embassy in Tokyo. As I walked into his office one time, the greeting I received from him was, "How are your boys?" No Japanese politician had ever said that to me. I can't say whether asking questions of a personal nature is unique to the Ambassador himself, or whether Americans just feel comfortable being that direct. Either way, I was moved by his open concern and interest in my family.

As I left that particular day, I glanced up at the municipal buildings surrounding the Embassy. I wondered if any of those buildings contained a single Japanese politician or government employee who could ask me a question like that and actually mean it.

~~~

One of my first decisions was to take down the hill across the city from the prefabricated makeshift City Hall. The goal was to allot that space to rebuild many of the city's essentials—a police station, fire department, emergency management control center, an apartment complex that would replace temporary housing, and a large community center. There would also be enough room for large parking lots as well as several businesses. For this to be possible, the trees on the hill needed to be cut down and the hill itself flattened. My staff at City Hall started to fill out the necessary forms as soon as possible.

I asked several departments within City Hall to prepare presentations that we could make to communities throughout the city. We held town hall meetings throughout the early summer after the disaster to share these plans with the locals. While ideally we would have complete buy-in from the residents, barring that they needed to at least be informed.

We had presented our plans in town hall meetings throughout the city by August of 2011, and we were prepared to submit our paperwork to the various government agencies. Government funds were going to be used for this, so government ministries needed to be contacted for budgeting and approval. First came the Ministry of Internal Affairs and Communications, who would approve the overall project. This took three months. Then came the paperwork for the Ministry of Agriculture, Forestry and Fisheries. They were the ones who would give permission to cut down the trees. This took another three months. Then came the Ministry of Land, Infrastructure, Transport and Tourism. They were the ministry that would oversee the actual process of leveling the mountain. This took four months.

Throughout all this waiting, I was becoming increasingly agitated. I had gone down to Tokyo multiple times to openly complain about the amount of time the paperwork was taking. Each ministry did their jobs at their normal pace. For them it was business as usual. I could not abide by this.

"Why is there no sense of urgency for you?!" I'm sure the staff outside my office could hear me yelling into the phone in my office. "These people need this construction done now!" My active complaints helped finalize the paperwork—no doubt sooner than if I had stayed silent—but the process still took another four months. It was November 2012 when all of the various agencies involved finally approved the plan and the city could begin laying out contracts bidding for the removal of the trees and the dynamiting of the hill, followed by dirt removal, followed by each individual construction project. The time it took to get here was ridiculous. Was this how it was going to go?

I was furious. I ranted to the press and anyone who would listen about the "temperature difference," as I called it, between the ministries and agencies in Tokyo and the ones in Rikuzentakata. We needed things done as soon as possible, but they showed no sign of speeding up the process to help reconstruction begin in earnest. Practically every municipal function of this city needed to be rebuilt, but they were prepared to let the paperwork alone take over a year. It was hard to stomach.

Even after permission was finally granted, my staff and I had more hurdles before us. When we received approval to use government funds to rebuild these buildings, it came with the caveat that the funds would only cover rebuilding to the original specifications of the building in question. If, for example, City Hall was built in 1968, funds would be allocated to rebuild to the specifications of the 1968 building. That meant if there was only one elevator in 1968, then the funds would cover only one elevator for the new City Hall. If I wanted to install six elevators, which a building of that size would realistically need, then the city would have to raise its own funds to foot the bill for the rest. What sense does this make?

The government essentially told us, "You want more? You go find the money." I didn't know if this was an oversight or if it was just bureaucracy as usual, but this wasn't going to work. Nursing rooms for mothers, bathrooms for people in wheelchairs, and changing tables didn't exist back when these buildings were built. Why wouldn't we want modern buildings? What's reconstruction without progress? Why allow us only to build what we used to have? It made no sense.

The worry I didn't dare express out loud was how much longer true recovery would take if we had to wait for the government's approval at every step and with every process.

~~~

Becoming known for being openly critical of the government in Tokyo, the media were the first to point out my reputation was taking a hit. "The newly appointed Mayor of a small, rural Tōhoku town has again complained to a ministry in Tokyo for their lack of support." Headlines began with similar sensational verbiage. It's true. I did complain. My job was to get this city functional as quickly as possible. That meant that municipal infrastructure, homes and businesses, money, expertise, food, education, physical and mental health, and general overall happiness of every citizen in town was my responsibility. It felt heavy. My sleep was starting to become erratic. But I had to make it happen. If I had to complain to get the job done, I would. I did.

I was unique in this. My colleagues, the other mayors in the region, did not criticize or openly complain about the pace of recovery. Granted, their cities suffered less damage than mine so perhaps they didn't have to completely rebuild like I did. But they should still know the challenges of providing shelter for their people while trying to clear away debris and salvaging infrastructure. They should still see the pain on the faces of their people as they try to grapple with the staggering loss of life.

Knowing what we've been through in Rikuzentakata, I had hoped these mayors would speak up alongside me. I longed for a collective voice. It was obvious there would be power in numbers. If more of us were vocal about our frustration, I believe things would actually change. Instead, they held onto the silent stoicism expected of them as men in Tōhoku. They were trapped by this pervasive idea that suffering is best done in private, and emotions made public only reveal weakness. The fact that I openly flaunted my objection to the pace dictated by Tokyo was seen as arrogant by the other mayors—although I secretly wondered whether they too would like to blow up at a minister or two. But I was young, and thus my arrogance and bad manners were tolerated, if not excused altogether. I did, in fact, have one or two mayors pull me aside and mention their frustrations as well. When I asked why they didn't complain, there were few words but heads were shaken as if to say, "You can't ask that of me."

I found a most unexpected group of allies. Rather, they found me. Out of the blue, I received a call from Yamanaka-*san*, Mayor of the City of Matsuzaka in Mie Prefecture.[6] Geographically, his city was nowhere close to mine. I didn't know him. He asked me to come down to Tokyo to a gathering of young mayors, all under forty. Together they had created what they called The Young Mayors Association. They were a support group of sorts, and they wanted to help me out as another young mayor in need. I went. Gladly.

Slowly, this group got the word out about just exactly how much help I needed. Soon municipalities across the country started sending me their staff on loan. They spoke and they acted. This was more than lip-service. Yamanaka-*san*, the Mayor of Matsuzaka, immediately sent his Deputy Mayor, Kobayashi-*san*[7] to Rikuzentakata. Kobayashi-*san* lived in town for several months—proof that help was available and ready to be given. He relayed the city's various needs to others in The Young Mayors Association who quickly followed suit. Hiwatashi-*san*, Mayor of the City of Takeo in Saga Prefecture[8] all the way down south in Kyūshū sent me his chief of staff, Koga-*san*, as a public relations expert. Koga-*san* ended up staying and helping for several years.

Already severely short-handed and with the mountain of work ahead of me and my staff, the actions these mayors took was a game changer. While never stated publicly, there was an understanding among these men, an unwritten sentiment of camaraderie: if the government can't or won't help us, we'll help each other. Soon, mayors from all over Japan were loaning me their staff for years at a time. In these men, I had a younger group of leaders to complain to and commiserate with. I desperately needed liked-minded thinkers who would both challenge and support me. This group was it.

Soon came a call offering an introduction to a member of the Prime Minister's Cabinet Office. The inner circle of power, this young man was described as up-and-coming, sharp, and would surely be of help. Was I interested in meeting him? It might be possible to arrange for him to be on loan to Rikuzentakata City Hall as Deputy Mayor.

In the twenty-six days before the disaster struck, there hadn't been time to designate a Deputy Mayor. This is partly why Kenta, my chief of staff, became the gate-keeper to my office, screening appointments and calls as he fielded requests and offers of help. I desperately needed someone else in a position of authority who could be me when I needed to go out of town. I couldn't do all of the work that lay ahead of me by myself. I knew this. I obviously knew this. But until this offer came, I hadn't gotten around to figuring out who my #2 could be, or where I might find him.

I met Takashi Kubota[9] in Tokyo. I liked him immediately and felt he would offer wise counsel, be a voice of reason, and a calming force the city and I sorely needed. He agreed to move to Rikuzentakata and in August 2011 he was officially sworn in as Deputy Mayor.

Maybe I complained a lot. Maybe I was angry. I didn't give it a lot of thought. I needed help. Takashi's presence made a significant difference. My schedule lightened just slightly, and then as if my availability became public knowledge carried by the winds, I was inundated with more work: requests for interviews, status updates, visitors, celebrities, countless meetings, and foreigners. Takashi spoke English well and handled as many of the foreigners as he could. Foreign media were told to bring their own interpreters so as to not burden those of us in the disaster region already overwhelmed. The least they could do was not expect us to find interpreters.

I was dealing. If I knew what to do, I did it. If I didn't, I tried to figure it out. If I couldn't, I asked for help. I was up late at night and up early every morning, mostly with fitful nights of sleep. I was dealing but I needed help. I knew as I won the mayoral election back in February 2011 that I would need a #2. I needed someone whom I could count on. That it took me months to actually get around to finding someone left a deep impression on me. Every day I triaged. Finding a Deputy Mayor just kept falling through the cracks. I had to rely on the suggestion of others to find the help I was desperate for. This is why when Mrs. Takahashi of the Liberal Democratic Party, our prefecture's representative to the National Diet, called me one day and said she had someone I needed to meet, I did as she said.

Part 2
Our Pain

Chapter 5

Amya Miller

I was being stared at. On the morning of March 11, 2011, I woke up to the unmistakable sensation of eyes nearby. When I could finally focus, I saw Jamie was sobbing, her face inches away from mine. Already startled, being jolted out of my sleep by the fixed stare of hers and barely awake, I mumbled, "What's wrong?"
"There was an earthquake in Japan," she said, still crying.
"There are always earthquakes in Japan," I said, rolling over, facing away from her. What time was it, anyway? Leave me alone. Let me sleep.
"And a tsunami. A big one," she said. I paused. Do I wake up? No.
"It's not like I can do anything about it," I said, and went back to sleep.

That was the beginning of my journey. When I woke up several hours later, vaguely remembering something about an earthquake and tsunami in Japan, I reached for my cell phone and rubbing my eyes, scanned the news. Sure enough, the headlines screamed at me in big, bold, black letters. Strong earthquake triggers massive tsunami in northeastern Japan. I read on, horror filling me. Oh no. Oh no, no, no. This was bad. This was very bad.

I had met Jamie in Tokyo several years earlier while on a business trip. Her husband's office was right across from mine, and he and I had worked on some projects together. A group of us gathered one night at a British pub in Tokyo, Jamie's husband among them. Halfway through dinner Jamie showed up and sat next to me. We said hello, chatted, and next thing we knew, we were instant friends. She and her family had returned to the U.S. in the following years and I had flown her to Boston where I lived to help with a job. I had clients in town and needed help. I had a friend in town, a business

deduction, and help with the clients all rolled into one person: Jamie. This
was meant to be a good weekend.

I grabbed my bathrobe from a chair and made my way downstairs. Jamie sat
at the dining room table, scrolling through her phone, her eyes red and wet.
I leaned into her hair and kissed the top of her head.

"I'm sorry," I said. She looked up at me with fury and sadness. "I'm so sorry,"
I said again. She stood up and we hugged. Japan was special to us. And, I? I
don't get to say, "It's not like there's anything I can do about it." Of all people,
I don't get to say that.

I was born and raised in Japan and grew up fully bilingual and bicultural,
comprehending Japan in ways only those dropped into the deep end can
grasp. My life had been focused on my identity as a white girl, a *gaijin* who
knew how to weave fluidly in and out of Japanese and American culture. I
spoke Japanese in public, and English at home.

By our looks alone, it was perfectly clear our family was not Japanese. At the
beginning, we were a Caucasian family in Tokyo. My parents rode around
our neighborhood with me in the front basket of their bicycle, my light
brown bobbed hair with ringlets flying in the wind. My gleeful squeals made
us stand out all the more. I was a cute little girl, quick to smile and always
wearing dresses made by my grandmother with fabrics unavailable in Japan.
Our obvious foreignness and my pinafores and other distinctly not-of-Japan
outfits drew even more attention.

In the late 1960s, foreigners were a rarity in Tokyo. A large metropolis even
back then, the streets weren't crowded with foreigners like they are today. By
the time our family moved to Hokkaido, the northernmost island of Japan,
we were even more of a rarity. In the early 1970s Tokyo was still a metropolis
of several million people. In Hokkaido, wide open fields could be seen all
over. Our city had a population of around 150,000. It was a city but one with
much more openness and nature. We could count the number of foreigners
in town: the Italian Catholic priest who only spoke Japanese and Italian, the
Kiwi missionary family with seven children, a few Chinese and Korean families, and later on several Mormon missionaries.

We were a foreign family in Japan by choice—that is, by my parents' choice.
Missionaries turned university professors; their careers were here so our
lives were here. My parents raised me to focus heavily on learning to speak,
read, and write Japanese as naturally as English. As well, they expanded my

cultural vocabulary. Intimate knowledge of customs, observances, history, folklore, local and greater societal expectations and norms all needed to be a part of daily life. I attended both public Japanese schools as well as international schools in Japan. I studied, watched, and listened, absorbing it all until Japanese culture became intrinsic. I may have had no Japanese blood in me, but in my gut I was all in. Japan was home.

This cultural immersion served me well through adulthood, all the way to a 35-year career as a U.S.-Japan business consultant. Language skills brought me work as an interpreter in both private and public sector organizations. In my consulting, my work was both hands-on and behind the scenes helping people understand each other, resolving problems, and calming tempers. Fluency in both languages and cultures allowed me access into the inner circles of otherwise off-limits job opportunities. And I was fluent in the social norms of expectations from both the U.S. and Japan, which allowed me to approach both cultures with a sense of everyone's expectations.

I made a career by building connections between Japan and the United States—my childhood home and the country where I made a life and built a family of my own. An early emotional connection to Japan had defined my life. So on March 11, 2011, when I first heard how a mega-quake released a monstrous tsunami that hit the Tōhoku region, I was gutted. The natural disaster that terrified me the most–my fear and hatred of tsunamis was real but difficult to explain–had struck the nation I thought of as my childhood home. So many people had lost their homes or loved ones. "There's nothing I can do about it" was entirely the wrong response. There had to be something I could do to help.

I had spent decades communicating on behalf of the country that meant so much to me. But now I needed to *do* more than talk. I had firsthand knowledge gained from facing crises and solving real, practical problems plaguing the Japanese. Not academic knowledge or information gleaned by listening to long talks, but street-smarts.

Long ago I learned that crisis management is best left to people who can think on their feet in difficult situations, not people who repeat theories learned from textbooks and lectures. Clearly, I should go. Maybe I could help coordinate large-scale relief efforts, or meet with local officials in affected areas and communicate their needs to foreign agencies offering aid.

The weekend went on as planned; I had clients I couldn't very well turn away just because the Tōhoku region of Japan had been decimated. Jamie and I came back from our meetings and hit our laptops and phones looking for updates and any sign the initial reports were wrong. By Sunday, we were both emotionally exhausted, weaving back and forth between work and devastating news, helpless and feeling utterly useless in Boston.

I started researching in both languages, reading every article and watching every video on the disaster. News updates poured in constantly as the death toll rose and the scope of the devastation became known. The fear began to creep in. If I wanted to help, I had to go directly to the people who had been affected. But that meant intentionally stepping into an active tsunami zone, rolling up my sleeves, and roughing it. This was my literal worst-case scenario—as far outside my comfort zone as it was possible to be.

Days passed. I took Jamie back to the airport, and came home to my laptop. With the clients gone, work could now wait. I spent the next several days alternating between my laptop and television. According to my husband David, I didn't sleep much and hardly ate during that time. He gave me gentle nudges now and then, breaking me away from the newscasts for a moment to deliver a meal or some words of encouragement. The week following March 11th, 2011 felt like a fog. I know I spent a lot of time walking around thinking and then flying back to my laptop to read the latest. I remember little else. David recounts when he left for work in the morning of March 16th and returned to find me unmoved from the kitchen table where I'd been that morning. The past several days had been spent watching more videos and reading more articles, bombarding myself with somber newscasts and horrific imagery while never changing out of my bathrobe and the 16th was no different.

Seeing me moping and helpless, he pulled me to him and spoke with concern in his voice. "This isn't like you," he told me. "If you're going to go, then go. If you're going to stay, then stay. But you need to decide. Just sitting here, seeing how bad it is, and wishing that you could be helping is tearing you up. This isn't like you."

I burst into tears. We stood there for a few minutes, my heaving sobs slowly quieting. He then whispered the right words, the exact words I needed. "You know you need to do this. You'll be so much more useful there than here. I know you're scared, but go. Just go."

That was the push I needed. Just go.

Chapter 6

I grew up with recurring dreams about tornadoes. In my dreams I'd be sitting in the den of my grandparents' home, looking out the window across the fields of beans and corn as the twisters drew steadily closer. Always more than one, occasionally they appeared in pastel colors, roiling cones of pink and lavender and pale yellow. Sometimes I was standing in them looking up at the blue sky above as the winds swirled around me, but I was never scared. I knew that tornadoes were terrible and frightening forces of nature, but in my dreams their awesome force was beautiful.

While tornadoes fascinated me, tsunamis terrified me.

It wasn't just the simple matter of not being able to swim, the fear of drowning, or not wanting to lose control. Whatever the reason, tsunamis were the most awful natural disaster imaginable. I had turned tsunamis into monsters. I had even anthropomorphized them. They were evil. If they were human, surely tsunamis were sadists. Their sole purpose was to destroy, and they enjoyed the pain they inflicted. I knew this made no sense. I also knew better than to go around talking about this fear. I was concerned I would come across as someone whose fear was irrational.

It was this real but unexplainable fear that delayed me in getting out the door to volunteer in the disaster region of northeastern Japan in March 2011.

David's words of support and his nudge toward action took hold. I started calling everyone I knew with the same question, "Who do you know who's going to Japan and needs an interpreter?" I started with the U.S. State Department, then the Red Cross, FEMA, USAID—every non-profit organization I found online who looked trustworthy. I had friends call their friends with the same question. Everyone was interested. Everyone was impressed with my qualifications, but I received the same answer from them all: "We need you on standby."

I don't do standby well. When I asked for clarification, I heard many different versions of the same thing. By this point the explosion at the nuclear power plant in Fukushima had occurred, and the unanimous consensus was that no one trusted the information they had in hand. The conclusion everyone was reaching together was to stay put until certain regions within Tōhoku were declared safe to enter. Until that all-clear was given, all anyone had to go on were the conflicting and somewhat sensationalized reports from international news outlets. The reports had many people concerned.

At one point I got a call from my 20-year-old child, away at college. "I read today that they detected radiation in rainwater all the way in Boston," they said, their voice heavy with concern. "They're saying it's from the Fukushima plant. Are you sure it's safe to be going over there?"

Their worry was touching, but I wasn't about to give up over this. I explained how unlikely it was that a rain cloud containing radiation specifically from the Fukushima power plants had traveled all the way up the eastern Japanese coast, across the Aleutian Islands, down through Alaska, all the way across Canada without spilling a drop anywhere along the way—or if it had, that no one thought to test that rain water for radiological contamination.

"Are you sure that's how rain works?" they asked. Though they still sounded worried, my explanation seemed to calm them a bit.

I laughed. "Oh, babe, nope, I'm not sure. But I'd bet neither are any of the news outlets reporting this stuff. Maybe they consulted a meteorologist for that headline, or maybe they just want to scare people into reading more. I don't know. But I do know that the people in Tōhoku need help, and I'm in a position to help them. I promise I won't do anything stupid. And I promise I won't work in Fukushima."

Maybe I'd put their mind somewhat at ease, but it would be hard to convince anyone that going to Japan was safe. I wasn't even sure I thought that, and certainly avoiding Fukushima seemed wise. But over the course of that conversation and many others like it, every time I heard myself talk about this, I knew what I'd decided. I wanted to be useful as quickly as possible. It made sense to go to Japan with the first group that called me and requested my help.

Finally, a nonprofit disaster cleanup organization reached out to me. This NPO was known as an on-the-ground relief group that would go into a city or region after a natural disaster and help with cleanup and basic carpentry. Could I go with them to Tōhoku, specifically two cities within Iwate Prefecture and be their interpreter? They could use help coordinating their efforts with local emergency services, as they assumed most of their volunteers would not speak Japanese. Over coffee with an NPO staff member, I heard how throughout the U.S. and abroad, this boots-on-the-ground organization went in after a natural disaster to help with clean-up efforts. The organization was an umbrella for volunteers who wanted to show up and help. That was all I needed to hear. I started to get ready.

I told my family of my decision. I followed this announcement by telling friends in town and beyond. Word spread quickly about my upcoming trip. Friends told friends. Soon, strangers started showing up on my doorstep with relief goods. I heard from many of the people I told and who came to my house that they wished they could go, too. Some had professional restrictions keeping them from going. Others had financial limitations or family obligations. I was in the highly unusual situation of having all three potential obstacles cleared for me.

Checks arrived in the mail. My doorbell rang with the same question, "Are you the woman going to Japan?" as people I didn't know handed me bags of items which I added to the already small mountain on our living room floor. "My dentist gave me these for you to take," a friend said, handing me a box of children's toothbrushes. Batteries, diapers, clothing, sanitary products, power bars, blankets, shoes, Band-aids, and toothpaste all covered the living room floor. Not having anything large enough to contain all of the donations, I asked for help in acquiring the largest duffel bags people could find, ending up with four. By the time all four were filled, they were grossly over the allowed weight and size for checked luggage. I had too many bags and they all weighed too much but the airline kindly agreed to waive all of the fees.

On the day of departure, I felt sick to my stomach with nerves.

"You don't have to go if you don't want to. It's okay to back out now," my husband said as he put my bags in the car. I shook my head and climbed in.

At the airport, I clung to David as I leaned up to hug him. What was I doing? Was this really a good idea? Me going into an active disaster zone? Alone? With people I didn't know? I cried as David said all the right things into my ear.

"You're going to be okay," he said. "You're good at thinking on your feet."

The flight was nerve-wracking. I already don't sleep well on airplanes, and thirteen hours cooped up on my way to the biggest solo undertaking of my adult life had me intensely jittery. But there was time to prepare: studying notes of the volunteer area, memorizing names, reviewing pre-disaster information on the towns. I looked through photos I had already seen online: a city full of mud and debris, and a few shells of concrete buildings still standing with windows and doors blown out. There were scenes of the Japanese Self Defense Force crews searching for bodies, photos of people putting their hands together in prayer and respect over a corpse covered in a plastic tarp.

Would I see dead bodies? What exactly does an interpreter for a nonprofit disaster cleanup organization do? Would I have to muck out houses while also doing interpreting work? What was "mucking" anyway? What had I gotten myself into?

~~~

After an interminable flight, I landed in Tokyo. I was met by a friend who assisted with my bags and we made our way to the apartment where I would stay for a few days before moving on to the disaster zone.

The NPO I was volunteering with made it clear they were not a relief agency, and I couldn't distribute the goods I'd brought. I gave away two whole bags to another friend in Tokyo who was taking a crew of volunteers to a different town, and kept two. I hadn't come here to hold back supplies that could help people just because of someone else's policy. Surely there would be a way to hand out items to people on my own time, away from the group.

An NPO staff member and I took the night bus from Tokyo Station, heading north to Iwate Prefecture to a train station inland. On the ride up I barely slept, preferring instead to stare out the window. The scenery was dark, with only pinpricks of lights here and there. Hardly any cars were on the highway. The landscape looked deserted. Were we driving through land damaged by the tsunami? Was that why there were so few lights? Or was Tōhoku just that rural? Even along the highway?

At an inland train station we were met at 5 am by another staff person. Sleepy and nervous, I surveyed the landscape around me. There was no obvious earthquake damage to any of the buildings, and I hoped this might be a good sign. Maybe things weren't as bad as I'd thought.

The three of us piled into a mud-covered jeep and drove through two mountain ranges, heading from inland Iwate toward the coast. The noise of Tokyo just eight hours ago and the rumbling of the bus on the highway had faded into the sound of a single car engine alone in the immense wilderness. The two NPO staffers took the time to catch up with each other, speaking about their fellow members. Not knowing any of the names or stories they related, I instead continued to look out the window. The fog blanketing the pine hills and the mist creeping down from the mountains made the scenery look like old Japanese paintings on scrolls. It was quiet and creepy and beautiful.

About an hour and a half into our drive, the staff person who had picked us up turned to face me in the back seat. "We're going to drive through Rikuzentakata. You should see it right away." I nodded but winced inwardly. This was it. I was entering an actual disaster zone for the first time in my life.

We drove down a hill. In the distance I could see the ocean. We were a fair distance from the water, but already I was seeing debris. My stomach sank. This was wrong. I couldn't do this. I'm not cut out for this kind of work. What was I doing? This was going to be harder than I thought. I dreaded what I was about to see.

Out the window to my right we passed a clump of houses nestled among dormant square rice paddies. In the middle of the paddy closest to me a crumpled shed lay on its side. When the water struck the building, it must have ripped it from the ground and fully flipped over. The shed probably wasn't even from this area. It had likely been carried here and left behind once the water receded. The paddy next to that had a banged-up car that had landed upside down, all its windows shattered and missing a tire. The vehicle was dented and crushed, as though the car had been chewed on by some massive animal. Its surface was covered in streaks of muck where the wave had dragged and rolled the vehicle along underwater. The ocean was still in the distance. How far inland were we? Three kilometers? More?

There was an odor of rawness in the air. Not quite rotten but somehow off. As we got closer to the ocean, we began to pass giant puddles of tsunami water and more debris laying cluttered around the landscape.

Around me I saw trees pulled out by their roots, telephone poles bent in half, cars and trucks and several buses all in varying states of destruction, sections of walls on the ground or propped up against the remnants of a building. Soon enough every surface except the road was covered in debris. It looked like a giant field of trash, except it wasn't trash. These were the clothes, bicycles, toys, books and photo albums of the residents' homes, signage from storefronts and merchandise from the shelves inside. Here were the remnants of windows and shards of pottery, the pots and pans and broken pieces of kitchen utensils. Not items discarded, but stolen by the wave and then strewn all over as it receded. Large concrete buildings still stood whole except for windows and some doors, but everything made of wood was splintered and in varying levels of destruction. Some houses had entire fronts sheared off. Others were skeletal, stripped down to beams and pillars. Some even showed gouges that looked like claw marks, leaving behind ribbons of electrical conduit and bent rebar.

At one point we passed a battered three-story apartment building. One of the first-floor corner apartments had borne the impact of an enormous pine tree that had been ripped from the nearby forest and rammed diagonally through the sliding doors in the living room and out the kitchen window. All over the building I could see stretches where the water had beaten against the walls and stripped away the siding. Three stories up there were gouge marks where a tree, a car, or a stoplight had scraped the building. The force of the wave had torn the doors from their hinges and every single window had been shattered. But as we passed, I saw curtains waving in the breeze. Looking from one hollow window to the next, I saw that even though the water had torn through concrete and wood, and flipped boulders like children's toys, the tsunami had left the lacey, delicate curtains behind. I saw these curtains in almost every house. Over and over. They fluttered gently, as if the owners had simply opened their windows to let the spring air in. It was haunting.

We drove on, passing small groups of men working five or six at a time, in and on what used to be houses. One group was walking on what was left of a roof. With long poles they gently prodded the material as they walked. These were the men I had seen in photos online. I knew instantly they were looking for corpses. These fields, these streets, this whole town was filled with death. It was all so quiet. No passersby, no pedestrians. Except for the large green trucks and jeeps of the Self Defense Force, there were few cars on the road. The silence was eerie, unnatural. It was a quiet hell.

~~~

We stayed in Ōfunato, just north of Rikuzentakata, a city also hit by the tsunami, but much less so. With twice the population and one quarter the destruction, it was still largely a functioning series of neighborhoods. Shops were open and houses and schools were mostly unaffected except for the inlet around the port and neighborhoods around the river and streams running through the city.

The NPO crew I was joining had come to the region with the aid of businessmen from Tokyo interested in assisting with the relief effort. Through a connection, one of them was able to get in touch with a member of the Diet—the Japanese Senate. This Diet member, in turn, arranged for us NPO volunteers to stay up in the hills in an evacuation shelter along with several locals who had fled there to safety. Eight of us were given a large room and a small kitchenette. We shared the bathrooms and the bath with the evacuees. The group was still trying to work out what they could do in the city. With little going on, I mostly sat around for the first several days trying to work out just where and how I could be helpful. I took walks by myself, getting the lay of the land, trying to make our presence in the community known and non-threatening. We were here to help. I tried to project that positive emotion as I passed houses still standing with doors shut tight and gates closed.

One night I dined alone in a neighborhood *ramen* shop, hoping to give my feet a rest. I had never owned hiking boots before, and after a few days of nonstop walking, my feet had begun to develop several painful blisters. I had resorted to wearing a pair of flip-flops I had brought along. It was far from sandal weather, but my feet were always cold anyway. At least this way I hoped the blisters would heal.

The front door slid open and a mother and her two daughters entered. I recognized them from the shelter we shared. I sat up on the *tatami* floor and quickly hid my blistered feet, bare and covered in bandages.

The woman and her children sat at the table next to mine. She offered me a quick bow and I smiled, bowing back.

"You're one of the foreign volunteers," she said, a statement and a question.
"Yes, I am," I replied.
"You speak Japanese," she said, and I nodded. "I don't know why I just spoke to you in Japanese. I guess I assumed you would understand me."
"That's okay," I said. "I'm the only one in the group that does."
"Still, that didn't make any sense. I should have said hello in English. Are you British?"
"American," I answered.
"Well, I'm glad you speak Japanese," she said and smiled.
We made small talk—what city I was from and how long I would stay, etc. I asked the girls their names and when they thought they might be able to go back to school. The girls—probably no older than 10 or 11—chatted and giggled. Their behavior didn't show any stress or strain.

Out of the corner of my eye, I saw the woman pointing to something on the floor. "Your toes," she said. I looked at my feet poking out from the other end of the table. Embarrassed because she was seeing the mound of bandages covering my feet, I thought about hiding them.

"I like your nail polish," she said. "I used to wear red on my toes, too. I don't think I'll be getting my nails done for any time soon."

It took a moment for me to process her compliment. It was an innocent comment, but it made me immediately self-conscious. Seeing my toes took her back to a time when her life was normal enough for her to get her nails painted. She wouldn't be able to do that again, indefinitely. Without even thinking about it, I'd reminded her of one of a thousand little things she'd lost. I felt painfully guilty. Would it be awkward if I pulled my feet under me? I decided it would.

My *ramen* hadn't arrived and she had just ordered. We would be here awhile, meaning I would have to sit in my guilt about my exposed beaten-up feet, a dainty foreigner who couldn't handle work boots. Yet, small talk was necessary. I would change the topic.

"Have you eaten here? Is the *ramen* good? What did you order?" I peppered her with questions.

We talked about food, what she liked, and what I liked. She told me her favorite *ramen* flavor—*miso,* mine as well. I slowly slid my feet under the table and out of sight and crossed my legs, careful to keep my actions inconspicuous. My food arrived and I ate quickly, wanting to leave the awkwardness. Her comment gnawed at me. I had something she didn't. What was once so ordinary, painted toes, was now a luxury I could afford but she couldn't.

Though our volunteer group's small accommodations gave us a place to call home base, the arrangement wouldn't be sufficient for the expected influx of volunteers over the next several months. My job was to find us a long-term base of operations in Rikuzentakata that would give the group more space. But with so much of the city gone, this was not going to be easy.

From my research, I knew very little about our volunteer organization. From their web page I knew they were focused on carpentry and boots-on-the-ground aid. They certainly came across as competent and experienced, but I didn't have much practical information to go on besides their own PR. In the first few days of working with them I found out three things. First, the organization needed several bases of operations; places for their volunteers to sleep. Second, they needed projects. And third, they knew practically nothing about Japan.

Directors went to Ōfunato City Hall to meet with officials, trying to see if and where they might be of use. The organization now labeled as the *gaijin dantai*, the "group of foreigners," became harder to ignore. I overheard plenty of conversations in nearby Ōfunato City Hall, indicating no one knew what to do with the foreigners. The group had shown up unannounced and uninvited. True, the mayor had given the NPO permission to work in the city, and obviously they were willing and eager to help, but Japan was unlike the other countries in which the group had worked. Donor money didn't go as far in securing food or goods, and the locals didn't fawn over the group for trying to lend people aid. No red-carpet treatment awaited them. They seemed to be a nuisance, a situation that needed "dealing with," as I heard one City Hall official say to another as we left a meeting. This wasn't a good sign. The foreigners I was with, myself included, collectively had a lot to prove before becoming accepted as a trustworthy source of help.

Nevertheless, every day, two or three of us would climb in our jeep and drive up and down the coastline looking for places that might become a project. There were massive shipping vessels perched on the concrete wall dividing the road from the ocean. Similar-sized boats had been carried ashore and left in someone's front yard, 400 meters from the coast. Another boat was perched on the roof of a three-story building. How were those boats going to be removed? All around was the logistical challenge of debris removal. I saw battered buildings, fields strewn with broken pieces of concrete and wood, and bridges missing chunks that looked bitten out by monstrous jaws. Sometimes we would get out of the car and walk through what was left over of small towns and villages.

What did we expect to find? Every hour or so the driver would pull over and we would get out to look around another small town whose name I didn't know and wouldn't remember. Every time, I contemplated staying in the car. Everywhere we went, the destruction was new, yet similar, and always somehow worse than before. One after another, I saw the same ruined townships, only with new buildings twisted and broken in different ways. The fact that they used to be different places didn't matter, because I could only see what was left behind. The common denominator was destruction, and with each new stop I could feel myself going numb.

Every time we pulled over, I tried to think of a reason to stay in the car. If I let the others wander around on their own then I wouldn't have to worry about coming across a body buried under a section of a roof, or a dismembered foot attached to a boot. Still, I knew I had to join in to not come across as antisocial. From the roads cleared of debris, standing a fair distance away from the others, I could let them talk on, explore or their own whatever they were looking for. I could have space to myself, to take in the emotionally jarring, the unimaginable scope of the landscape.

Whenever I walked, I looked for the remains of gardens. Gardens offered peace and soon I found them. Places of reprieve, gardens offered calm. They gave off feelings of tranquility, even though many of them were utterly destroyed. The houses beside them were often ruined, skeletal, or torn down to their foundations, but some remnants of the garden usually survived. It was an eerie sight—broken branches of small bushes festooned with streamers of plastic—and yet I felt oddly connected to the gardens and the houses that weren't there. The gardens connected me. The leftover trees and shrubs didn't look the same as before; that much was clear, but I could still imagine their simplicity and elegance. I could visualize the house still standing, with a couple my age sitting in their living room sipping tea as they looked outside at their garden, proud of its modesty and grace. At least the little shrubs were alive. Barely, but alive. A pathetic and small comfort, I took what I could from the barrenness around me.

It was on one of these excursions along the coastline that I stepped on a fish the size of my foot. Before I saw the fish itself, I felt its softness give way under my foot with an unmistakable squish. I let out something between a gasp and a scream, yanking my foot up to see a mess of long strands of intestines and organs scattered on the ground and clinging to my boot. Immediately I was hit with the stench of sour rot. I felt bile rising in my throat and started to gag. I stomped my foot onto the ground, trying frantically to wipe the rotten fish and putrid odor off my boot. To an onlooker I must have looked possessed—a strange foreign woman doing some sort of wild dance, her arms flailing and her foot kicking the ground over and over.

I knew the fish had been dead before I squashed it, washed up onto land by the wave. But I still felt as though I had killed it. My foot crushing it had taken away the last remnants of its form. Now it no longer looked like a fish. Now it was just rotten guts and entrails splattered on the ground.

I didn't sleep well that night. In my sleeping bag, I kept telling myself "It was already dead." I felt myself becoming numb to the landscape comprising Ōfunato and Rikuzentakata. Hating that, I tried to look deeper. Don't let one town blend into another so much that you can't tell them apart. Everyone's story is different. Not all pain is the same. Don't go numb and be dead inside to the pain around you. Notice the pain. Do your job. Be aware. Don't be that fish.

Chapter 7

I found an ally. I made contact with a man named Fuchigami-*san*,[10] a city councilman from one of the enclaves in Ōfunato. He was receptive to the fact the *gaijin dantai* felt stymied. He had a reputation as a kind and comfortable man, and when I met with him, I could see why. He was always bowing and always smiling, and had a relaxed aura that put me very much at ease. His cell phone rang continually, and he bowed to the invisible person on the other end of the phone as he listened to their needs. Once he ended the call, he would immediately make another call to some other unknown party pursuing the favor that had just been requested. When the person on the other end picked up, he'd bow to them too. Here was someone who made things happen.

After our first several meetings I resolved to schedule more time with him, hoping he'd be able to help me and the NPO find work in the area. He did one better. As the only one from the organization who could communicate in Japanese, I found myself invited out for drinks one night along with a group of young leaders from the community. This was the kind of environment I was accustomed to, and I recognized how big this invitation was. I was not only foreign but female, and a complete stranger in town. My invitation to a social gathering carried an implicit level of trust—Fuchigami-*san* was welcoming me in the hopes that others would follow.

"We'll meet at my house," he told me. I nodded, wondering which *izakaya*, a Japanese pub, we'd walk to from there. When I arrived that night, however, it was an entirely different story. Fuchigami-*san*'s garage door was open, and smoke from multiple *hibachi* grills poured out into the night. A group of businessmen and middle-aged community leaders—all men—sat on plastic chairs and upturned buckets around a series of card tables, laughing and drinking. This was a first for me. I'd never been invited to a garage-party before. But it made sense. Although much of Ōfunato had survived the tsunami, the city had still lost a significant section of homes and businesses, especially in this neighborhood. Some shops were still open but resources were very limited, and people had to make do wherever they could. Fuchiga-mi-*san* was working with what he had.

On arrival, there were smiles and waves, and I was quickly introduced as the interpreter for the "group of foreigners" in town. I joined several of the men at one of the tables. When the alcohol started flowing, they began talking about how they had never gotten drunk with a foreigner before and how nice it would be if they could do this more often. The foreigners they had seen in the area were either Russian sailors who were docked at their port or English teachers who lived in the area. Neither were people my new friends were comfortable reaching out to. But I was someone who spoke Japanese and understood Japanese culture. What were the chances such a person would show up in their town? I was an anomaly, but an interesting one. They bombarded me with questions and requests.

They asked my age, but I rolled my eyes and deflected that one. Well, I countered, how old did I look to them? They all agreed they knew better than to try to answer. Then they asked how this anomalous foreigner felt about Japanese food. Did I like *natto,* the smelly fermented beans, and did I eat raw fish? They found out I loved *takoyaki* and *yakiudon,* and I made sure that my child had developed an early love for *sushi.* That got their attention. But, no, I didn't like *natto.* "Ah," they said. "*Yappari,*" or "we thought so." On came new rounds of food, offerings of local cuisine to see how the foreigner would react. They were delighted when I consumed homemade pickled vegetables, drank local grape wine, and enjoyed the most delicious hot pot filled with vegetables and *miso* and massive chunks of locally harvested oysters.

Then the men singled out one of their number, Junji. His birthday was only a few days away, and he needed cheering up as his mother had recently died in Rikuzentakata Hospital. Would the foreigner sing happy birthday to him? At first the request seemed unusual. Was this request meant to make me into Marilyn Monroe, singing happy birthday in public? How much was this request a test, designed to put me on the spot? But as I looked from one face to another, I realized that the request was genuine. In rural Tōhoku, there was a dramatic scarcity of foreigners they could communicate with. They had very little connection to the outside world, and found the differences in our cultures fascinating. This would be the first and probably only time anyone would sing to Junji in real English.

For his part, Junji was mortified. A shy man turning twenty-four, he was not at all interested in having this strange foreign woman sing happy birthday to him in front of his peers and elders. The older men, now happily drunk, offered him no choice. I sang to Junji. His cheeks flushed scarlet and he smiled shyly as the men around him clapped him hard on the back. Everyone cheered and applauded, and Junji very reluctantly stood up and took a bow of recognition. I chuckled inwardly. Why was *he* bowing? I was the one who did all the work.

After the success of this night, I decided I could approach Fuchigami-*san* with a new pitch. How about introducing the councilman and his friends to the directors of the NPO I was working with? I would be present too, so that they could communicate. It would be another opportunity to loosen up and get to know more foreigners. We could all go for drinks, just like tonight. They could ask questions, maybe teach the directors all about the local *sake*.

That got his attention. When I mentioned *sake* I could see Fuchigami-*san* start to deliberate in earnest. This was a big selling point, a bit of local pride that was sure to win them over. Many of the men who the councilman had invited that night worked at the local *sake* brewery, Suisen. As I got to know their faces over many more outings like this one, I quickly committed their names to memory—Suzuki-*san*, Ando-*san*, and Taniguchi-*san*.

Nine of their fellow employees had been lost in the disaster, as well as their building, which had been nestled away at the base of a hill in Rikuzentakata. The only bit of the structure that had survived was one barrel, miraculously the first barrel ever made, which they found clinging to a steel beam that had been bent at a 45-degree angle protruding out of the base of the facility. The barrel was damaged with a big dent in its side, but the label survived enough to be identifiable. This was seen as a huge point of pride for the locals, a fortuitous moment that let the people of Rikuzentakata salvage a bit of hope. In areas as rural as Tōhoku, rice farming is widespread. Plenty of rice meant plenty of *sake*, and like any town with a brewery, they insisted theirs was best. The *sake* inventory, just about ready to be released for the year's shipments, was entirely lost. If anyone wanted to drink some particular brand of *sake*, whatever the local shop owners had in stock was it. These men—Suzuki-*san*, Ando-*san*, Taniguchi-*san*—went from one *izakaya* to another, drinking up their own brand.

My plea to the councilman and his friends worked. An invitation was extended. Fuchigami-*san* invited me and two of the directors of the NPO, along with a few of the local leaders he trusted, to a local *izakaya*. We gathered around a small wooden table, so small that the plates of *sashimi* and *yakitori* soon overflowed onto the empty table next to us. We dragged it over and spread out, ordering more and more. The Pacific saury was technically out of season, but the owner of the pub had frozen some. He brought out dishes piled with this grilled fish, long and silver and left whole, with grated *daikon* radish on the side.

I had sworn off eating fish after having stepped on one, but I hadn't told anyone that particular story. As this whole grilled fish was placed in front of me on the table, I felt suddenly nauseous. Whole meant it still contained innards and bones. Sheepishly, I slid the plate over to Fuchigami-*san* and asked if he would clean the fish, eliciting guffaws from the Japanese men. Never before had they met a woman who couldn't gut her own fish.

The men peppered the NPO directors with questions. What makes someone want to volunteer? Why would someone do such a thing? Is their concept behind volunteering rooted in Christianity? Is the NPO a Christian organization? One of the directors shook his head. Maybe for some Westerners volunteering was a faith-based practice, but the NPO wasn't an explicitly Christian group. They were just here to help. I could see the community leaders starting to nod, and some exchanged looks of relief. Religion—especially Western faiths—could be polarizing in a small community like this.

At one point, Fuchigami-*san* said something that put the barrage of questions about volunteering in context. "When I was growing up, the kind of thing you're describing was used as a punishment," he said. "If we acted out in class, we were told to go stand outside in the hallway and then volunteer after school."

The NPO directors gave Fuchigami-*san* a quizzical look. "Is that volunteering, if you were made to do it?" one of them asked. It confused me too. I'd never heard of this before, the idea of volunteering as detention.

But Fuchigami-*san* nodded. "That's what they called it. 'Go volunteer after class,' our teachers would say. They'd make us clean the school grounds or walk around the neighborhood picking up cigarette butts. So, for my generation, volunteering is something we would only do because we'd been bad."

The directors looked to one another, suddenly understanding why their "group of foreigners" had created such a stir.

"On the other hand," Fuchigami-*san* continued, "for the younger generation volunteering isn't seen as punishment, but rather a box to tick on a resume. Everyone applying for a job these days has to be able to list at least one volunteer activity they took part in. So it's still not something we do because we want to. It's a task to be completed if we want to look good on paper."

This key bit of cultural context suddenly put a great many things into perspective. There was no precedent in this region that tied volunteering to anything positive. It was either an outright punishment or a prerequisite to get in the door for a professional career. No one willingly volunteered. To the people of Tōhoku, the idea that these foreigners would choose willingly to volunteer didn't make sense.

An important barrier had been breached. The locals understood what the NPO wanted, and the foreigners had some context for the cold shoulder they'd gotten on arrival. With copious amounts of alcohol consumed, there was an honest, albeit drunken, plea from the NPO for a place to call a home base closer to the downtown area. Could the city council and these local leaders help? Fuchigami-*san* agreed.

A few days later, Fuchigami-*san* talked his constituents into letting our group use the second floor of a commerce building as base camp. The space had two large rooms, one small room, a co-ed toilet, and a serviceable kitchen. We would move several people from the facility up on the hill down to the commercial building, but first Fuchigami-*san* had to get the approval of the local elders. He convened a meeting.

Two NPO directors and I entered the room to find ourselves facing a half-circle of old men, all at least in their seventies. Dressed in sweaters and cardigans and jackets of gray and brown and black, I could see they were wearing layers. There was no heat in this building. I suddenly realized my feet were cold. Early April was spring only on the calendar. In reality, there was a distinct chill in the air.

Fuchigami-*san* who had arranged this meeting, still older than us three foreigners, was the youngest of the Japanese. The councilman explained to the elders who we were and why we were in Japan. He assured the elders that the foreigners would not cause problems, and spun our arrival as a chance for the grandchildren in the community to make friends with foreigners. How many times in their lifetime would they have an opportunity like this to interact with people from so many different countries? He concluded by asking the men for their blessing to use the second floor of the commerce building.

The elders exchanged a loaded look with one another as if silently asking, "who's going first?" Slowly, the eldest-looking among them started to ask questions. "Where have you worked before? How many people are coming?" Soon others followed with their inquiries. "What projects do you see yourselves doing?" All questions were answered by the NPO directors, with me interpreting. I saw the elders slowly starting to warm. Heads began nodding. The councilman asked for any final questions. One of the elders who hadn't spoken asked, "What are you going to eat?"

One of our group directors laughed. I cringed. It was a good question; there was nothing funny about it. The director explained that we were respectful of local food customs and that we would not ask for anything out of the ordinary. Indeed, we would eat whatever the locals ate. Japanese food, if that's what was available. The elders' faces went blank and I saw the warmth drop from their expressions. Some shared looks of disbelief.

The director had essentially just said the volunteers would be shopping at the local grocery stores, taking food off shelves that were already bare. In other words, the NPO did not have its own food supply. "We'll eat what you eat" was thoughtless, and exactly the wrong answer.

The councilman jumped right back in, deftly sliding past the comment. "Does the group have your permission, elders, to use the base? Could we vote, please?" He knew, too. He couldn't let this gross oversight hang in the air. I respected him all the more in that instant. He was asking his constituency to let their food supply dwindle due to the influx of volunteers. The elders voted and all raised their hands in unison. The volunteers could have the second floor.

I felt a mixture of surprise, relief, and disillusionment. After that last misstep, I was prepared to have the elders refuse. I would have to thank Fuchigami-*san* profusely, and acknowledge the significance of what he had just done. He had made a masterful job of emceeing the meeting—and he had helped the NPO dodge a massive bullet.

Likewise, the two directors needed to come to terms with what had happened. I wanted to turn to them and scream, "Japan isn't like the other countries you're used to helping! Things are different here. You essentially just said you're going to compete for what little food is on the shelves, when it's being rationed for a town in disaster!" I said this, more toned-down, and less screamy.

"Thanks for the insight, Amya, but we know what we're doing. This isn't our first disaster experience." I recognized the cue to shut up.

~~~

Tensions were mounting in Ōfunato. It was slow going to get assigned actual projects. Half the volunteers were sleeping in the evacuation shelter up the hill while the other half remained downtown at the new base camp. I had hoped our meeting with Fuchigami-*san* and the elders would help move things along, but three weeks after my arrival, the *gaijin dantai* still hadn't been assigned a concrete act of cleanup or assistance mission of any kind. The NPO staff didn't understand why people weren't knocking on their door for help, and were irked at having to sit around and do nothing.

Once I moved into the base camp in the city, I found I desperately wanted space and time to myself. But with more volunteers arriving and the building becoming cramped, if I wanted to be alone, I had to leave the premises. Being in a central part of the city, even though some sections were destroyed, I could find places to walk to, stores to peek in. Most of all, there was access to the people in town who I was slowly getting to know.

The first evacuation shelter was a community center located up in the hills. Staying there, the isolation would get to me. I craved anything resembling a community, the sense of intimacy and the closeness of neighbors and friends. But I would have to walk a fair distance if I wanted to reach a neighborhood. Down in the second building, at base camp, I had much more access to people, food, and shops.

Much of my time was spent with Fuchigami-*san*, asking him again and again if he could help find work for the volunteers. I found myself stuck in the middle between the City Hall officials who weren't thrilled about having this group of foreigners on their hands, and the NPO, unaccustomed to doing nothing. I heard complaints from both sides. This, combined with the images of destruction all around, contributed to disillusion. Was this what I'd signed up for?

To clear my head and to get time to myself, I went on walks in the neighborhood. There was no gym in town, so for any kind of exercise, I had to walk the streets. It wouldn't raise my heart rate, but at least it was something.

During these walks I would call my friends in Tokyo and have them talk to me. It could be about anything apart from my situation: their day, their dog, their taxes. I would listen to whatever they had to say. If they could make me laugh, all the better. These phone calls were my connection back to reality outside of this place, giving me perspective physically and emotionally. I needed to laugh. I needed the outside world. I needed, for just a few minutes, to not think about where I was and what I was seeing. If the time zones lined up, I would also call my friends back home. My cell phone bill would be astronomical but I would deal with that later. I reserved calls to my husband for the most dire of days, afraid I would hear him say he wanted me to get on the next flight back. As uncomfortable as I was, I wanted to see this through.

One day walking on a sidewalk near the river, talking on the phone with a friend in Tokyo, I sensed I was being followed. I turned around to see a small boxy car slowly following, eventually pulling up next to me. I told my friend to just stay on the line, please, I needed to figure out what was going on.

A man got out of the car. He looked at me and I looked back at him.
"You're on the phone," he said.
"Yes," I said.
"You're the interpreter for the foreigners."
What was going on? Who was this guy?
"I am. Who are you?" I asked.
"I live nearby. I was wondering if I could talk with you."
My friend on the other end of the line asked what was going on. I didn't know. Was I safe? What did this man want? Other than to talk?
"Okay," I said. "What did you want to talk about?"

He looked at me for a moment, then sighed, his face cracking with sudden emotion. Then, it was as if a dam burst. I stood there for what must have been twenty minutes while he poured out all of his bottled-up guilt. He told me he had read in a magazine somewhere how vulnerable this region was and that the city's preparedness wasn't up to par. He should have warned people, he said. He should have spoken up. If he had, maybe all these people wouldn't have died. He had also had a dream. Was that dream an omen? Did I know? Should he have said something about his dream? He should have, right? What would I have done?

All the while I held my phone to my ear, staring dumbfounded as he unburdened himself of all his fears. What if there was another tsunami? With all these aftershocks, it was just a matter of time, wasn't it? Before one of them triggered another massive tsunami?

Somewhere in the overflowing wall of words coming at me, I told my friend I was okay and that I didn't need him to stay on the line. This guy wasn't going to hurt me.

Eventually the man's energy ran out. "Well, that's what I wanted to say." Depleted, he got back in his car and drove off. It was as if he had found a priest walking down the street and stopped to ask for an impromptu confession.

How did he know who I was anyway? And, how should I feel about what had just happened? On the one hand, I was glad he got this off his chest. On the other hand, he hadn't made much sense. He read about the tsunami danger in a magazine? He had dreams? And it was his fault for not warning anyone? Was he ill? Did this incident mean I should stop walking around by myself?

A shrine with long and steep steps stood on a hill near the center of town, about a five-minute walk away from base camp. This spot, this holy site was a place of emotional refuge. I would climb up near the top, out of breath, and sit on those steps at night and look down at streets below me. And it was here that my feet led me after this uncomfortable encounter. I climbed the steps and called another friend in Tokyo and explained what just happened.

"Did I do the right thing?" I asked. "Was I safe? I was, right? That guy wasn't going to hurt me." The last part came out as a statement, sounding more certain than I felt.

"This happened during the day," my friend observed. I pressed the phone against my ear as his voice crackled. Cell service in the area was still spotty. "If he had tried to do anything, and he wouldn't in broad daylight, you would have been able to call attention to yourself. No, you weren't in danger. What bothers me is that he knew who you were. Find out how. How did he know you were the interpreter? That's the part I don't like."

The next time I saw Suzuki-*san*, Ando-*san*, and Taniguchi-*san*—the guys who used to work at the *sake* brewery—I asked them point-blank. I told them about the man following and stopping me.

"Everyone in town knows about you and the other volunteers. 'The group of foreigners'," Suzuki-*san* said. "And most people know about you, personally. You're known as the 'white woman with short black hair.'"
I was stunned. Why didn't I know this?
"Because I'm the only one who speaks Japanese?" I asked.
"Obviously."

So there it was. I was under observation. Not for doing anything wrong, but there were eyes on me. I would have to be even more careful going forward—best behavior all day every day. This was unwelcome added pressure. How does one try to blend in when we're the obvious outsiders? It seemed best to throw myself into work and not think about it.

Knowing I was under observation left me unsettled. I craved time alone, but I also didn't want to go about town aware that my every move was being scrutinized. Back to the steps leading to the shrine, not wanting to think about what my cell phone bill would be when I got back home, I called my child.

"I used to tell you stories when you were little," I said as soon as they answered. "Now it's your turn. I need to hear something funny. Distract me. How's college going? I need something that will take my mind off," I waved around in the air knowing they couldn't see, "all this."

"Um, sure," they replied. "That's kind of vague. Let me see what I've got," My child thought for a moment. "All right. I helped set my friend on fire the other day."
I balked. "You what?!"

"It's okay," they said. "He's training to be a stuntman, like for action movies. And it was only on his arm. He just learned a technique for doing this safely and wanted to test it out."

We talked a while longer, my child explaining to me how this could possibly have been safe. After half an hour I still wasn't convinced, but our faux-argument had done the trick. I noticed my shoulders weren't hunched next to my ears anymore. For a long moment I was successfully distracted. When they finally got around to wishing me a good night, I paused, letting out a long and deep sigh.

"What was that about?" they said.

"I'm not looking forward to trying to sleep. I'm just not the kind of person accustomed to waking up staring into the eyes of someone I don't know," I said.

I could hear my child's confusion in their silence. "What are you talking about?" they said finally.

I told them how I slept on the floor in the sleeping bag I had dug out of our garage, next to a bunch of people I didn't know well or at all. New volunteers kept showing up, so I would see a new pair of eyes first thing in the morning every now and then.

My child started to laugh. "My mother, who refuses to go hiking because she's afraid she'll see a snake or get bitten by mosquitoes. Who hates camping and won't go anymore because of that one time ten years ago—do you remember this, when you almost stepped on that skunk? And now you're out roughing it in a sleeping bag waking up next to strangers," they said. "C'mon, it's pretty funny."

They were right, of course, but there was no way I would tell them so. "I'm right," they said. "Admit it."

My child started to laugh again and this time I joined in.

~~~

The leaders of the NPO made the rounds of various municipal buildings looking for ways to help, but every visit was met with a polite but firm rejection. At one hospital we couldn't meet with the director because he was attending the funeral of his wife. At many of the places we visited, we were told they weren't prepared to accept volunteers because they didn't have the staff to delegate. Too many other issues had to be resolved before they could even think about delegating work to strangers, much less foreigners. "We have an unemployment problem here in the city. A lot of people are out of work right now. We can't just let you do work we could have them do." I was obliged to interpret these words over and over.

In the meantime, more and more volunteers arrived and the rooms in the bases filled with sleeping bags full of strangers. Not all of the volunteers were foreign. One third or so were Japanese, some from the area near the disaster and others who heard of this organization's work through the grapevine. There was little to no notice of who was showing up on any given day. But for every volunteer who showed up, the agreement was the same. The NPO would provide lodging and food for six days a week, and all the necessary tools and gear to do any work they were assigned. On their one day off, the volunteers were responsible for their own food, and everyone was expected to find their own transportation to get themselves to and from the city, though transportation to the project sites would be coordinated by the NPO.

I headed out of base camp and started my walk. I didn't have a destination in mind. I wanted silence, peace, and to be left alone. I wandered around the neighborhood, taking the narrow back streets on purpose. I had decided to avoid the main routes, especially those with sidewalks. I didn't want to be followed by a random stranger who needed to purge his or her guilt. I hoped the narrow roads connecting the neighborhoods were less traveled by cars and there, I could find the quiet I craved.

I found myself walking toward Ōfunato Bay. As I rounded the corner I heard the sounds of construction up ahead, and noticed an older woman sitting on a row of concrete blocks staring intently at a house being torn down. The claws of a front-end loader raked through the walls, tearing away small chunks. As I approached, I realized the woman was crying.

"Are you all right?" I asked.
She nodded, hurriedly dabbing at her eyes with a handkerchief. I stood watching her. Suddenly, she moved over on the concrete, opening a space for me and patted the block she had just vacated.

"Please join me," she said.
I sat down next to her and looked at the house across the street.
"Is that your house?" I asked.
She shook her head. "My friend lived there. She's not been found yet. They're tearing down the house one piece at a time because it's too dangerous to go inside. They think she still might be in there," and the woman pointed to the house.

I felt a cold chill. I had managed to avoid seeing any dead bodies so far during my time here, and I didn't want today to break that record. It was one of my biggest fears, along with that of another massive earthquake triggering a tsunami. While the constant aftershocks and the possibility of a tsunami were now a way of life I had become accustomed to, the fact that the region was still mired in death wasn't in the foreground of my mind. I was deeply entrenched and focused on getting through each day. I was engrossed in my life in the disaster region, and again I found myself being here but not *of* here.

I didn't know what to say so I just sat down next to the woman, leaving a foot of space between us. Silently, we watched the crew of three or four men take pieces out of the second floor. Piece after piece fell away as the massive hydraulic claw tore plaster and snapped rafters with surprising finesse.

Finally, the machine powered down, and a man in a hardhat came over to the woman. He looked at me with passing curiosity, but before he could ask who I was, the woman spoke.

"Did you find her?" she asked. The man shook his head.
"I don't see where she could be in the house," he said. "There's nowhere else for us to look. We've taken down all of the walls on the second floor. We can see into every room now. She's just not there." He bowed and walked back to the remains of the house.

The woman put her face in her hands and started to quietly cry. I didn't know if these were tears of relief, confusion, or sadness. What were the chances her friend had escaped? Perhaps she'd left town and not had a chance to call and report her whereabouts. Or had she been sucked out into the ocean like so many others? I didn't have the words to comfort this woman, and I didn't want to say the wrong thing. I ran my hand up and down her back, and sat there as she wept silently. Slowly her breathing calmed and she looked up at me, nodded, stood up and left. I never learned her name.

I sat on the concrete block a little longer, my walk no longer restful or quiet. I felt like I needed another walk to calm down from this one. It was starting to get dark, and it was time for me to head back to the base. I stood up, stretched my legs and shook out the stiffness, knees cracking. I began to walk. I had gone fifty meters up the road when a man I'd never seen before came rushing out of a building on my right. I stopped, startled. Was he going to unburden himself with stories as well? Had I been wrong in taking back roads? I looked around to see if other people were nearby.

"You're from the volunteer group," he said. I nodded. "You speak Japanese, right?" I said that I did. "I was wondering if your group could help clean out my house," he said, pointing at the building behind him. The wall facing the street was gone, and I could see inside the house, a layer of thick mud covering the *tatami* mats on the floor. On the left was a kitchen with shelves of pots and pans. The second floor looked untouched. It took me a moment to process the man's request—he wanted the NPO to do something for him. Finally. A job. I told him I would ask the group, but was sure they could help. We would come back later in the evening with a reply.

Finally, the NPO had a request for assistance. After dinner, one of the directors and I returned to the man's house and listened to his request from the day before.

"Clean out the remains of my house and find two items for me," he said. He wanted the small urn of ashes that he had placed on the Buddhist altar to honor his ancestors, and he needed his *inkan*, a stamp that took the place of his signature. Both were vitally important to him, and the rest of the house's contents could be thrown out, since he planned to tear the place down.

The director jumped at the request. Telling him that we could start right away, we returned to the base and brought the news to the eager volunteers. The following morning we loaded up shovels and arrived at dawn, prepared to muck. The group assumed he simply wanted a thorough cleaning of the first floor and they offered to shore up and reinforce many of the walls. With a little reconstruction this place could be perfectly livable again. "No," the man said. "Get rid of everything. I want nothing to do with this house ever again."

This was the first time I came face-to-face with someone in an apparent state of prolonged shock. He was coherent, but some of his behavior caught me off guard. Why tear this place down rather than rebuild? Why fixate on two specific belongings while insisting that the rest of his possessions were expendable? It didn't make sense. I hadn't seen enough of these patterns of grief to understand why someone would want this. So at the time, along with my fellow volunteers, we didn't give the request a second thought. The idea of challenging him or asking him to explain his reasoning never occurred to us. He could easily have kept most of the kitchenware but it was connected to a bad memory. Everything had to go.

We loaded dishes and *daikon* radishes, heads of cabbage, and other produce out into the trash, even though the dishes were fine and the food still perfectly edible, if perhaps a little salty. At the man's request, we threw it all out. We found the urn, although the stamp—a soapstone cylinder the size of your little finger—was lost for good. We shoveled mud and hauled soaked bedding and heavy ruined furniture out of the house. It was surprising to learn how heavy a shovel of mud was to carry.

Within an hour, the press showed up. They swarmed over the site and bombarded us with questions, quickly finding that only one of us spoke Japanese. My first awkward morning interview commenced. Who were we? Why were we here? What was our connection to Japan?

That was the last time I mucked. Now that the press had their angle on this group of foreigners, and knew one who could speak Japanese, the requests started to flow. The work poured in and more volunteers showed up wanting to help. Local women wanted to help the helpers and organized a cooking schedule. Now there were volunteers helping the volunteers. As the NPO had a food budget, it was left to the women volunteering to feed everyone with the allocated money.

This "group of foreigners" was now getting requests left and right, and they seemed ready to resume their usual routine. They'd overcome cultural barriers that had made it hard to help the way they were used to. Now they could roll up their sleeves and lend a hand the way they did in their other worksites around the world.

One day, a staff member of the NPO pulled me aside and asked me to help her with working out a menu. She explained they had a project to deliver enough food for the 10,000 or so people living in shelters in Rikuzentakata. This was news to me. The NPO had already informed City Hall of their plan, and now they needed to find 10,000 people's worth of food. The staff member needed my help putting together a menu of food the evacuees would likely eat. I was thrilled. Food was scarce, and a tangible project of this scale would make a huge difference for these people.

I sat down with the staff member and came up with a list, suggesting a few menu options. We did research into the bulk costs for chicken, rice, vegetables, noodles, *miso* paste for soup and seasoning, and other staples. As we worked, a worried look crept onto her face. The numbers piled up before us, and it was clear that the budget she'd been given wouldn't cover food for that many people at these prices. It wouldn't even come close.

"Can we increase the budget?" I asked her. "Whom do we have to talk to?" She shook her head. "This is what I've been given. I guess our money went a lot farther in the other countries where we've worked. We're probably going to have to abandon the project."

I was stunned. Just like that, abandoned. There were people here who needed this food—food which the NPO had already promised to Rikuzentakata City Hall. People in town were counting on this food. The NPO had money, just not enough for the number of people they'd committed to. In the end the project was scrapped, and City Hall was never informed of its cancellation. I was embarrassed and livid. I was growing weary of being shocked by what this NPO didn't know.

It came to a head one night in the dinner queue. One of the NPO staff members yelled at the volunteer crew who were in line to fill their plates with rice and chicken and vegetables. "If you take more than one piece of chicken, I will name you and shame you!" I repeated her words because that was my job, but inwardly I was disgusted. Ostensibly, the deal was that the NPO would feed the volunteers. Food costs more in Japan, even rural Japan compared to the places this NPO had worked in before. Clearly, they didn't budget for that. How is that the fault of hungry volunteers? These people were performing manual labor for eight hours a day. They were coming back dirty and sweaty and hungry. How, after all this, could the group chastise their own volunteers for wanting to eat the food that was their responsibility to provide?

I left the line. Someone else could have my piece of chicken. I walked to a nearby grocery store and bought an apple, cheese with almonds, a bottle of water, and a cup of yogurt. I needed Plan B. I needed something meaningful and impactful. Dinner in hand, I climbed the stairs to the shrine and as I sat on the steps I started to think about where else I could be of use.

Chapter 8

Mayor Toba and I don't agree on when we first met. I'm certain I ran into him in the parking lot outside the school lunch center during the first week of April. He was making a simple public appearance, taking a moment to be accessible and raise the spirits of his constituents. I saw a long line of people coming up to speak to him one by one. Some thanked him, others just bowed as they held back tears. Many of the people he spoke with were elderly and easily a head shorter than him, and Mayor Toba had to lean down to their ear level when he offered his condolences. At a glance this startled me; it almost looked like people were lining up to hug him.

I had heard of Mayor Toba. I was familiar with bits and pieces of his story. I was also keenly aware of the differences in devastation between the two cities of Rikuzentakata and Ōfunato. Every day I heard stories of people who had died in Rikuzentakata—so-and-so's cousin, that man's mother, a friend-of-a-friend. I would sometimes scan the local newspaper and read the number of missing people noticing a steady climb.

As I passed, I bowed out of respect and greeted him, but I didn't wait for a reply and didn't expect anything in return. The Mayor was busy. He didn't know me and I was clearly not a local. There was no reason he would remember me walking past him. To this day, he still doesn't.

In hindsight, I wonder if those who were lined up chatting and bowing to Mayor Toba were being consoled or doing the consoling. Early April was when the body of his wife Kumi was discovered.

I had made numerous trips to the school lunch center before, but this time I wasn't sure why we were here. I'd made the trip with a staff member of the NPO, and when we passed Mayor Toba, he confirmed my suspicions. The NPO had sent us to ask around about work.

When the staff member with me suggested approaching Mayor Toba, I said "no." I put my foot down. Not only did we not have an appointment, but we were also witnessing here a moment of grief and consoling. This was not the time to ask for work. I made it clear that I wouldn't interpret for him if he went up to Mayor Toba. There were lines of cultural decency one does not cross. We didn't have an appointment, and that was that. Want to meet with City Hall staff? Figure out how to make an appointment.

As we stood beside the school lunch center, I observed people coming up to the long bulletin board that covered the outside wall. It was easily ten meters long, and every square inch was covered with photographs and handwritten notes. "This is a picture of my father. He was last seen at this location, has anyone seen him?" "The kids and I are staying at this shelter. Please come and find us." "Papa, I'm safe. Where are you? Please find me."

Locals gave the wall a respectful distance, making room for people to scan the photos and read the messages written by family and friends. Others waited on the steps hoping to locate missing loved ones. It was a difficult scene to watch.

Nearby stood two women, huddled together with handkerchiefs to their mouths and reading the postings on the wall. They wore dark peacoats and dark pants, which made me think of mourning clothes. Had they just come from a funeral? Both were in their fifties, and they looked similar enough that I guessed they had to be sisters. They stood by the bulletin board, scanning the photos of hundreds of names and faces.

Suddenly, from out of the crowd burst a young woman who could easily have just stepped out of a nightclub in downtown Tokyo. Her curly brown hair bounced around her face, and her exquisite makeup might have taken hours. She wore a chic silver down jacket and white miniskirt that stood out against the sea of woolen black and navy coats worn by the locals. She clipped up the steps on a pair of strappy high heels, crying as she called out to one of the two women with the handkerchiefs. The older woman turned and the young woman fell into her arms.

"I thought you were dead!" the younger woman sobbed.

The other woman now whipped around and gasped. "How did you get here? I can't believe it, I'm so happy to see you!"

The wails from the three rejoicing women descended into noises of joy and confusion and sorrow. I couldn't tear my eyes away. The three of them hugged, the young woman openly crying and her two elders trying to control their emotions but slowly failing. I glanced at the crowd. Everyone else was watching them, too. It was hard not to. I couldn't help but feel like I was invading a private moment, like an emotional voyeur.

Even though I knew these were tears of joy, their reunion still represented a familiar heartache for everyone gathered on those steps. For these women, this open display of pain and loss had been building for weeks. These tears were a release of hurt that must have lingered while they waited to be reunited, not knowing if the others were alive or dead. This bawling young woman's emotions had straddled a terrible divide, wanting to hold out hope that her loved ones had survived but knowing she had to prepare to accept their loss. Now, in this moment of rediscovering each other, their eruption of emotion was both beautiful and traumatizing. It was raw. It was glorious. It was awful.

~~~

As I stayed longer in Rikuzentakata, I started hearing stories about how people around me were dealing with pain. One friend told me, "My dad told me never to show tears in public. If I needed to cry, I did it in private." He, in turn, told his 5th grade son the same thing. Men don't cry. Boys don't cry. If you do, there better be a damned good reason. Over and over there were variations of this. One man at City Hall who cried during the earthquake was talked about behind his back in front of me and the message was clear: his tears were an unacceptable sign of weakness.

The more I talked with people about this, the more stories came up about kids acting up at school. Disobedience and rudeness is certainly one way to release pent-up emotion, just like cutting school or rebelling against parents' discipline. In the schools in Rikuzentakata, this mostly came from the boys. Girls were allowed to cry. They were scolded when they whined, but crying was accepted.

One day, combing the internet in search of local news articles, I came across a series of posters released by a Japanese relief organization. All showed smiling faces and slogans of reassurance, reminding the people of Tōhoku that "We're going to get through this," and "Stay strong, we have people supporting us." One of them stood out to me. A young boy of ten or eleven on his bicycle, grinning ear-to-ear with a mountain of debris in the background. The caption read, "I'm not at all the least bit sad."

So there it was. We are not sad. We are fine. Smile, don't cry. Everything is alright. The image of this boy and the message the poster was sending broke my heart.

Mayor Toba himself is no exception to the boys-don't-cry rule. His 12-year-old son became more and more withdrawn, distant while living at the mayor's uncle's house up in the hills. When the mayor would go there to bathe, sleep, and check in with his sons, even then sobbing was not allowed. One particular instance when his 12-year-old burst into tears, the mayor yelled at him. "Shut up! You don't get to cry. I'm sad too, but I don't get to cry. Neither of us get to cry!"

When the mayor and I discussed his outburst at one of our dinners many years later, he asked me if he's a terrible father. It's a thorny question to which he has obviously given a lot of thought. I want to shake him and shout "You think? Yes, you were a terrible father! How could you say those things to your son?!" Instead, using a little more tact, I said, "Pain is complicated. You had to hold your pain in. I can only imagine what that does to you."

It took Mayor Toba years after the disaster to realize he had been in a prolonged state of shock. At the time he had no one around to tell him that—everyone else in the city had experienced the same trauma and was grappling with the same emotional turmoil. Having asked his staff to put on a brave face, he had to do so as well. In hindsight, he recognizes that pain can only be held in for so long. Cracks started emerging in his staff.

"We were all barely hanging on," he said. "Everything needed to be done now, and then we'd accomplish things only to end up with double or triple the number of items that needed doing the next day. The workload, the newness of it, the trauma, the reality, it was inhumane. I see it now. The only way we survived was to stay in shock mode. It's unreal, when I think back on it now. I don't know how I did it."

He and I talked about this concept of "barely hanging on" and how it manifested itself in people differently. I thought back to my first few months in Tōhoku, and the things I did to cope.

Aftershocks were a common occurrence in the region. I quickly came to realize how much I dreaded these surprise earthquakes. They were often prefaced by a low rumbling sound as if a train was passing. Then the aftershock would hit. There was a Japanese word for this low growl, *jinari*, translated as "ringing earth." After the first twenty or so I came to realize the loudness and the duration of the rumbling had nothing to do with the severity of the aftershock that followed. Every time I heard that sound— the precursor of impending doom—I'd find my body locking up. When the aftershock actually hit and the room shook, I'd freeze even more. Though these quakes were fairly common, I never got used to them. Every single one terrified me, bringing to mind unbidden thoughts of crumbling buildings or walls of water.

I even started to feel phantom quakes, a sensation as though the floor or the building was moving. In the middle of a meeting I would suddenly find myself petrified, clutching a table edge or the arms of a chair only to realize moments later that there was no shaking. Yes, I was hanging on, and more than barely. But there was a sense of slipping, that I wasn't fully myself.

It came to a head one night in April, around 11:30 pm. I'd been in Tōhoku only a few weeks, and at that time the NPO group hadn't yet received permission to move into the second floor of the commerce building. We were still sleeping in the cramped evacuation center up in the hills of Ōfunato. With over a dozen people crammed together in one room, sleeping bags lining the floor like a carpet, I found myself quickly needing my own space.

I announced to the rest of the staff that I was going to sleep in the closet. I told them I just needed a bit of privacy, that I had started craving space for myself. What I didn't tell them was how bothered I was by the lack of privacy. I was in the most rural part of Japan. I couldn't just up and leave. All around me was death and destruction. The only way to get physical, mental, and emotional space to myself was at night. Sleeping in a closet seemed like the perfect solution.

The floor of the closet was just barely long enough for me to put down my mat and sleeping bag. If I crammed myself in at the right angle I could fully lie down, nestled among shelves on three sides with a sliding door along the fourth wall. I cozied up and was just drifting off to sleep when the building began to shake violently.

Canned supplies and heavy storage boxes fell from every shelf, raining down on top of me. Panic and confusion combined with pain as shelves buckled and dumped their contents onto my sleeping bag. Bruised by cans and the sharp corners of boxes, I bolted up and threw open the door, scrambling furiously out of the closet.

The power went out, and the fluorescent lights throughout the building all died at once with a static popping sound. At the same instant my cell phone rang. A friend from Tokyo was calling.

"You okay?" he asked.
"Yes," I replied, although I was still panting. I probably sounded panicked.
"Were you asleep?" he asked.
"Mm-hmm," I said sleepily.
"Do you need to get out of the building?"
"Maybe," I said, not sure what was going on.
"Hey!" he yelled. "Pay attention! Are you safe?" That snapped me into full engagement.
"I'm fine," I said. "I'm on a hill. No tsunami can reach this place. I'm way inland. I'm okay."
"That was a big one, we felt it all the way down here too. They're saying it's easily an M7. You're sure you're okay?"

The line went dead. I had lost my signal. I looked at my cell phone in my hand, dumbfounded. Did this just die on me? Obviously. Still, it came as a shock. Just like that, I had no phone.

It takes a specific kind of stress to push a person into a mindset where they think that sleeping in a closet inside an active earthquake zone is a good idea. My need for space overruled the obvious need for safety. I had become numb to the landscape around me—seeing debris and muck and pain every day, driving through remnants of a city where I knew the dead were still buried under fragments of their former life. It had become so routine that it all blended together. I'd just wanted space, and I'd wanted it enough that my judgment was affected and I didn't know it until that night.

Was I also barely hanging on? Why was this so normal here? Why were we all suffering together, in silence?

It comes down to the Japanese idea of *gaman*. Translated into English, *gaman* means perseverance. It's seen as a state of mind as well as a verb. *Gaman* is stoicism, suffering silently by bottling up your pain and hiding your emotions. It's considered noble. I heard people saying "Do *gaman*." They said it to each other, to their children, and to themselves. This idea is deeply entrenched in Japanese culture, and any behavior to the contrary is considered highly taboo. Boys don't cry. Girls don't whine.

I had long since embraced the American in me that didn't believe in *gaman*. I felt exempt from this expectation. In the West, people are much more willing to directly acknowledge and express emotions. Pent-up feelings fester and cause harm, but the process of releasing those feelings can help with recovery. Japan's idea of *gaman* is the exact opposite. In painful or extreme situations, you must behave stoically and control your emotions at all costs. It's the cornerstone that holds together mental health in Japan. If you can do *gaman*, you can survive anything.

I had cried once when I first came face-to-face with uncontrollable emotion—mine—within the first ten days of my arrival. In the NPO's search for a second base camp, we drove to Rikuzentakata one day to Hirota Peninsula, the southeastern corner of the city that surrounded the bay. High on top of the peninsula was a campsite that had huts and enough open space for volunteers to spread out in tents. Could we use this place? The directors of the NPO were getting the runaround. The campground manager was not the least bit thrilled his space had been "volunteered" by someone higher up in the community without his approval. The manager was hesitant to agree but couldn't produce a concrete reason to turn the NPO away, so the NPO directors kept going back to examine the area.

On one trip to the campsite, another attempt to convince the manager of the grounds, he asked us to accompany him in his car to the highest point on the peninsula. We reached a lookout over Hirota Bay. The manager led us to the lip of the overlook, and I stood beside him ready to interpret. We stared down at the city laid out in its horrid state of debris-strewn destruction, a ghost-town except for the few concrete buildings standing.

"I stood here and watched the tsunami hit the city," the manager said. "The wave got higher and higher and I just stood there watching it take over everything in sight. I couldn't do anything. All I could do was watch. It was the worst feeling in the world."

As the interpreter it was my job to repeat these words, but I couldn't. This was the first person I'd encountered who had actually seen the tsunami do its damage. I heard the quaver in his voice as he spoke, trying to keep a level tone while replaying through this painful memory in his head. The lump in my throat felt like a rock. I couldn't stop my tears. I had to excuse myself, turn around, and walk away. In that moment I saw what he saw. I felt his sorrow, his powerlessness. It was deep and too intense. After a few minutes, I composed myself, walked back to the group, apologized and repeated his words.

On the drive down to the campsite, the manager found me in the rear view mirror and said directly to me, "Your tears back there. You don't get to cry. We don't have the *yoyū* to cry. You're not from here. You certainly don't get to cry."

Yoyū is a word that has no direct equivalent in English because it changes based on context. It could mean anything from, "I don't have the luxury of," to "I don't have the energy to," to "I don't have it in me to." The implication is there's a void. The context could refer to money, time, ability, emotional capacity, energy, or wherewithal. When used, it's a dead stop. *Yoyū ga nai*, "I don't have *yoyū*" has no comeback. When someone tells you that, you can't push or cajole them with "Sure you do." It shuts down the conversation. If you don't have the *yoyū* to do something, that's that.

When the campground manager said he didn't have the *yoyū* to cry, he was telling me he had to shut off his emotions to go on—that he didn't have the time or capacity to sit around and cry, that he didn't have the luxury of releasing his emotions. It was all knotted up in that one word: *yoyū*. His point was clear. If he didn't get to cry as a local, I certainly wasn't allowed tears as an outsider. Rightfully or not, I stopped crying in public that day. I held it in, knowing it wasn't a healthy response, but accepting that it was necessary for now. Just for a little while until I could go somewhere safe to release it. I was battling the stigma of mental illness in Japan and applying the societal expectations to myself as well.

On that particular day my emotions had boiled over. From then on, on seeing the same broken landscape day after day, the imagery didn't register the way it first had. I was getting used to seeing the destruction, but I had to shut down a part of myself to get through each day.

It took an aftershock and a shower of canned food to jolt me into realizing how deep that shutdown went. This stress was affecting my judgment, and I needed to focus on my safety. I asked myself, how did I let it get that bad? Was I taking on the expectation of participating in *gaman*?

No, I tell myself. Partially because I was able to walk that line between Japanese and American values. I could see *gaman,* which meant it couldn't be my whole world. But more to the point, this wasn't my pain. It hadn't been my community that was destroyed. Technically, this wasn't even my country. But if this was true, why was I not myself? Was I just barely hanging on because I had subconsciously embraced *gaman*?

~~~

The headlines kept referring to "The Patient and Resilient Japanese." The international press had extensively covered how polite the Japanese were in the face of a disaster—quiet and organized queues by pay phones, waiting to call home to check in with loved ones. By contrast, disasters in the U.S. were often faced with looting in their aftermath. "It would never occur to us to steal from a store after a tsunami," I was told by women and men of all ages in Japan.

In my first several months in the two cities I now called home, there were plenty of examples of strength and courage, acts of bravery and kindness from people of all ages. On a visit to the school lunch center in Rikuzentakata, I saw a boy no older than eight or nine giving a younger girl, his sister perhaps, a piggyback ride. Struggling to keep going, he walked up a hill, an old man at his side, the young girl on his back. He didn't complain. He didn't say to the girl, "You're heavy. Can you get off while I rest for a minute?" He cheerfully called out greetings to everyone he passed on the sidewalk, myself included. Here was resiliency. On the part of a child. The boy was doing what he could. He was stepping up, helping, carrying someone else's weight on his shoulders. I choked up and willed myself not to cry, nodding and saying to him as he passed, "Good for you." He smiled back.

The more I read various articles about the resilient Japanese, the more I felt conflicted. Initially, I witnessed acts of resilience, but over time, these public displays of patience and bravery seemed to wash out. It was like a rote exercise. People were going through the motions of saying the right things, but their eyes were glazed over. Their faces and bodies looked heavy with exhaustion, but their words about their situation projected strength. It was an odd and awkward contradiction.

Many journalists, delegates, academics, and visitors alike came up north to Tōhoku to meet and briefly interview people. For these visitors, their take on the situation tended to reflect the best about whom they met or saw. From these limited observations, they would give reports or write articles lauding the ability of the Japanese disaster survivors to bounce back—to adapt, to cope well, be tough, and return to pre-crisis life in a remarkable way. The resiliency of the Japanese people was described and praised.

But there was a stark divide between what came out in the press—the Japanese survivors are resilient and on the road to recovery—and the layer of deep and profound pain just below the surface day to day. True, many people exuded this resiliency that outsiders noted. But often, these same people would get drunk at night and complain. The unfairness of it all. The exhaustion. The lack of clarity. The need to find hope. These were their coping mechanisms, themes that didn't make it into columns and articles coming from the press.

Those of us closer to the ground couldn't help but see that, unless part of "resiliency" could be called lying, saving face, and deliberately holding in pain, few people could truly be called resilient. More and more evident over time was a deeply disturbing trend of undiagnosed depression, of people going through the motions day in and day out, with little in their lives that could be described as positive. While outside societies might observe that Japanese people in general were capable of admirable "resilience," of a coping that displayed humility, self-control, and lack of fuss, the disaster survivors were actually deep into a state of *gaman*.

For instance, people would repeatedly respond to questions with a polite rejoinder, *daijōbu desu*, "We're fine," mouthing what they knew was expected. One could say that the Japanese consider *gaman* to be highly appropriate in a situation of pain or discomfort. The idea is to consider the other party first in what one reveals. If I say I'm in pain, it reminds you of your pain too. Whereas if I keep my pain inside, it can't spread to you. Those who serve as icons in Japan uphold this image. No sumo wrestler, the modern-day *samurai* of Japan, would ever say in a television interview that he was in pain. His *gaman* was expected and would be praised, revered, and respected. This makes perfect sense because it maintains harmony, doesn't focus on the individual, and is evidence of a quiet and stoic strength.

Back in my Japanese elementary school days, above the classroom blackboard, framed in gold on a white background were two large letters in calligraphy: *chōwa*. Harmony. Life is better harmonious. If we all play by the same rules, if we have the same expectations of each other, then we all know what's coming. Life is simpler when the rules are clear. Blending in is preferred to standing out. Strive for this harmony. Harmony is about the collective. It's about the group, the school, the organization, the family unit. It's not about the individual. In the context of Tōhoku, this meant no one individual's pain was worse than anyone else's, especially when everyone was hurting.

The Westerner inside me had little patience for *gaman*. I might have learned all about it when I was young, but I soon abandoned any rule that "keeping feelings inside is good." Rather, you talk things out, don't let your pain fester or bottle up. Release your emotions. Cry. There's nothing wrong with talking to a therapist. Why would anyone suffer alone and in silence when there were people around willing to help? Why do *gaman*?

Perhaps the press with its problem of recognizing *gaman* and its lauding of "resilience" confused the latter with what they saw as a commitment to routine. It was apparent that people were engaging in a day-to-day emphasis on getting back to normal activities as quickly as possible. Get the children back in school. Give them something to do. You may not have your home, and you may not live with the same people anymore, but what you can make normal, you make normal. Adults as well. Take the unemployed and put them to work. Give them jobs. If full-time jobs aren't available, give them part-time work instead. Something. Keep people occupied, and that will take their minds off the disaster. Politicians, teachers, and friends articulated this sentiment. Did the press think busy people were resilient people?

The Japanese language recognizes there is a public face, *omote*, and a private face, *ura*. In Rikuzentakata, on the surface, on the *omote*, people acted as if everything was "*daijōbu desu.*"

A major crisis had uprooted everyone, but they would figure it out.

In private, *ura* mode, the talk turned to the disaster—especially with some alcohol. Complaints about local government, trash-talking about someone they knew who had behaved badly, conflicts between traumatized people who weren't thinking clearly, and tears of frustration and confusion. This wasn't resiliency. This was deep loneliness, intense anger, and profound pain. It was this *gaman*, not resiliency, that the journalists were seeing.

~~~

"They say she just walked into the ocean," Matsumoto-*san* said at dinner. I had met Matsumoto-*san* through a friend, and she had invited me to her house for dinner. We sat around a low table covered in small dishes of *edamame*, a variety of pickled cabbage and vegetables, and large plates of *yakitori*, skewered chicken from the smoky grill just outside.

The table was long and packed with Matsumoto-*san*'s friends and family. Some spoke loudly, but others used the clamor to converse in hushed tones, a rare moment where *gaman* could break down and locals could share pain. Who were they discussing? I pricked up my ears. Eventually, it became evident that they were discussing an elderly woman who had lost her husband in the tsunami, whose body hadn't been recovered. She just couldn't take it anymore, and decided to join him in the water. Someone driving by saw her in the ocean, her head barely bobbing above water, but by the time they called for help, she was gone.

"It's hard for people who are older," Matsumoto-*san*'s father explained. "They're already at the end of their lives. Finding a reason to keep going, to live, to hope. It's hard." He was probably in his fifties and did not yet consider himself old. Did he have hope? Did he believe his life would improve? Did resiliency have an age cutoff?

What journalists were writing about and what was going on behind the scenes were two very different realities. The locals were projecting stories of *gaman* to the journalists so that's what they reported. They had no way of knowing that the truth was far more complex and resulted in stories like that of this old woman. As a result, the press ended up misconstruing *gaman* as resilience.

I wondered if there was something I could do to change the narrative. The world needed to be let in on more than some journalistic sound-bite about Japanese disaster victims' apparent ability to bounce back. What if I could take a more direct approach? What if I outright asked people what they needed most? Aside from those whose loss included life—the ultimate in the unrecoverable—what did people need in order to start over?

Chapter 9

"Of course, someday I'll have to leave," I said to the businessman whose home we had mucked out several weeks prior. "I can't stay here forever." It was shocking to see tears in his eyes. Was he crying because I was leaving? Surely not. So caught off guard by his display of emotion, I put my hand on his shoulder and asked, "Are you all right?" He brushed my hand away and turned around, his square back a clear signal. I backed off.

Volunteers kept arriving every week, with more and more bilingual people among them. I finally started getting help with the interpretation and translation work. My role in this nonprofit organization had never been to muck out houses. I was supposed to be an organizer, a verbal and cultural conduit. As these other volunteers began to show up, my role was no longer a one-person job.

Now that the NPO had other people who could help them with the language barrier, I could finally start looking for other places to work. I wanted to be useful, but where could I go and what could I do? It was a matter of finding an organization that would take me on as a consultant or an advisor. I started by asking Fuchigami-*san*. He quickly put me in front of other councilmen and word started to spread. "She's serious about helping at municipal level," I heard one say to another. Soon enough, I was soon sitting in front of Ōfunato city officials in a conference room.

"What do you think you can do for us?" one of them asked me. I went through a list.

"I can raise money for you among the foreigners in Japan who want to give. I can connect this city with foreign media. I can also bring in donors and delegations and help keep the city and the region in the news, making sure the awareness and interest don't wane."

They looked pleased. Our chat was going well.

"When can you start?"

"Well, first I need a work visa," I said. As a foreigner, I needed permission to stay in Japan long-term. I needed a visa sponsorship. Their faces fell.
"Ah, well," one of them said. "That complicates things."

The same conversation took place in numerous other city hall conference rooms, all with the same result. In the best cases, a city wouldn't have the time or resources to petition for a visa. The government was taking long enough to approve local matters, and would certainly not consider one woman's visa a priority. In some cases, my pitch was met with open disdain. One mayor said frankly, "I don't need help from outsiders, and certainly not from foreigners."

Encountering this brick wall was frustrating and disheartening. By now, I had been in Ōfunato and Rikuzentakata for two and a half months, coming up on the end of a 90-day tourist visa. I felt my time with NPO was over. I knew I needed a change of scenery in order to let myself make such a big decision, a possible major change in my work here in Japan, if indeed I was staying on. Was the consistent rejection I was getting from one city after another a sign that I was meant to go home? Did I even believe in signs?

Although I wasn't ready to go yet, I had no choice. I took the bullet train back to Tokyo, hauling now one of the four large duffel bags I had initially brought with me, the last one significantly lighter as I had left behind my woolen socks, work boots, fleece jackets, and all other items I promised myself I would never wear again. As much as this was a departure, it was just as much a starting over. I liked change. I liked morphing. I was eager to see Tokyo again, as I needed skyscrapers and concrete around me instead of rotting fish and sprawling destruction.

Once in Tokyo, I went straight to the 26th floor of a high-rise apartment building where a friend had given me access to an extra bedroom. I was met at the door with a plate of cheese—exactly what I had asked for. "Can you get real cheese?" I had asked. "Not the fake cheese I get up north. I want Gruyère and Brie and Gouda. White Stilton with apricots if you can find it. The good stuff." He didn't disappoint.

Here I had a private room with a bed and a bath. In Ōfunato I had bathed using baby wipes and had washed my hair in the sink. Once or twice someone in town had extended an invitation to their home to use the bathing facilities. But the lack of bathing had gotten to the point that it no longer fazed me, another new experience for me. I had become used to my messy hair and smelling just a bit off—everyone else was in the same boat. In Tokyo I craved the scent of soap as I soaked in a bathtub. I was clean again. I was desperate to revert back to my old self and this apartment was where I would start.

Now there was something soft to sleep on. I would gladly have accepted a friend's fluffy sofa if someone had offered, but this apartment was a godsend. I had a real bed, all to myself. I could toss and turn without worry about bumping into someone else. Above all, it was thrilling to have access to a real washing machine and clothes dryer. While volunteering in the disaster zone, I had to wash my clothes in a bucket. Never having done laundry this way before, I learned the hard way that I didn't have the wrist strength to wring out wet blue jeans or sweatshirts. These stayed on hangers for days, the dampness lessening but never fully going away until I was forced to wear them anyway. Here was access to a washing machine plus a dryer. I could wear dry and soft clothes again.

The first several days in Tokyo were spent walking around, losing myself in the din and buzz of the metropolis. For the first time in weeks, I was part of a crowd instead of standing out as the foreigner always on display, exposed and vulnerable, constantly minding manners and being on best behavior. I craved anonymity. Tokyo was where I could have it.

Tokyo was full of friends from long ago—international high school buddies, people with whom there was history, rapport, and trust. Enjoying that familiarity, I let myself revert to being me as I sat with them and relaxed, with no expectations, nothing to achieve, no best-behavior business.

Everyone wanted an update. For every story told on these frequent social occasions, there was the reward of great food, good coffee, chocolate, a massage, an evening watching movies, eating salsa and chips together. I peppered these friends with questions of my own. What could I do? What should I do? Who might sponsor me? Why was this so difficult?

Alone in the comfortable bed, I tossed and turned at night, existential questions about motivation and purpose of the trip buzzing through my mind. Had I been of any use, accomplished anything, after all? Yes, helped the NPO find a place to stay; mucked once; found the volunteers some projects to do. Did that count as being useful? It was a painful reality check: volunteers come in with their own agenda and expectations, myself included. I had done what was best for the NPO, but hadn't done the most I could, based on my skill set. I was just now starting to feel myself again after feeling numb and beaten down.

Flying back to the U.S., I spent the next month at home, recovering and trying to let go. I wasn't always having to be careful. Being around David, I could be myself. I could exhale. I slept. I relaxed. David and I went on long drives. We were together and we were good. We drove to our neighborhood bakery on Saturday mornings to line up for fresh croissants. We went to our favorite diner so I could eat a Reuben sandwich. I was sleeping next to my partner, someone I loved and wanted to be with. Everything around me was familiar. I was home.

Just like in Tokyo, people in the U.S. wanted to hear what I had done and seen. During the weeks that followed back home, friends and acquaintances sat in our living room as I told them what I had done, seen, and heard. I was contacted by people who had offered the supplies that had filled my four duffel bags when I first left. Everyone wanted to know what I had been doing, and what things were like in the disaster zone. I found myself speaking at organizations, churches, companies, and schools. Story after story left people in tears. Everyone except me.

No matter how many times I related what I'd seen, images of destruction and pain, I found that I couldn't cry. I did everything I knew how to release my tears. I watched sad movies, I listened to Tchaikovsky's 1812 Overture. (The part with the church bells always got to me.) Except now, nothing seemed to work. Was I so accustomed to keeping my emotions bottled up that I had lost the capacity to let the tears flow? It was my husband who made the suggestion.

"You're not done with Tōhoku. There's a part of you left behind." He said that over dinner at our favorite pizza restaurant, reached for my hand, lowered his voice and said, "I think you need to go back and figure out what it is you want. Go get that piece of you that you left behind and either let it go completely, or leave it there forever. Put yourself back together. Or, find something you can do there. You're a doer. Find a project you can believe in. But you can't figure that out here. Go back."

He was right. Five weeks after I had flown home, I returned to Japan determined. I was either staying and doing something much more practical, tangible, and applicable, or I was going home to David, my husband.

Part 3
Our Resilience

Chapter 10

Amya Miller

A blast of wet heat met me as I walked out of the airport. After a brief time in Tokyo seeing friends, after a trip back to the U.S. reconnecting with David and with friends there, I was back in Japan again, determined to make it work up north this time, whatever that took. The NPO was still there operating out of the same bases, but I wasn't working with them, I told the staff. On the flight to Tokyo I had decided what I needed to do. I had to confront the ocean. This, I knew, would either make or break me. I would begin to heal, or my tears would stay inside me forever and I would never be able to release my anger and raw pain.

I took the bullet train to Ichinoseki Station. There I rented a car as I wanted the freedom to take off on my own. I drove to Rikuzentakata and on to Ōfunato. The day after I arrived in Ōfunato, I drove to a scenic coastal park called *Goishi Kaigan*. I parked my car on the side of the road and walked with purpose to the water.

My rage was aimed at the sea. I knew this made no sense but I had decided the ocean was at fault. I didn't share this with anyone––no one would understand. I had to let the ocean know just what I thought. Picking up rocks as I went, I started cursing at the vast spread of water facing me. I hurled at it every name I could think of. I threw the rocks into the water, one after another. I knew it didn't hurt, my words and the rocks. The ocean has no skin, no feeling, no capacity to emote. I knew this. Still, I wanted to blame something, someone, to release the frustration of everyone around me including mine. I wanted to aim it at something specific.

I walked up and down the coast. I kicked the sand. I stomped on small marine creatures I couldn't identify. Everything associated with the ocean was bad, at least today. I had to take my anger out on whatever showed up in front of me. I cursed at the ocean all the while I walked, using the language I reserved for the most heinous. Eventually I sat down on the wet sand, drained, completely spent from sobbing and yelling.

It started to rain. My feet were already soaked from the waves I didn't bother to move away from. Now my clothes were soaked. Good. Now no one who sees me will wonder whether my face is blotchy from crying or from being out in the rain. They won't know whether I'm shaking with rage or cold. I couldn't remember the last time I was soaked through from head to foot. It was cleansing. I felt washed. I felt better.

I was going to be okay.

~~~

I spent the next ten days asking questions of the locals I had met along the way.

I started with Fuchigami-*san*, asking "What do you *really* need?" I posed the same question to the people at his dinners. I found myself face-to-face with business owners, restaurant operators, and men in various positions of local government. These were the people who would know the needs of their community. The consistent answer I received was "money." Both short- and long-term economic aid was necessary for true recovery to take place. There was already a slow but steady influx of cash at municipal level from the central government. But individual organizations, companies, schools, and projects were all competing against each other. Economic development: here was something specific and tangible.

David and I had several long virtual chats where we hammered out logistical details of what it would mean for me to move to Japan long-term. What would it be like for us to live apart, and how would that affect our marriage? We agreed we were strong enough as individuals and as a couple that we could handle a long-distance relationship for a little while. We made the choice for me to move to Japan to continue working in the disaster region.

This time I would get a work visa from a private organization that would give me the permission to stay in Japan but also the freedom to let me more freely move around. This was asking the near impossible I knew, and soon enough it became evident. One organization after another had slowly shaken heads and said, "Sadly, we're not prepared to help." Frustrated, one day I vented to a former international school classmate who lived in Tokyo. He had introduced me to a prominent CEO earlier in my stay and now pushed me to call him to ask this favor.

I rolled my eyes. "I've met the guy once and it wasn't particularly memorable," I said. "You two did most of the talking. He's not going to want to sponsor me."
"Just call him," my friend said.

Frustrated and out of options, I did. Mr. Michio Kanamaru, the CEO of Onizaki Corporation, at that time, agreed to meet me for lunch.

I spent the next several days preparing my pitch. There would be less than a minute to make my case. It needed to be short, to the point, powerful, and convincing. Concocting a 45-second speech, I memorized it complete with gestures at the right moments and emphasis on the right words. Nervous and excited, I headed to lunch with Mr. Kanamaru.

"So, what is it you want?" he asked me as he picked up the menu and started to read. Was he listening? Did he mean I was to make my case while he was reading the menu? I decided to dive in. I would leave the part of the pitch, "...and that's why I need a work visa sponsorship" to the very end of my 45-second speech.

I began, hitting all the blocking, the emphases and gestures (not that he saw them) perfectly on cue, just like I'd practiced. But about thirty seconds into my monologue, Mr. Kanamaru lowered his menu and said, "You need a visa? I'll sponsor you."

Euphoric and yet thoroughly annoyed that I didn't get to finish my well-rehearsed speech, I thanked him profusely, still in shock with a mixture of amazement and incredulity that it was this easy. Why hadn't I complained to my friend sooner?

We ate our meal, chatting as if we were old friends. To fulfill requirements, I had to fly back to the U.S. while he processed the work visa application, but within four weeks, a work visa was stamped into my passport. Both Mr. Kanamaru's speed at getting things done and his openness to letting me develop my own work schedule in Tōhoku were awesome beyond measure.

"Just report back every month so I know what you're doing, and I'll let you know when I have a project you can help me with from time to time, but other than that, go do your work in Tōhoku."

Carte blanche. Just like that. What an unbelievable stroke of luck and an unheard-of act of kindness and generosity. I hit the ground running. Weeks later, when I had returned to Tokyo to report on my work, I asked him why he had agreed so nonchalantly.

"You made it sound as if it was the most natural thing in the world, sponsoring me," I said.

"It was," he replied. "My company is headquartered in Kyūshū so sending my employees into the middle of Tōhoku wasn't an option. I gave money personally, I gave money on behalf of the company all to the Red Cross, but it's an entirely different feeling to be able to send someone there who can and will commit to helping. I'll of course tell people that I've sent one of my employees to Tōhoku to volunteer. But, I'm also willing to help you do what it is you came here for."

Next on my list was a real project. I decided to go to the most prominent person I knew. I asked for a meeting with Takahashi-*san*, the Diet member who had helped the NPO to get access to the first evacuation shelter as a base immediately after the disaster. She had said, "Call anytime." I hadn't until now.

We met for dinner and I told her my dilemma. I had tried to offer my services to a variety of organizations but no one seemed interested.
"Let me make a call," she said and picked up her cell phone.
"Toba-san?" she said, and chatted away. "I have someone here you should talk with right away."

I knew she was calling Mayor Toba of Rikuzentakata. She was calling the one man I had not reached out to. I had avoided calling Mayor Toba about working for the City of Rikuzentakata because I sensed they were in over their heads and asking for an appointment from anyone at Rikuzentakata City Hall was simply asking too much. I knew his story. I knew just how overworked people were at that particular City Hall. While volunteering with the NPO, I was in Rikuzentakata easily half of every week. I knew he and the city needed help, but didn't want to go as far as to ask for his time—especially since getting visa sponsorship from a municipality had proven more difficult than I had hoped.

As I explained why I had not reached out to him myself, Takahashi-*san* said, "I understand. We decide certain things in a disaster and even though in hindsight we know it doesn't make much sense, we stick with our initial reaction. You should ask him, though. Now is different from when you first came here. He'll have more mental and emotional space, more *yoyū* to work through how to use you."

Indeed, I did receive a call from Mayor Toba's staff at Rikuzentakata City Hall and within days he and I met. This was our first official meeting. We still don't agree on when this was, but the mayor came right to the point.

"Can you help me?"

I had prepared a pitch with a list of my skills and qualifications, like the one I'd given to others from the various cities in the region. But in that moment I saw the quiet, desperate pragmatism in Mayor Toba's expression. He didn't have time for that. He just needed an answer.

Swallowing my speech, I replied, "Yes, I can."

He nodded slowly, considering for a moment. Then his next words caught me off guard. "Good. I just need you to make things happen. Press coverage, donations, support, whatever you can get. I don't want you to come to me with every little thing. I don't have time to listen to every idea or approve whatever it is you want to do. I need you to act. I need you to make good decisions. Call me if it's something really big and you're absolutely certain you need my input. Or if someone is offering the city a lot of money. Other than that, you decide. I trust your judgment."

What was going on? I was a foreigner, and essentially a stranger. Mayor Toba was handing me permission and access to tell his story and to make something out of this blank check. Carte blanche again. I was flattered and touched, but the trust he placed in made no sense. Go make something happen? Who was this man?

Back-to-back I had spoken with and received unbelievable support from two key men: my new visa sponsor, Mr. Kanamaru, and Mayor Toba. Both offered free reign. Both had brought in a foreigner—and a woman, at that—

to take on a project with no precedent. Never in my 35 years of working with the Japanese had I experienced such a shocking turn of events, much less the same level of extreme generosity back-to-back.

The word *goen* came to mind. A word in Japanese with near-magical connotations, rich in meaning, *goen* says five things at once. The term represents luck, fate, miracles, synchronicity, all things wild and beautiful converging at the same time. It's the best-case-scenario that comes out of nowhere. These men had presented an incredible gift which I, in turn, would repay by doing everything possible to raise awareness and bring joy to a community and region distraught and broken.

Chapter 11

Futoshi Toba

This was going to be interesting. The American woman sitting facing me is offering help. Do I want her help? Yes. Should I get to know her before asking? Yes. Will I? No. She was certainly polite, and when she started to speak, she exuded a natural calm. But the dichotomy between her whiteness and the fluidity of her spoken Japanese was so jarring that it took me a few moments to stop staring. It was as if she thought a white foreign woman speaking flawless Japanese—just chatting away with me offering to help— was normal. As if this happened every day. On good days I could see these strange new experiences as positive. On bad days, these new developments were weird and off-putting. Had it not been for Mrs. Takahashi's introduction, I don't know that I would have met with Amya. It turned out, Amya would change people's lives in town. Mine included.

I realized quickly I didn't have the time to tell her what to do. She wasn't the right person to negotiate with government officials to expedite. She was, however, the perfect person to put in front of foreign visitors. It was a risk and I knew it. If she didn't work out, I would figure out a way to part ways. I didn't know her. I wasn't sure how well Mrs. Takahashi knew her. But I decided to risk it.

I told her to get press coverage, get donations, bring in foreign visitors, anything that would help keep the city relevant in the eyes of people not of here. I couldn't have her coming to me for permission for every little project. She had to be able to make these calls, to use her best judgment and just make something happen on her own without my input. Telling her to just get things done wasn't helpful and I felt bad for not being able to give her a specific assignment, but I had neither the time nor the inclination to specify how a foreigner could help. My words were less a test and more a testament to the fact that I was overwhelmed. Figure it out. Make something happen.

The next thing I knew, she was translating my daily Facebook posts. I had found refuge and comfort in being able to complain online to a largely unknown audience. Their anonymity helped me feel less guilty in venting. Amya took my posts and translated them into English. Then she found translators around the world who translated my posts into Arabic, Korean, Spanish, German, and French. Within a matter of days, the city's Facebook page had several thousand additional followers, all foreign. At first I found her initiative off-putting. She hadn't asked my permission to translate my personal Facebook posts. Then again, I realized I was used to being asked everything by everyone. Hadn't I told her not to come to me with every little thing? She had listened. I decided to trust her judgment.

One day I saw her name on my list of appointments. She was booked into my calendar for five minutes. Five minutes? I was surprised the secretaries even booked a meeting that short. Normally the shortest meeting I had would have been thirty minutes. Amya's ideas and plans and methods were new. No one spoke their thoughts about her out loud when she was at City Hall but if I was reading the faces of my staff correctly, there was certainly a buzz that came with her in the room. She exuded energy.

Three knocks on my office door, and I said "Come in." Amya popped her head in and walked toward my desk, started to speak. There was no preamble. No small talk. She dove right in.

"How would you feel about being a speaker at a press conference? At the Foreign Correspondents' Club of Japan?" She said as she pulled out a chair at the conference table and sat down.

I obviously knew of the Foreign Correspondents' Club of Japan. Their indigo felt banner with gold embroidered letters was a familiar backdrop for press conferences of well-known speakers from around the world. News outlets showed up when speakers were booked there. Press conferences at the FCCJ were a big deal. I told her I would go. Gladly.

"Good!" she said. "Thanks. I'll make it happen. Well, that's all I have for today. I figured this was a big enough venue that I should ask your permission before just booking you." She grinned. I couldn't help but grin back.

"And I wanted to say hello," she said. She waved her hand at me and said, "Hi" in English. I laughed. It felt good to laugh.

Soon, we had foreign media in town. For a while, it seemed every time I saw Amya, she had a different camera crew in tow. Amya had cast a wide net, covering news outlets from a variety of countries. Sometimes the news crew wanted to interview me, other times Amya had arranged for them to meet the locals. I liked her approach in helping the world to understand both perspectives; mine differed from that of the residents in town. I was a victim and a leader, the one in charge. The residents were all going through varying degrees of trauma, and none of them felt the responsibility to rebuild the way I did. Some handled their trauma better than others. Showing all of this, what life was really like here, helped people understand us better. I wanted to make sure others didn't have to endure what we in Rikuzentakata had gone through. Getting the word out was of paramount importance.

City Hall started receiving letters of support from foreigners all across the globe. Word was getting out. I never wrote any replies, assuming Amya would handle that, which she did. I was informed only if we received a letter from a noted celebrity or politician, someone whose name I would recognize. Amya told me later that for those letters, she wrote back as me. I remember signing a series of letters in English but it didn't register how unusual this was. I watched in fascination at the speed in which she operated and how comfortable she seemed to be about asking for help.

Whom to trust, when, how, and why. In a crisis—when defenses are down and nerves are fried, tensions mounting and endless bullshit paperwork that makes us think someone is enjoying making us go through all of this—trust is scarce. Trusting a stranger, a foreigner, even someone with the obvious knowledge Amya had, this trust I placed in her didn't sit well with everyone. Did she sense there was jealousy? Perhaps. Although I made every effort I could to introduce her to the residents in the area, not everyone knew who she was. The announcement I had formally hired her on as a consultant without pay all made the news, and at the formal ceremony there were just as many Japanese journalists present as there were heads of various City Hall departments.

Still, her obvious foreignness startled some people in town. In a city the size of Rikuzentakata, there just weren't many foreigners. Those in town were known. Amya's presence became known only with time. Even then, the assumption from everyone who met her was that she spoke little to no Japanese. It took several minutes of stunned silence for shopkeepers to realize that they were speaking to a foreigner in Japanese.

She seemed to blaze ahead with little or no input from others. By the time late 2011 came and the wet chill settled in through the long, dark winter months, Amya had made herself at home in Rikuzentakata. When the first memorial service came in March 2012, Amya was in attendance, sitting alongside others in dark coats. When I saw her crying, I got it. This pain, our pain, was real for her. She hadn't lost anyone in the disaster, but still she understood our grief.

I decided I was right to trust her.

Chapter 12

Amya Miller

Rikuzentakata was the only city in the disaster region that brought on a foreigner, specifically an English-speaker, to be their spokesperson. My position was unorthodox, a one-of-a-kind job. There was no template or precedent. I could do what I wanted. I knew with my presence I could help draw attention to the city. I was as much a coordinator as a curiosity—I was a contact point for the international media, as well as a unique story for the Japanese media.

The fact that the city had been so profoundly flattened had made it a powerful visual tool for the press. That, combined with a mayor who was willing to be brutally honest and outspoken, meant that it hadn't taken long for journalists to begin flocking to Rikuzentakata. My presence at City Hall meant I could coordinate with the media who wanted to make contact with residents, as well as people who wanted to make donations, conduct research, and volunteer. More and more foreigners started to show up in town.

I went to Mayor Toba requesting a formal title to use when contacting the press.

"I can't very well say I'm a volunteer calling from Rikuzentakata City Hall," I told him.
"You're right," he said. "What do you want to be?"
"I have to come up with the title? Isn't that your job?" I grinned.
"You want me to give you a title?" he said, his head cocked to the side. "You'll be okay with whatever title I give you?" Now he was the one grinning. This was a test, his private joke on me.
"Scratch that. I'll come up with my own title."

"I thought so," he said, and we both laughed.

Soon there was a new Director of Global Public Relations.

Dozens of publications began to contact me, some foreign and some Japanese. They asked to have conversations with the locals, to inquire about their experiences, and document the ordeals they'd been through. I contacted the people who had told me their stories and set up interviews. Here, finally, I was in a position to discuss resilience as I saw it. Everyone around me had stories. It was a matter of finding those who were willing to go public and talk openly.

The presence of foreign media resonated among the locals. Before the disaster, few people from Rikuzentakata had had any interactions with foreigners. Many locals were astonished and moved by the fact that strangers from all over the world—people who they would never have met—were interested in their struggle, so much so that media organizations were prepared to ship entire camera crews overseas. Although some of the locals were less enthusiastic about sharing their town with swarming camera crews, they also understood that press coverage drummed up interest in the city and encouraged people to come to town and spend money. Economic recovery was connected to press coverage. A mixed blessing. Talking and dealing with the media became part of the landscape of recovery.

"It's proof we're not forgotten," Mitsu-*san* said. Introduced to me through a city council member in town, she was a former sales manager for one of the companies in Rikuzentakata. She had already carved out a path for herself in her youth—women were not sales managers in the 1950s and 60s—now at 80 years of age, she was still formidable. Mitsu-*san* wasn't outspoken but was instead more of a hands-on personality. Age gave her the comfort of not having to edit her words and Mitsu-*san* took full advantage of this.

"We know when foreigners are here, because unless they're Asian, you foreigners don't blend in," Mitsu-*san* told me one afternoon, chuckling. "We also like it because someone cared enough to bring them, or they cared enough to show up. Either way, it matters to us," she said.

Mitsu-*san* decided she wanted to help with the town's recovery any way she could, so she rolled up her sleeves and did just that.

"I'm going to teach myself to sew," she told me during one visit. I had brought persimmons and little tubs of vanilla and caramel custard, the former for her and latter for me. Mitsu-*san* knew she was past the age to be considered as a candidate for volunteer work, so she would have to carve out a new niche for herself. So she bought herself a sewing machine. I asked if she'd ever sewn before.

"In middle school. Maybe high school as well. Home Economics class, I think. We all had to learn," she said. "But that was sewing by hand."
"What are you going to make?".
"Dresses," she said, and before I could comment, "Do you want one?"
"Of course!" I said. "I absolutely want one."
"Good," she said. "I'll practice on you, and then when I get good enough, I'll donate the dresses to people who need clothing."

~~~

With so many foreign journalists coming to town, some of the stories started to sound similar. Competition led to constant pressure to find a new angle, a different and compelling story that was bigger and more dramatic.

One day the owner of a local pub came to me after his interview, frustrated with the way he had been treated by a reporter. "The guy wanted to see inside my house," he said. "He wanted me to call my wife and ask if they could come over right then. No preparation, no warning. Did you know about this?"

I shook my head, confused. I hadn't authorized anything like that, and the journalist hadn't cleared it with me. He'd just said he wanted an interview in the man's pub.

"My wife was livid. She felt like she couldn't tell them no. It didn't matter that they were a major newspaper; she didn't want them in our home. She ended up allowing them inside, but she was still furious."

It turned out that many of the journalists and writers were asking this of their interviewees, all unannounced. After the questions were done, they would spring a request to see inside the person's home, the temporary housing provided. How small were the rooms; what were the living conditions? What was it like to have such thin walls? Did they miss their old homes? That last one question was infuriating. Of course, they missed their old homes. Questions like that, designed to elicit tears, felt like the journalists were baiting these people. "I thought you painted the Japanese as resilient," I wanted to say. "What's with trying to get them to cry on camera?"

Battles with the journalists were more common than I would have liked. After the incident with the pub owner, I had to tell all journalists that homes were off-limits. I started asking to see a list of their questions ahead of time, knowing this would be turned down—and it always was. But I had to keep on asking, keeping the subject out there and building a reputation. They needed to know that I cared about having some control over what kinds of questions were going to be put to the residents.

One major international newspaper asked to show up and meet with Mayor Toba two days before the city memorial service planned for March 11th. It was to be a large and complex affair, a time for remembrance, tears, grief, and reflection. The mayor's schedule around the memorial had been booked months in advance. Two days was not nearly enough lead time. I turned them down.

"What about before he leaves the house?" the reporter asked me. "Can we visit him the morning of the memorial, first thing? At his home?"

Were they serious? No, they absolutely could not do that. The mayor wanted family time with his sons. The boys needed their father as they remembered the day they lost their mother.

"No, the mayor is booked solid."

The journalist wangled a meeting with the Deputy Mayor and grossly misquoted him. The Deputy Mayor, thoroughly annoyed, showed me the article. I, too, had been shocked at the freedom with which the journalist had twisted his words. I called her and complained and told them they weren't welcomed back, my first experience banning a publication from writing about the city.

As complex as the residents' relationship was to the press, things got even worse when it came to tourists. Rikuzentakata is off the beaten path. It's a minimum seven-hour drive from Tokyo, or a three-hour ride on the bullet train plus a one-hour drive across the mountains. For foreigners to have spent the time and money to get here was proof they knew of the city, and cared enough to make the trip. Tourists were also the ones who would leave behind money. Economic survival of shops and restaurants was dependent on the influx of cash from visitors.

Still, not all visitors demonstrated the kind of sensitivity the residents needed. Locals consistently expressed their frustration and irritation to me about tourist buses and cars driving through temporary housing complexes gawking and taking photos.

"It's as if we're in a zoo," Ozawa-*san* told me. "Like we're on display. I hate it."

The reluctance toward welcoming guests, even those who left behind money, came to me through a friend from City Hall. I had just pulled into the parking lot in front of the prefabricated City Hall and this woman came walking toward my car. I waved as she approached, but she only gestured for me to roll down the window.

"Guess what someone said to me today?" she asked. I could hear the tension in her voice.
"What?"
"They said 'Oh, the disaster must have been so hard on you,'" she said, her voice mockingly high. "Must have been! Past tense! She said that in the past tense!" The woman was visibly angry.
"She wasn't from here, I take it?" I asked.
"No, some visitor from Tokyo," she replied. "They come here, seeing what they want to see and assuming we're all fine? What, because we live in temporary housing now as opposed to sleeping on the floor of a gymnasium? That makes it all fine now?"

I didn't respond.

"Sorry," she said, still fuming. "I just had to tell someone. I felt like I was going to explode."

This was not the first time I heard this complaint about the use of past tense, suggesting people's ordeal was over. The tourists and visitors and the Japanese press all urged the people they saw to *ganbatte*—a catch-all Japanese phrase of encouragement. The word meant everything from "hang in there" to "do your best" to "you can do this" to "go, go, go!" I could tell that people around me were sick of hearing it. Maybe *ganbatte* was well-meaning, but the people here couldn't help but want to respond, "What? It looks like we're not trying?"

Saying "it must have been hard" came with an implied follow-up: "But you're all better now, yes?" In those days, I knew of no one in Rikuzentakata to whom that applied.

Chapter 13

Amya Miller

I approached Mayor Toba with a bold idea. How would he feel about being a speaker at a press conference? At the Foreign Correspondents' Club of Japan? Their headquarters was foreign-media-central in Japan. All major foreign publications as well as freelance journalists called the 20th floor of a building in Yūrakuchō (central Tokyo) their hub, at that time.[11] Press conferences held here were notable. Dynamic and well-known speakers had graced the podium—the Dalai Lama, Ai Weiwei, Muhammed Ali, several Japanese Prime Ministers, as well as a high-profile sumo wrestler.

Surely getting Mayor Toba on the same stage would garner press. And the foreign media in Japan were certainly known for publishing facts the Japanese media couldn't or wouldn't touch. Here was an excellent way to get the word out about what was really happening in the disaster region. It was time to start taking real control over the narrative. It was time to take the power back.

"Go for it," Mayor Toba said. "That's good. If you can get me in, I'll gladly go."

I quickly called and secured an appointment. I knew Mayor Toba was a dynamic personality who spoke without a script. He had compelling stories and was open to sharing them. He had also started to say publicly that he had made mistakes, a highly unusual move for a Japanese politician. Having the foreign media as an audience, I was sure, would get the word out: Tōhoku still needed help, the past tense didn't apply, *ganbatte* was the wrong word. The world needed to know. I pitched my case for having Mayor Toba as a speaker and was quickly approved. His reputation already solid among the foreign and Japanese media, here was a chance to hear directly from someone known for his bluntness.

The press conference was packed. Standing room only. The Mayor did not mince words, and dove in. He got straight to the point.

"I've been labeled in the foreign media as a troublemaker," he began, and I saw backs stiffen in the audience. "But if being a troublemaker is what it takes to get noticed and improve the situation in Rikuzentakata, then I won't let up." Inwardly, I gave him my own private standing ovation at that moment. This was going to be good.

Mayor Toba blasted the two prime ministers of the Democratic Party of Japan, criticizing both of them for being unable to make any changes in protocol or policy that were helpful to the disaster region. He criticized the establishment of the Reconstruction Agency during their tenure. The agency was meant to be a point of contact for municipalities in the disaster region needing permission to move forward on their various projects, coordinating the paperwork. Instead, it became just one more agency to report to—a burden that Mayor Toba pointedly told them he did not have time for. The establishment of the new agency, meant to be a through point that simplified the process, instead created more work and did no streamlining.

Then he said something unexpected, something I'd never heard him say before. He denounced Prime Minister Naoto Kan,[12] who had been in office when the disaster hit. Mayor Toba's main objection with Prime Minister Kan was his abrupt announcement of resignation in August 2011, just five months after the disaster.

"What leader of a country just resigns in the middle of a disaster and then is not held accountable? He went on a pilgrimage. Our nation needed a leader, but he chose that moment to go on a pilgrimage to find himself. Was he serious? Why was he allowed to walk away without taking any responsibility for the things he left unresolved? What country lets this happen?"

The mayor was going full throttle. After Prime Minister Kan, he started in on the next Prime Minister Yoshihiko Noda.[13] Neither prime minister understood the severity of the disaster. Mayor Toba held them personally responsible for the ineptitude and lack of understanding of the needs of the people in the disaster region. He spoke out against their inability and unwillingness to adjust the normal rules and protocols in acknowledgement of the disaster. He told the world how, by spinning their wheels over paperwork, the Japanese government had inexcusably slowed recovery for the regions that needed help the most.

Here again, Mayor Toba was not shy about criticizing the government's lack of priority. Tōhoku, he said, had not been a priority because it had no economic or fiscal power, and its population was dwindling and aging. If the disaster had occurred somewhere else—somewhere that mattered—the sixteen-month processing time for paperwork alone would never have been tolerated.

How many times that afternoon did I imagine myself standing and applauding? Mayor Toba made a powerful impact on people. He concluded the press conference by saying he had two missions in life. The first, to see the reconstruction of Rikuzentakata through to the end. And the second, to raise his two sons. I had heard this reference before—to be a good father—and I had repeated it for him many times as I interpreted his words. I had to fight tears every time he said this. Yes, all else mattered, but this mattered most. Japanese politicians, indeed many Japanese men, do not express that sentiment very often and certainly not in public.

The Mayor's entire speech was unheard-of in the realm of Japanese press. Nobody went that deep or public in their criticism of the nation's government or heads of state—and certainly nobody was that openly emotional. Mayor Toba thanked the onlookers for their support of Tōhoku, and the room erupted into applause before the interpreter could finish relating his final words. He'd struck a chord, and the response was tremendous.

Mayor Toba made his point. He criticized and stood firm. He made a case for more and better support. His story was poignant and gripping, and he made a powerful statement through the humanity and character he brought to his work. He was a man who was hard to ignore, and the press knew it.

We were about to have another influx of press coverage by major international media.

Chapter 14

Futoshi Toba

The level of disconnect between the disaster region and the central government in Tokyo was exhausting and never-ending. They found new ways of infuriating me. They constantly asked us for more mountains of paperwork, more explanations for very straightforward projects, more updates and trips to Tokyo to deliver my report in person—it was as if they thought I had nothing better to do than to justify everything to them.

With the media I had been open about my frustration with the central government, and in some of the English publications I'd been labeled "The Angry Mayor." I was fine with that. I was definitely angry. I was tired of doing everything at the unnecessarily slow pace dictated by Tokyo. I was tired of watching the government not even pretend to care. I was tired of waiting.

In one of my speeches somewhere down in southern Japan I made the comment that if the Tōhoku disaster had happened anywhere else in Japan, recovery would have been completed by now. The Japanese press jumped on that. My comment made headlines. I received several phone calls from people in Tokyo with stern warnings that my words had gone over poorly among the senior ministers. I didn't care. If it took negative press coverage of the government to get things moving, I would gladly continue speaking up.

When I was away from town, I found myself expressing my misgivings publicly in my speeches, but back in the city I had bottled things up as expected. It was a strange balance. I knew that my people needed to see me as collected and in control while I oversaw the town's recovery, just as I told my staff they couldn't appear openly sad on the job in the first few weeks after the disaster. The principle was still true. I could be the angry mayor on the road, but while I was here, I had to stay even-tempered.

With all the media attention on Rikuzentakata and all the visitors arriving, I was most frustrated that my level temper in town was seen as heroic. I recall I once snapped at a foreign visitor when they made a comment about how incredibly resilient I was. Amya was interpreting for me at the time, and she looked at me and said, "there's not an easy equivalent in Japanese." She tried to explain the word resilience, stringing together a few descriptive words. I recognized what they meant, but I didn't see it as a compliment at all.

"I'm not resilient. I'm exhausted," I snapped at the person who'd made the comment. "What you see as resilience is a cover. I'm annoyed and tired. You see me as resilient because you're seeing what you want to see, that the Japanese are born with a national trait of patience in our DNA. But under this mask is exhaustion."

The Japanese praise the idea of *gaman*—pushing down our true feelings in order to persevere through difficult situations. Seven times falling down, eight times getting back up. Not complaining is a fundamental aspect of Japanese culture. But for disaster victims, this attitude isn't helpful. In situations like ours, *gaman* is stifling and repressive.

The Japanese government offered us help with posters bearing slogans like "*Ganbare Tōhoku!*"—asking the people of Tōhoku to "hang in there." But that didn't solve our problem at all. My people are depressed, confused, and beaten-down. Telling us to "hang in there" is like offering a handshake while we're drowning. These simple words of encouragement only served to absolve the rest of the nation from any responsibility to actually help. They upheld the status quo and shifted the burden of recovery onto us. It was on us to make the best of our situation, to hang in there. These slogans told us that by doing *gaman* we could overcome anything, and that idea was supposed to comfort us while we slept behind thin walls among the ruins of our former lives. Anyone who doesn't hang in there, who dares to speak up and admit they're miserable and needs help, is labeled a dissenter. Or an Angry Mayor.

Speaking up about the pain we're supposed to be hiding was especially hard to do for people in Tōhoku, not just for me. It's an open secret that there's an inferiority complex among those from Tōhoku. This part of Japan is so rural it was considered almost backwards. There's nothing romantic about being from this part of the country. The regional dialect and accent is mocked, and there's a general assumption that those from Tōhoku are uneducated and lacking in sophistication. These stereotypes are hard to dismantle.

This inferiority complex kept us downtrodden. Open opposition to authority was still shunned. Traditions were upheld to a fault. Rather than examine alternatives, we defaulted to tradition because "that's the way we've always done it." Where the rest of Japan has moved on, Tōhoku was a place where time stood still. I imagined this place as a time capsule, similar to what Tokyo was like in the 1960s and 1970s.

This was why the locals objected to my frequent business trips, to my outspoken speeches and comments criticizing the central government's pace. "None of the other mayors in the region complain," they said. I wanted to shout back at them, "Exactly! That's why it's going so slowly! That's why I have to!" But I knew I couldn't.

If my projects were going to succeed, if the pace of reconstruction was going to speed up, and if real progress was going to be made in this city, I needed more allies. I needed the younger generation to join in in raising their voices. I focused on those in the community who did understand what I was trying to do and encouraged them to bring their friends and family into the fold.

City Hall staff fielded complaints about the pace at which reconstruction was progressing. "Why doesn't Ōfunato have this problem?" they would ask. Really? I wanted to get sarcastic and say, "Oh, I don't know. Because they have double our population? Because they have a functioning city center and city hall, a big hospital, multiple schools, supermarkets, and fire departments? Because the damage to their city is much much less than ours?" I didn't. Prolonged shock and grief, exhaustion and restlessness, loneliness and the lack of joy were evident in questions like these.

I had begun rebuilding my house. I decided to prioritize the health of my sons. We needed to learn how to live together, the three of us. We needed a routine. We needed to be a family. Still, with Kumi gone I couldn't very well leave them at home for extended periods of time. My uncle offered the land behind his house and said I could build there. This was a generous and remarkable offer. The boys could continue going in and out of my uncle's home where they'd been staying since the day of the disaster. We would live right next to them, in their backyard practically. I could travel, work late, have dinner meetings, drink with constituents all as I was expected to as the head of the city, and the boys would have dinner at my uncle's. Here, Kumi's absence was real. Again. There was a hole in the fabric of our family. There would always be. But at least our sons were safe, cared for albeit by others, and I could continue doing my job. I was trying. Having a house of our own was the first step. I believed, in time, I would be able to make meals for them, and be at home at a reasonable hour. Be dad. Until then, we all pitched in and did our share of *gaman*.

Chapter 15

Amya Miller

In order to understand what tangible deeds were possible for the city and its residents, the place to start would be connecting with the people of this town. Anyone and everyone's story needed to be heard and some collected. What were people feeling? What did they want? How could the outside world help?

So began various kinds of little "occasions," for tea and cakes, drinks and dinner. With chefs, businessmen and businesswomen, shopkeepers, housewives, young mothers, employees from the sake brewery, teachers for kindergarten and high school—anyone who would agree to meet and tell me their stories. Some wanted dinner. Others just wanted to drink. A restaurant in a temporary facility, an *izakaya*, and sometimes a small coffee shop became my new meeting spots. All three of these venues were made out of the same prefabricated material as City Hall—metal sheets on the outside, plywood walls on the inside.

Friends brought friends, invitations into homes came, each new voice revealing a different side of the disaster. Although their trauma source was mutual, each of these people had been through something different, and all were ready to talk.

At first it was surprising that these people opened up so quickly, displaying an unexpected level of honesty with a complete stranger. But the more encounters, the more what was unique about this experience became evident. As a foreigner, I was the furthest thing from a local that anyone could find living in this town. Also, people noticed they were talking with a volunteer who had stuck around and was fluent in Japanese. I was even picking up the local dialect, to everyone's amusement.

For these people, there was safety in being able to open up to a complete outsider. The community was so tight-knit that the locals wouldn't dare share these raw emotional stories with each other. That would violate the deepest taboo, the understanding that people were not to compare pain with one another. So when they sat down with me, an outsider, and shared coffee or drinks, the words poured out.

I heard stories of all kinds. Genuine and intense. Gut-wrenchingly horrific losses, acts of grace, survival by sheer luck. Some were private joys or sorrow, and the grief and trauma and elation needed no sharing with a global audience. Others confessed moments where they had made split-second life or death decisions, and now they had to live with the consequences of their choices.

"I was in Rikuzentakata when the earthquake hit," a local rice seller told me. "I wanted to get home to my parents, but I wasn't sure I could make it back safely because I didn't know how well the roads held up. I'd also heard the emergency broadcast and was worried about the possibility of a tsunami. So I decided to go to a designated evacuation shelter downtown. The closest one I could think of was the city gymnasium. When I got there it was already full. Someone turned me away at the door, saying they couldn't take in anyone else. It turns out it was a good thing," he looked down, slowly stirring his coffee. "You know what happened to the gymnasium."

I did. The gymnasium was designated as one of the city's evacuation buildings. People fled there when the waters started rising, but the building quickly filled with water all the way to the rafters. Once the water pressure became too much for the walls to handle, the back wall of the gymnasium blew out and everyone trapped inside was sucked out along with the water. Between 80 to 100 people who had evacuated there died.

Then there was Mana, an outspoken single mother of three young children who lost the nail salon she owned and operated. Unafraid to stand out in a town of gray sweaters and drab clothing, she wore red and gold and believed in lipstick and of course, painted fingernails. Every day after picking up her daughter from preschool, the four-year-old girl would ask, "Mama, can you drive past your salon?" Mana would drive her to the exact location and park the car. And then, the daughter's face and hands would be glued to the window as she stared at the empty lot where her mother's business used to stand.

"I don't know what that was about," Mana said. "I just know it was important to her. Then one day, my daughter says that she doesn't need to go see the spot anymore. She says she's okay now. Then she tells me, 'Mama, if a tsunami comes to this town again, I'll protect you. I'll beat it up for you.' I picked her up in a big hug, thanking her, while I fought back laughter and tears."

Mana had a friend that lost everyone but her father-in-law. Her three children, her husband, both parents and mother-in-law, all gone. "What am I supposed to say to her?" Mana asked me. I could find no suitable words.

A city councilman, Shimizu-*san*, discussed how he lost his wife. He was the one of the few exceptions of a man who would openly cry. Shimizu-*san* would drive me through town in his small squarish car pointing out spots that were important to him. "I'm told there was a group of people standing here, a bunch from the neighborhood who had escaped together," he tells me on one such drive. "Then suddenly, one of the women sees her dog near her house and calls out to it, but it doesn't hear her. Before anyone can stop her, she runs down the hill toward her house to get her dog. By this time, people on the hill see the tsunami coming toward them and start screaming at her to leave the dog and come back. She doesn't. She didn't make it. Neither did the dog." He used his white handkerchief to wipe his eyes.

Rikuzentakata City Hall had a disaster preparedness plan and there were committees designated ahead of time, filled with members who knew their roles. One man's job was to go out into the town in the event of a disaster and get people moving toward the shelters. Hearing the tsunami warning, he did just that. He saw that a large group of people had congregated in a park near City Hall—exactly as they were supposed to—and called out to them to evacuate to the civic center across the street from City Hall, a three-story building that he was sure would keep them safe. How many went inside? He doesn't know. The civic center had four survivors.

A young man told about the red claw marks that appeared on his arm every time he took a bath. "This is where the person I was trying to hang onto slipped through my fingers. Before I lost him, his fingers gouged me. I don't know why it turns bright red every time I take a bath. Am I going to have this scar the rest of my life?"

A man went from shelter to shelter, looking for his elderly mother. Unsuccessful, he kept on hoping one of these times he'd be told "she's here." On one such trip to yet another shelter, he came across a group of older men in their 80s and 90s smoking outside a short distance from the front entrance. One of them gestured to the man to come over. "I'm looking for my mother," he said to the elder. "Have you seen her?"

"I was just going to tell you," the elder said. "She..." he stopped. The elder looked up at the sky. The man followed his gaze. What was he looking at? "She..." the elder started again and made a circular motion in the air followed by a noise like, "*pudapudapuda*."

Completely lost, the man decided the elder meant his mother had gone up to the skies. She had died. She was gone. What the noise was he didn't know, but the circular motion must have meant she was making her way upward. She was in heaven. "She's had a good, long life," the man thought. He thanked the elder and went inside the shelter. He said later that he didn't know what he was looking for in the shelter, now that he knew his mother was dead. He had been headed to the shelter when he encountered the group of old men, and it felt like the right thing to do, to go on in. Once inside, a young woman came running up to him.

"Your mother," she said, out of breath, "the Self Defense Force took her."

"Do you know where?" he asked her.

"I think to a hospital inland," she said.

He stood looking at the young woman. Why would the Self Defense Force take his mother inland? To a morgue, he decided. That had been kind of the Self Defense Force guys. A bit weird, though. There were morgues all over town in the school gymnasiums. Still, it was a nice gesture, to take her to a hospital morgue instead of laying her out on a cold floor somewhere. As the man was thinking this, the woman suddenly said, "Oh! I have something for you." She dug in her coat pocket. "Here," she said, handing a man a folded piece of paper. "This is the number of the hospital your mother is at."

The man went to City Hall where there were telephones available for the public to use, and dialed the number of the hospital. He reached a hospital receptionist and gave his name, asking if his mother was in the morgue. He then gave her name. Before he could ask to be transferred to the morgue, he heard a series of clicks and then his mother's voice.

"Hello?" she said. *Moshimoshi*.

"Ma?" the man said, stunned.

"I was wondering when you'd find out where I was," she said.

"Ma?" the man said, again. How was she not dead? The elder said she was dead.

"What?" his mother replied.

He didn't know what to ask next. He couldn't very well ask why she wasn't dead.

"I rode on a helicopter," he heard her say. "I fell and broke my hip and they had to move me in a helicopter," she said.

The man wanted to laugh. His mother was alive. The "*pudapudapuda*" sound and the circular motion of the elder's hand were not the mother's soul ascending to heaven. It was a helicopter flying her away for surgery.

He made his way back to the shelter the next day and found the same elder outside, smoking again.

"Thank you for telling me about my mother," he said. "I'm glad the Self Defense Force helicopter came and got her."

"Helicopter!" the elder said. "That's the word! I couldn't remember the word. That's why I made that noise. *Pudapudapuda*," he said again, beaming. "It was bugging me all last night. I just couldn't remember the word. Thanks for telling me." The elder put out his cigarette, clapped the man on his shoulder and walked away.

At one point, Mayor Toba, too, weighed in with a significant anecdote. He revealed that he refused to delete on his cell phone the phone numbers of over a hundred people, friends and colleagues whom he'd lost in the disaster. While he would never speak to them again, deleting their numbers was an act of finality he couldn't bring himself to take.

There were dozens of stories like these. Collecting certain ones, I could call on major international media outlets, ask for appointments with bureau chiefs as well as independent journalists. These stories could remind the world that the people of Rikuzentakata were still human even though the disaster was fading from the headlines. They had suffered an unthinkable loss, and they needed anything and everything the world could give.

I made sure the stories didn't overlap. Two different news agencies reporting on a story about the same person wouldn't do. The stories were deep and intense. I wanted coverage. Broad coverage. Casting a wide net seemed prudent.

Mitsu-*san*, my mother figure in Rikuzentakata, the woman who taught herself to sew at age 80 was someone whose story I saved for the journalist who I felt would cover her the best. I enjoyed chatting with her. Her skin was flawless, tight on her face as if she'd had multiple facelifts. I knew she hadn't and couldn't understand how with her crinkling eyes as she laughed and her increasing years hadn't taken a toll on her outlook, her skin, and her attitude. Several weeks after she had told me she had bought a sewing machine, I had a few minutes between meetings and called to see if she was available for a chat. Knowing what little she lived on, it would be an excuse to deliver some food—fruit, vegetables, rice, and other staple foods she liked.

"I'm running to a meeting, but could I swing by? I just want to say hi."
Mitsu-*san* laughed. "Sure, I'm home. I'm not going anywhere."
"Are you okay?" I asked.
"Yes, just my knee."

Before the disaster Mitsu-*san* lived in town, close to a steep ridge on top of which perched one of the local middle schools. When the ground began shaking on March 11, she knew she had to get to safety, so she ran out of her small house and started climbing the ridge. Feet slipping, fingernails breaking, the 80-year-old woman clung to tree roots as she pulled herself up the hill.

"I started to lose strength in my hands or arms, so the going was slow. But, more importantly, I didn't want to die, so I just pushed with my feet, up and up, a bit at a time. I had to make sure my footing was solid. That wasn't easy on a steep ridge of dirt. I finally made it though. I never imagined in my lifetime that I would tell anyone about having to flee for my life. That it was up to me to save myself. We just don't grow up that way anymore, do we? We're so used to everything being low-key. We're spoiled by peace."

What Mitsu-*san* didn't know as she was fleeing for her life was that she had twisted her knee during the climb. Shock masking the pain, she didn't realize this until she was in the shelter, completely covered in dirt, that her knee was throbbing. She's had problems with her knee ever since.
"Do you want to go for a walk?" I asked over the phone, as I made my way to her house. "Stretch it a bit?"
"No, it's better if I stay inside today. I walked yesterday. I have to pace myself."

I pulled into the unmarked parking lot behind the row of metal temporary housing where she lived.

"I'm almost there. Don't come out. I'll just run up quickly and pop my head in." I grabbed the grocery bags full of fruits and vegetables, *miso* paste and a small bag of rice. I slid her front door open and stepped inside. "Mitsu-*san*? I'm coming in. No need to get up, I won't stay long."

The hallway leading from her front entrance of her temporary housing was perhaps two meters long. Her kitchen was to the left: countertop, sink, a stove with two burners, and a refrigerator. I saw her sitting in her living room that doubled as a dining room as well as a bedroom. Her sewing machine perched on her bed made out of sturdy cardboard boxes. She looked up at me, beaming.

"You seem well," I said, "and happy."

"Look," she pointed to the wall separating her bedroom from the kitchen. There I saw a row of three dresses on plastic hangers. One was a plain but bright purple, another brown with white flowers. The last bore a print of bold, horizontal lines that alternated black, yellow, white, and green lines.

"They're for you," she said proudly. I whipped my head around.

"Did you make those?" I asked, turning around again and walking up to the garments and admiring the fabric between my fingers.

"I did," she says. "I even surprised myself!"

"They're gorgeous!"

"Really? I wasn't sure you'd like the brown one or the one with all those colors. I didn't have a lot of choice," she says, suddenly shy. "The fabric was all donated. I used what I could find."

As I admired these homemade clothes and the tenacity of the woman sitting before me, I thought of the other people throughout this region who were stepping up just like Mitsu-*san*. There were plenty more stories like hers. My job was to convince the media to tell these stories the way we wanted them told.

Months after the disaster, these people were still learning and growing and trying to rebuild their lives. If the only way to get the press to focus on the disaster in as accurate a way as possible. There was a lot of journalistic emphasis on the nuclear meltdown, on the reactor in Fukushima. There had been plenty of demeaning headlines in print and online, implying all of Tōhoku was radioactive, speculating about potential fallout disasters with skull and crossbones and mushroom clouds. It was cruel—the recourse of a global media that had gotten bored admiring the resiliency of people like Mitsu-*san* who still lived in the so-called radioactive area the press was trumpeting about. Somehow, we had to humanize the disaster, reclaim control of the narrative, centering the story of recovery on the people who actually were needing attention and the aid it could bring. It was time we insisted on telling the stories we wanted to tell and that meant putting the human element front and center.

I turned back to Mitsu-*san*. "The dresses are lovely," I said. "I'll wear one next time I see you. It'll be a surprise which one." She beamed.

Chapter 16

Futoshi Toba

As Amya collected stories from the locals and wrote them up for the global audience, and as more foreign journalists came to town and our stories became known, I felt a strong urge to add a new element to these stories. Sections of my city were largely flattened because of the tsunami, but more specifically the height of the tsunami. Earthquake drills and neighborhood tsunami evacuation plans had not prepared us for a disaster of this magnitude. We had to start talking about how to prepare ourselves for another disaster, and we had to do this now as we rebuilt the city. No future generation of Rikuzentakata residents would ever go through what we had just gone through. I was relentless in conveying this message and called for a complete overhaul of our disaster preparation and evacuation manual, and policies.

We had to create a new evacuation plan, practice drills that would ensure our safety, and rebuild the city at the same time. I might not be able to guarantee everyone would survive the next disaster but I had to at least try. The new city had to be built in such a way that it offered concrete plans for security.

In order to add safety and security into our plan, we had to understand what happened that led to such a high death toll in the city. We had all grown up knowing about and practicing drills. Still, almost one in ten people in town had died. Why? Did they not evacuate? If so, why not? And who were these people who had not evacuated? I decided to conduct a massive data-collection project. Not repeating mistakes meant I first had to know what mistakes had been made. I tasked Takashi, my Deputy Mayor, with this data-collection project. I knew in order for this information to be useful to a wide audience, the report from the data collected would have to be written up in a certain way. I wasn't much for writing academic papers but Takashi could. What he lacked in know-how, he would bring in specialists to complete the write-up.

Soon we had data. Takashi and the experts he brought in created an extensive questionnaire covering a variety of topics. Now we had a better sense of what happened. We had numbers. We learned the reasons behind why decisions were made. If we were going to protect future generations of residents living in this city, then the documentation of what transpired had to be a part of our learnings. My goal was to incorporate this data into the plan for rebuilding the city.

We learned, for example, that while approximately 60% of the residents heard the tsunami warning siren and the announcement that followed, 33% did not. Here was our first problem. What good are emergency announcement systems if people don't hear them?

Soon, we identified another problem. Of those who heard the siren, only 55% thought they should evacuate. What's the point of having a siren announcing an impending tsunami if people who hear it don't bother to evacuate? And, what if this reflected a wider Japanese sentiment? What if we, as a nation, had become so complacent, used to life just plodding along with no real crisis or impending doom that when something did go wrong, we were too busy or lazy to do anything about it? The answers we found were telling. They ranged from: I'll play it by ear, I thought I lived high enough that the tsunami wouldn't reach me, I lived far enough inland from the ocean that I didn't think it would come this far, family and friends said we were safe, I thought the seawall would keep it at bay, and past tsunamis never reached this far inland.

There was more. We asked if people knew where to evacuate to. The city had long ago designated certain parks and buildings as evacuation sites. Our message in conveying this information was to say "go here and you will be safe." Over 70% of the residents knew their closest evacuation site. But, here again only 40% of the residents actually made it to that site. Why? The answers included: it was too far, I went to check on my loved ones first, I went home, I went to get the kids, I tried to evacuate to a higher point, I was driven in a car to another location, I was told to go somewhere else, the tsunami came too quickly, the road was blocked, and finally, too much traffic.

Possibly the most upsetting discovery was the realization that only one quarter of the residents in town had actually discussed with their family what they would do in an emergency. In essence, it seemed to me the high death toll might have something to do with the fact there were scattered reactions. Although as a city we called upon neighborhoods to practice drills, and schools and businesses and municipal buildings had their own evacuation procedures and routinely rehearsed them, there still had been confusion. It got worse. When we asked about whether they had participated in the drills, easily one third to almost half of the residents said they hadn't. What was going on? Why was there such a blasé attitude toward emergencies?

During this process, the questions lingered. How do we move on as a city when death is everywhere? How do we deal with our grief? No one in the outside world knows how we feel. Even the residents in other cities who lost family and friends don't understand. Our grief is collective. We have no one to blame and no one to forgive. These deaths were cruel and took people away seemingly at random. As we mourned privately behind closed doors, we wondered what we would do differently in the next disaster. If people didn't evacuate this time, would they next time? Did the death toll and our palpable pain give us the ammunition we needed to do better and save more lives next time? Is this how our psyches work?

Could it get any worse than the answers we had gotten so far? It could and it did. When asked whether they thought the location they were at could be hit by a tsunami, of those hit 22% thought a tsunami wouldn't ever reach them, and 12% didn't even give it a thought. Were we or weren't we a nation aware of impending natural disasters? Where was this complacency coming from?

When our questions dug deeper, we got more specific information. Of those who had lost family members, when asked about their family members' previous participation in evacuation drills, around half had practiced once a year but 30% had mostly not. Again, why?

One interesting but troublesome fact emerged. The number of those who died because they were people who required assistance was disproportionately high. Of those who perished who didn't have the proper help needed included the bedridden, people in wheelchairs, those with physical/mental disabilities, pregnant women, young children under the age of six, and foreigners. This would not do.

Also troublesome was the fact that the Japan Meteorological Agency, the entity responsible for issuing weather- and emergency-related warnings, had officially issued a tsunami warning for a three-meter tsunami. What hit us was a fifteen-meter tsunami. A three-meter tsunami is survivable if one evacuates to the second or third floor. I was on the roof of a four-story building and almost didn't make it out alive. Many who didn't evacuate must have thought the same. A three-meter tsunami is big but doesn't sound nearly as terrifying as six or ten or fifteen meters. How were we, a small coastal town in rural Tōhoku, supposed to get the national weather and emergency management entity to change their policy? Was that even worth taking on? Surely they were the experts. But if that was the case, how and why did they get it so wrong?

It was profoundly humbling to review the data and see the massive gaps in our evacuation plans. It was also frustrating to see how a national entity we all relied upon had severely underestimated the size of the tsunami. What could I do to ensure future generations would actually take part in drills? Would there be more interest and willingness to emphasize preparedness now that we all had this collective memory of grief and trauma? Was I going to use this latest disaster as a constant reminder of what happens when we aren't prepared? On the one hand, that felt almost cruel. On the other hand, it was a powerful and undeniable fact: we needed to be better prepared. Whatever plan I would put in place had to be more thorough.

We needed a reality check. We needed to face up to the fact there had been complacency. I needed to take people back to that day without traumatizing them or making them feel guilty to drive home the point we could and needed to do better. I sensed I was right. But how do I do that?

Chapter 17

Amya Miller

A large national supermarket chain was building a shopping mall in town. Half of the citizens were ecstatic. Now they didn't have to drive to Ōfunato for daily essentials. Clothes, cosmetics, food, over-the-counter medicine, shoes, and toys would all be sold under one roof. Life was slowly, very slowly, starting to return to normal. The other half of the citizens were livid.

At dinners and over drinks with friends I heard a variety of opinions. As with everything else in town, the consensus was split. Half were for, the other half against. Neither side would budge. The argument in favor was that food and other essential items would all be available in one location. A one-stop shopping experience. Convenience was important, now that we were all living in a town destroyed by a tsunami. We had to start over anyway, so why not make things easier on ourselves?

The argument against it was based solely on the fact that the presence of the giant supermarket would shut down mom-and-pop shops. But no, countered those in favor. We had a large supermarket in town before the disaster. That didn't wipe out the mom-and-pop shops. Why would this supermarket be any different?

The debate was endless. I mostly sat and listened as tempers rose, often in proportion to the alcohol being consumed at the time. Sometimes one of the more sober people at the table would try to change the subject or suggest *karaoke*. It seldom worked.

"Where is this new supermarket going to be built?" I had asked the table one night, trying to do my part to calm tempers. I was given a description of the location and after a few questions clarifying the exact spot, it hit me. That spot was currently occupied by the dormant rice paddies, the first things I had seen when driving down the hill in the jeep on my day of arrival into Rikuzentakata. My mind went back to the beaten-up shed on its side and the dented car that had been tossed onto the square patch of mud, a remnant of what used to be. I spoke without thinking.

"That was the first thing I saw on my first day in town," I said. I told all assembled about the shed and the car. Heads nodded.

"I remember those," Yoshida-*san* said.

For a few seconds, the table went silent. I hadn't meant to blurt out what I had seen, but it felt like too much of a coincidence not to share. And because I wanted to change the subject back to the supermarket without starting another round of arguments, I said, "I promise I'll shop at the supermarket *and* the mom-and-pop shops."

When that was met with more silence, I searched the menu for a way out. "What do they serve here that has cheese in it?" Soon, menus were handed from one person to the next and we began an earnest search for cheesy food.

In our chats, Mayor Toba had voiced his concern over how to get people thinking back to the day of the disaster without traumatizing them all over again. Perhaps subconsciously I remembered the point he was trying to make when I brought up what I had seen on my first day in town. The potency of the subconscious mind, I thought.

My gut told me the subject of the new supermarket was going to come up repeatedly. With this in mind, the next time I had time on the phone with Mayor Toba, I asked him for the backstory. Why was this new supermarket so contentious when it was desperately needed?

"The man who owned the land sold it to the supermarket chain," he said.

"I don't get it," I said. "So?"

"There are people who think this is a city-sanctioned project. That I suggested that the supermarket chain contact this land owner."

"I get it," I said. "So, it's your fault that mom-and-pop stores might not survive."

"Except they will survive," he said. "They survived before. If they don't survive now, I'm not prepared to say it's the fault of the new supermarket."

"Let me make sure I understand," I said. "People in town-"

"Some people in town," he clarified.

"Right. Some people in town think you told the supermarket chain to get in touch with the land owner and ask him to sell his land."
"Right." "So what if you had?"
"Then I'm on the side of big business and not the smaller family-run stores."

Something felt off. This didn't sound like a story or rumor that would cause this much friction in town. I decided to probe. If it was truly just that, I would drop it and stay out of future alcohol-induced arguments about this. Before I could push for more of an explanation, Mayor Toba spoke.

"And the national supermarket chain that's coming in is a direct competitor of the supermarket that was here before. It's somehow become my fault that the new supermarket is coming to town. I didn't have anything to do with it. The farmer who owned the land was contacted directly and asked to sell. I believe him. It's the owner of the supermarket that was in town before who's angry. His dad didn't get along with my dad so there's a grudge."

There it was. Small town politics strikes again and the fall guy is the man in charge.

"What does your dad have to do with this?" I asked.
"My dad was from Rikuzentakata. His family were pig farmers. They were poor. People like that had no say. No power or voice. Back when he was growing up, there were a social strata here in town based on status and family finances. Things were run by the merchants, those with wealth. Dad didn't like that. He thought politics was the only way to get things done. To make change. So he ran to be a prefectural assembly member representing this region. After a few losses he won. Dad, a lowly pig farmer, suddenly had power. He got into a few arguments with the owner of this supermarket chain, the pig farmer standing up to the big-shot businessman."
"And this is still playing out? The sons are now going head-to-head?" I said.
"Traditions die a slow death here, if they die at all," said Mayor Toba.
"This is stupid," I said.
"It is, yes. But you can't say that out loud around here. To people who only know this part of the country, local history, traditions, and ancestors all play a huge role in daily life," he said.

If I were to tell the foreign press about how petty local politics—generational politics at that—was causing friction and hindering progress and redevelopment, they would be all over it. Friction in local politics transcended cities. It was a well-known fact that the relationship between the cities of Ōfunato and Rikuzentakata was anything but amicable. This, too, went back generations.

If I went out to dinner with friends in Ōfunato they would badmouth Rikuzentakata, the residents, and Mayor Toba. Dinner with friends in Rikuzentakata might, on occasion, include a complaint about the people in Ōfunato. But with more immediate worries facing them on a daily basis, the animosity was less open.

Still, there was tension. When a drunk man I didn't know complained one night at a dinner party in Ōfunato about all the press Rikuzentakata was getting, several men snuck glances at me. I was largely responsible for that press and they knew it. The drunk man evidently didn't.

"It's not as if they're the only victims in the area," he slurred. "We got hit by the same tsunami here as well."

Was he serious? What was he saying? That there is disaster-envy? You got hit worse than we did so now you're getting all the attention? We want press coverage, too? I managed to not snap at the drunk man, but my annoyance must have shown on my face as several around the table started to talk over the man, changing the subject entirely. One asked who needed more drinks and another asked for the remote control to turn up the volume on the television; a local baseball hero was up at bat and he wanted to hear the commentary.

I had picked up on the tension between the two cities early on in my stay when I arrived with the NPO. On occasion I would tell people in both cities what I thought of this generational feud, pushing city council members and both mayors when I could to just put aside their differences for five years, work together just for five years. It would be so much easier to pitch stories to the press and donors of two cities working together, joining hands, and supporting each other. I felt strongly it was a matter of time before the foreign media sniffed out this juicy story of a tale of two competing cities.

"You can go back to hating each other after five years," I said one night to a city council member in Rikuzentakata. I was tired of hearing complaints about people I knew in Ōfunato. "I get that there's bad blood," I said. "I'm telling you now, if the foreign media gets wind of this, it's going to be ugly. Donors aren't going to be sympathetic to what they'll perceive as petty competitiveness in a time where the survival of the region is at stake."
My comments were not well received.

"You're not from here," I was told. "You don't understand."
"It's because I'm not from here that I can see things you can't," I said.
"You're foreign. You'll never get it."

The last sentence had shut me down. No matter how long I lived in Japan I would always be foreign, and thus never "get it." I couldn't argue with that. Comments like these didn't keep me from going back and forth between Rikuzentakata and Ōfunato. I had friends in both cities. People in both communities had adopted me into their families and I relied on this generosity and the friendships to keep myself going. Ignoring the decades-long conflict was the only way I could get anything done. Precisely because I wasn't from this region, I decided I could put aside and essentially ignore the history between these cities. It wasn't my job to make these two communities get along.

Chapter 18

Amya Miller

On occasion, I would find someone who rose above the tension between Ōfunato and Rikuzentakata. Mamoru was one such man.

Mamoru's head was large and peanut-shaped. He had shown up as one of the local volunteers on the first day the NPO had mucked out the businessman's house looking for the urn and *inkan*. And he kept showing up.

At first glance Mamoru came off as a bit intimidating—bald, big-boned, and full of muscle. Once he spoke, however, there was an immediate and obvious difference between his outer appearance and his soft, poetic voice. Mamoru used the most elegant *keigo*, the Japanese mode of speech reserved for addressing respected individuals in the most formal situations. He took it one step further and wove deftly between the various structures of *keigo*—the form that exalted the person being addressed, the form that humbled the speaker, and the most difficult form that accomplished both simultaneously. Few people I knew did this so well. It was like he spoke in calligraphy. The dichotomy was both entertaining and jarring: the visual did not match the spoken words.

Mamoru's outfits were on the verge of garish—shocking pink and neon yellow socks inside purple Crocs, with an emerald green basketball tank top over a sky-blue t-shirt. The more he came to volunteer, the more people were struck by his presence, the mismatch between his clothes, his demeanor, his size, and the way he spoke.

As someone else who stood out, I immediately became fast friends with Mamoru. We would sit out on the benches long after dinner talking about anything that came to mind. This is how I learned that Mamoru was also a rapper. On several occasions he showed me videos of Buddhist monks who had adopted rap music as a new way of reaching Japan's younger generation. In one video, a monk in a full robe and shaved head stood next to a man dressed much like Mamoru. Both held microphones and swayed before a crowd as a hip-hop rhythm played on speakers somewhere nearby. The complexity of their Japanese poetry was amazing, the way they restructured classic prayers into rap verses. It was fascinating that this was even allowed.

But why was Mamoru volunteering here, I asked. As it turned out—much like Fuchigami-*san* had said in the NPO directors meetings months ago— Mamoru was volunteering as a way to help fill out his resume. He knew that the people of this region needed help, and he genuinely wanted to stay here as long as he could. But he also had to think about his future. Mamoru was at an age where he would soon need to commit to a career. He knew he was good with numbers and was considering becoming an accountant, though he was not particularly enthusiastic about this.

I thought about what I'd seen of Mamoru's personality in the time we'd been here. Mamoru and I saw each other off and on, getting together for meals and joining the same groups of people who were out to dinner. His personality was both impressive and reassuring. He was always respectful and careful to give his full attention whenever anyone was speaking. He seemed wise, and I was sure he would do well at whatever he chose. Even if that was accounting.

I pointed out that he was just as good with people as he was with numbers, and that was more of what the community needed. There were already plenty of accountants in town. A community organizer, someone with a sympathetic ear, a key individual who could both understand pain and help people through it.

So when Mamoru told me he was going to enter a monastery and train to become a Buddhist monk, I was elated and stunned. I was elated—it fit him so perfectly, and he had already shown me monks could rap. But his decision also stunned me. I had heard that entering a monastery was a grueling experience, the training said to be excruciatingly harsh. Still, with his innate ability to listen, his calm demeanor and his eloquence, he would make a perfect monk.

~~~

"One of my biggest regrets is that I didn't stop my friend from driving to pick up his kid," Mamoru told me one night as we sat out on the bench outside of base camp. "I passed him on the bridge," he continued. "I was heading home to make sure my mother and grandmother were okay, and he was on his way to his kid's preschool. He didn't make it. He got too close to the wave and he didn't make it."

We sat in silence.

"It's not like he would have stayed back if I'd told him not to go toward the ocean," Mamoru continued. "We all protect those we love. He was a dad. Of course he would protect his kid."

I didn't know what to say.

"Still," Mamoru said, "I wish he wasn't gone."

I reach out and take Mamoru's hand and squeeze it.

"You like to protect people," I said. Mamoru nodded.

"You're right," he said.

We sat in silence a little longer and Mamoru finally said, "Like my mother."

"Your mother?" I asked.

"Yeah, my mother. When I was fourteen, I kicked my dad out of our house. I was tired of him beating up my mother. Back then I was already big for my age, and after one night when he got particularly violent, I told him I was either calling the cops or he could leave. For good. So he left, and I haven't seen him since."

"That must have taken incredible courage," I said. Mamoru was quiet, and I let a long moment pass between us. Finally, he spoke.

"My mother, I admire her. I admire her strength. What she does with the kids in her preschool really inspires me. She's a preschool principal. She's dedicated her life to kids."

Suddenly, he turned to me. "Would you go to her preschool?" he asked. "I'm sure the kids would have fun seeing you."

"Because I'm foreign?" I asked. Sheepishly, he grinned.

"I didn't mean that to offend. I just thought you might be good with kids. You seem like you would be."

"I'm not offended," I said. "I just want to be clear why I'm going. If I can help, I'll gladly go."

"I'll talk to my mom when I get home tonight," he said, and we agreed this was interesting enough to pursue.

Mamoru was the first person outside of the NPO volunteers whom I saw the next morning. Clearly eager and a bit antsy, he was pacing back and forth on the front patio of the base camp where I stayed. He put out his cigarette as soon as he saw me.

"I spoke to my mother," he said, breathless. "She thought it was a great idea. Would you go to her preschool someday this week? She's eager to start."

A few days later, I drove up a narrow and winding hill to one of the preschools in town. I knocked on the sliding glass door that led into the teacher's room. I saw metal desks pushed together, filing cabinets and a large whiteboard on the wall. Mamoru's mother was petite, ten years or so older than me, with short-cropped black hair and glasses. Her face was a mixture of exhaustion and determination. Her thin lips formed a straight line on her face and she looked tense, but her eyes were welcoming.

In the background I could hear a wide range of squeals—babies crying and kids yelling. Right as I said hello and introduced myself, starting our chat about what kind of help she needed, a group of four-year-olds poured out onto the school grounds, running for the swings and slides and the sandbox full of plastic pails and half-built sand castles.

"Why don't we start now?" Mamoru's mother said. Before I could answer, she pulled my arm and led me back out the sliding glass doors onto the playground. She clapped her hands and called the children to her. We hadn't discussed details. What did she have planned?

"This is Amya-*san*," she said to the mass of tiny heads looking up at her, pointing to me. Several kids looked at each other, some in shock and others whispering, "*Gaijin!*"

"Amya-*san* is going to come and visit you from now on, as often as she can. She will teach you English, and she'll play games with you." She looked at me, and nodding, said, "Won't you, Amya-*san*?"

That was my introduction to a new job description.

"Yes!" I said. "Is it okay if I come and visit? Will you play with me?"

Some of the children were much more vocal in their "*Hai*" than others, obediently agreeing to play with me as asked by their principal. Some were clearly unsure. I was likely the first foreigner they had ever seen in person. One of the girls nearer to the front said just loud enough for everyone to hear, "You smell like marshmallows."

"Do I?" I said, sniffing my wrist and shoulders.

"You do!" I heard. Others said, "You smell like a candle!" and "You smell like vanilla ice cream!"

My perfume became the perfect ice-breaker. I mentally noted what scent I was wearing today and vowed to wear that with every visit.

I taught the children sardines—hide-and-seek where everyone hides together in groups of sixes and sevens as one person tries to find the hiding spots. We counted to ten together in English, most kids already knowing *one, two, three, four, five*. They were thrilled to learn that these words were actually English. They knew colors in English; also, pineapple, donut, cake, penguin, lion, koala, bus, taxi, cheeseburger and trampoline. They were thrilled to learn that these were all English words. "See! You already speak English!" It never occurred to them that these words they knew weren't Japanese. Once I told them the words were English, and that meant they already spoke a foreign language, the kids were eager for more. Each week I added words, soon introducing other foreign words like pizza, crêpe, and croissant. We extended our numbers from ten to twenty. Once they had mastered that we went on to numbers in Spanish, French, and Italian. Soon I was making weekly visits to Mamoru's mother's preschool.

Over time, I heard stories from the teachers on how the children were processing my visits. Teachers had walked in on groups of two or three children "speaking English" except their conversation wasn't any language the teachers recognized. The teachers laughed as they recalled these moments. A private moment between two boys was overheard and relayed to me during one visit.

"One boy would say, 'Mwa-moo-ju-popi-ni-panda?' and another would reply 'Gee-two-may-lala-no-gorilla' as if this was completely normal. They were mimicking you, Amya-*san*. Pretending to have a conversation in English with you about animals. At least, we think that's what was happening. What an experience these children are having. Who would have thought the disaster could produce something so positive?"

Slowly it became clear why this new project of mine meant so much to me. My reasons were based in my childhood. My kindergarten memories weren't necessarily traumatic, but rather specific. Okuno-*sensei* was the only male kindergarten teacher in my school—and for the next thirty years, the only male kindergarten teacher I had ever known in Japan. Teaching preschool and kindergarten was largely a woman's job. That's one reason why he remained firm in my memory.

He was also large. Or rather, he seemed large from my kindergarten perspective. He would walk down the hallway, two kids on his back, one kid hanging from each arm, and make roaring sounds as the children screamed and ran away. For some reason, the man terrified me. I know it wasn't his fault, and I don't blame him. After all, I was five. But I distinctly remember hearing one of my classmates refer to him as Okuno-gorilla-*sensei* and decided that was a bad sign. Gorillas were monstrous, fierce, frightening. They could have called him Okuno-lion-*sensei* and I would have been equally terrified. To my five-year-old self, his roars were awful. I remembered little else from kindergarten.

I would be the opposite of Okuno-gorilla-*sensei*. I hoped to be a positive memory. I wanted these kids I was playing with to remember at least part of their childhood with happiness.

Wanting to do something special and memorable, the first Christmas after the disaster, I approached the foreigners I knew in Tokyo and asked for donations of foreign Christmas candy. I asked people back home to send me a box of Christmas goodies as well, hoping to make the rounds of as many preschools as I could. By now, word had spread to the other preschool principals in the area and I was visiting six kindergartens a month. What had started out as a plan to go to Mamoru's mother's preschool for a big Christmas celebration turned into five additional preschools also holding Christmas parties. Clearly, I needed to go all-out.

One night, invited out to dinner again by Fuchigami-*san*, I brought up the plans to visit the preschools before Christmas. By this point, I considered the Ōfunato city councilman a close friend.

"I want to do something big and bold for the Christmas parties at the local preschools. Can you help?"

I laid out my plan. I would wear a Mrs. Claus costume with gray hair pulled into a bun, silver-rimmed glasses, an apron with frills all making me look 70 and not 40. I needed a reindeer or two, and an elf if possible. Would some of the guys at the table help out—Akira and Kazuki, the brothers who always fought, as well as Suzuki-*san*, Ando-*san*, and Taniguchi-*san* from Suisen, the sake brewery? And could we get a sleigh, if possible?

At the request of a sleigh, the entire table burst into loud guffaws. A sleigh? Where were they going to find a sleigh? But if they could, surely they would ask some of the local hunters to go round up some deer from the mountains and we could make the deer pull the sleigh. More laughter followed. The consensus reached was "no sleigh" but they had fun trying to decide what the sleigh might look like. Could they use one of those small pickup trucks and string lights on the back? Would they make the two men dressed up as reindeer pull this little truck? Who were the two strongest among them who could pull a small truck? What about a throne? Didn't Mrs. Claus need a throne?

"We'll take care of everything," Fuchigami-*san* said. "You just get your costume and however much American candy you can gather." A deal was struck.

Hopping on a bullet train to Tokyo, I ventured out to collect the boxes of Christmas candy that had been donated by various local expats and spouses of embassy workers who'd been informed of my mission. With over a dozen stops all across the city, I knew I would need to rent a van. But by the fifth house, the boxes were starting to pile up, leaving me with a dangerously low amount of free space. It wasn't all going to fit. I drove back to the rental agency and secured a larger van to complete my run. By the end of the day, I packed thirty massive moving boxes and several bags into the back of the largest rental van I could afford. Now armed with a truly staggering amount of candy, I started the seven-hour drive back to Ōfunato and Rikuzentakata.

By now, eight preschools had asked me to show up as Mrs. Claus. I wasn't sure who else was coming along to help, as Fuchigami-*san* was being oddly cryptic about details on his end. The morning of the first Christmas party, I donned the gray wig and put on my rectangular silver-rimmed glasses, added a thick green turtleneck under my large matronly dress, and tied an apron around my waist. The outfit was completed with what looked like a cloth shower cap. I looked nothing like me.

Showing up at the designated meeting spot Fuchigami-*san* had told me about, I felt highly self-conscious and yet convinced my disguise would work. I stepped out of the large van to thunderous applause and side-splitting laughter from the men Fuchigami-*san* had lined up as helpers. I was patted on the back, complimented, chided, told the chunky turtleneck made me look fat and the gray hair and glasses old. "You're a perfect Mrs. Claus!" They congratulated me for pulling off something only a foreigner could do. "The children will not recognize you," Fuchigami-*san* assured.

In order to make sure my disguise was convincing, I would play a monolingual Mrs. Claus. Clearly foreign, the character of Mrs. Claus didn't speak Japanese, thus needed an interpreter. I asked which one of the guys would be my interpreter, and Akira's hand shot up.

"You don't speak English," I said.

"None of us do," he said, defensively. "But out of all of us here, my English is the best."

There was more laughter and Kazuki, the younger brother shook his head as if to say, "You're the only one who thinks that" and "You're going to embarrass yourself." I gave Akira all of my lines ahead of time.

None of the children recognized me, and all of the children got over their initial shyness very quickly. They flocked around this new foreigner. The children marveled over this *bāchan*, this old woman, who had mysteriously shown up claiming to be Santa's wife. As promised, Fuchigami-*san* had recruited several of the men from the community to dress as reindeer, and in full-body suits they helped distribute the candy among the hundreds of preschoolers who were dressed in their own versions of Christmas costumes. Snowflake hats, trash bag coats with Christmas trees and gold and silver stars pasted on. I patted their heads, blew kisses, hugged the ones that were brave enough to come forward.

Mamoru's mother insisted that the two reindeer who showed up at her preschool—Kazuki and Taniguchi-*san*—needed to have red noses. She proceeded to cut round circles out of felt and taped them onto the faces of the two men. More laughter ensued and the mood was merry. Fuchigami-*san* took his turn in the reindeer costume, creeping down the hallway as quietly as his large frame would allow. He walked past the doors of the preschool classrooms and began to ring a mass of small bells strung together. Doors flew open one by one as the children heard the bells and a flood of excited preschoolers burst out into the hallway, screaming with joy at the strangers in even stranger costumes who looked funny but fun. They all gathered in the gymnasium where I handed out candy with the help of the two or three reindeer.

At one preschool after another, I told the children gathered how proud Santa and I were of all of them. Santa and I knew how hard this year had been, that they had all been so brave. Santa and I knew all this because we had been watching them from the North Pole all year. Santa couldn't show up himself today because he was still working on making their presents, it was right before Christmas after all. But, he would arrive on Christmas Eve. Because he was so impressed by how good the kids were this year, Santa had asked me to show up a few days before Christmas Eve to hand out special presents. "You were all so wonderful, kind, patient, and strong," I told the children. "We're so very proud of you. And, most of all, Santa and I love you very much."

Each preschool had a different flavor, personality, and character. I don't know whether that was a regional trait, or stemmed from the teachers' personalities, or if it was something else altogether. The preschools I visited as Mrs. Claus all gave me different insight into how kids were coping.

I felt tugging on my skirt. I turned around to see a boy around four years old holding out two sheets of paper. "Please give these to Santa," he said. "What do you have there?" I asked in English, frantically glancing around for Akira, my interpreter, who was nowhere in sight. One of the reindeer, seeing me almost speaking in Japanese and completely breaking character, came running over.
"Hey, buddy," he said. "What's this?"
"It's money," said the boy. "I want Santa to have it."
"Wow," said the reindeer. "How much money are you giving Santa?"
"One ten hundred thousand million billion gajillion," he said.
I looked down at the money. Sure enough, there were more zeros on these two bills than I had ever seen in my life.
"Okay," I said and tried not to cry.
"You're a good boy," the reindeer said to him as he high-fived him. I bent down to squeeze the boy into a hug but after five seconds he squirmed out, back to his desk where the candy I'd given him still remained, a sticky mess of melted bits of sugar and squishy chocolate.

"Ma'am, Ma'am!" I heard, and not thinking it was me that was being called, I kept walking. It was a boy's voice. I felt a tap on my shoulder and turned around to see one of the teachers with a little boy next to her.
"This little boy has something for you," she said in Japanese and I panicked. Do I speak in Japanese to her? She realized my dilemma and nodded. She told the boy to hand me his artwork. She looked at me and pointed to the Christmas tree made out of toilet paper rolls.
"For Santa," she said, in slow and deliberate English. "The boy, uh, *tsukuru*, uh, make! Make. For Santa."

I grinned and she grinned back. I reminded myself to thank her and compliment her next time I show up as myself.

"Okay," I said to her, and to the boy, "Thank you so much." I pointed to the Christmas tree and said, "For Santa" and nodded. He looked up at me and beamed.

That night I got a call from the preschool principal where I had been given the homemade Christmas tree. She had never called me this late before.

"I'm so sorry to call you at night," she said.

"Is everything okay?" I asked, recognizing how unusual this was.

"Yes, well no. I'm fine, but…" I cut her off.

"What's wrong?" I asked.

"Well," she said, "the boy who gave you that Christmas tree today," she paused.

"Uh-huh," I sensed something was wrong.

"Well, he needs a bit of help."

That could mean a lot of things.

"He needs help at home?" I asked, taking a stab at the canvas of all the issues it could be.

"Yes," she said. "It's fairly bad."

"Okay," I said. "What can I do?"

"It would mean so much to him if Santa were to send him a letter thanking him for the gift," the principal said.

"I can do that," I said and then realized it wouldn't reach him in time for Christmas. There wasn't enough time for me to write the letter and turn around and send it. I was heading to Tokyo on the first bullet train in the morning and even if I sent it by express it wouldn't arrive for Christmas.

"Don't worry about that," she said. "If you could just send him a letter in Santa's name. And then since that'll be in English…" she trailed off.

"I'll translate it. I'll use my name. Say I'm friends with Santa or something. Will that work?"

"Perfectly."

Santa did write a letter, which I translated, and I managed to send it by overnight express. The boy got it in time for Christmas, and the next time I showed up at his preschool, he came running up to me.

"Amya-*san*! Guess what?!" he said, waving Santa's letter.

"Oh my!" I gasped. "Is that…"

"A letter from Santa Claus!"

"How lucky are you?!" I said.

"I know," he said, his chest thrust out.

"It's because you're such a good boy," I said, messing up his hair with my fingers. He giggled. I knelt down so I was eye-level with him.
"You're a good boy and Santa knew that," I said. "If you ever need any help, tell your teacher or your principal or me. Okay?" "Will Santa help me?" he asked.
"All kinds of people will help you," I said.
"Okay," he said, nodding. He stood there for a few moments, looking down at the letter I had written as Santa.
"Can you read this to me?" he said.
"It's in English," I said. "Is that okay?"
"It's okay," he said and he crawled up into my lap.

The joy and season's tidings fresh in mind, I vowed to celebrate as many holidays as I could with these children.

~~~

Months before Mamoru would be joining a monastery as a monk-in-training, a group of us went out to dinner one night. As others got drunk and sang *karaoke*, he and I sat in the corner eating liver and garlic chives. I had been feeling faint and dizzy from a lack of nutrition, and I worried I was becoming anemic. I'd even blacked out once or twice. He was trying to build up stamina for an upcoming *karate* competition. We both hated liver but decided if we ate it together and kept talking throughout, it might not taste as bad.

"I just realized recently why I'm going to be a monk," he said. I looked up at him, startled.
"You didn't know until now?"
"Not really," he said.
"I don't get it," I said.
"I didn't want to," he said. "It's hard work, being a monk. But, the more I listen to people in town, the more I realize people need a leader who's not a politician. Someone who's separate from the town. Not a businessman, not someone in politics, not a teacher. A monk. Monks are respected and trusted. It made sense to me that I should become a monk. I didn't want to, though. Two years up in the mountains with harsh training and eating very little—I don't know if I can do it."
I sat stunned. I hadn't known he didn't want to become a monk. I thought he felt it was a calling, something only he could do.
"It hit me one night a while back. I went to a local neighborhood meeting where the City Hall guys were talking about how they were going to rebuild

the city. Several older guys stood up and said they wanted the city rebuilt just as it was. They didn't want a thing changed. They wanted their old town back." He looked down at me, and I could see the bewilderment on his face. "But that makes no sense. If I have kids someday, I don't want them to grow up in a city that's been rebuilt to look like some old, dying town. I want there to be joy and optimism. Hope."

Mamoru stared past me.

"I have to be someone who can stand up to these older guys, our leaders and our *sempai,* the elders, and say, 'We have to have a community where hope runs in our veins.' And the only way I can think to do that is to be a monk."

"I'm so proud of you," I said. "I admire your strength."

Mamoru and I stood at the edge of town. A black sedan pulled up and a monk emerged, fully bald and wearing the traditional robe of his station. Mamoru was going to a temple notorious for its strict but thorough teachings, and in two years he would be allowed to return to his community ready to work at one of the local Buddhist temples where he might eventually work his way up to the head monk.

"You can write to me but you can't call me," he told me as I stood by him, not wanting to see him go. "I won't have access to my cell phone or the internet while I'm in training. I also won't be allowed to write back to you, but I'm told I'll receive all letters sent to me." He handed me a sheet of paper with the address of the temple.

"Please write," he said as he hugged me goodbye. I promised I would.

My letters to Mamoru became another calming ritual during the time I spent in Rikuzentakata. I told him again how proud I was, how I knew his mother was also proud of him. I wanted to take part in a Zen meditation session led by him when he returned.

As he was driven away, I reflected back on the conversation we had early in my stay where he had talked about becoming an accountant. I had encouraged him not to pursue that line of work. I had said he was better suited to being a community leader. I was suddenly keenly aware of the role I played in his decision. A mixture of discomfort and genuine pride swirled in me. What had I done? It was his decision. I had told him I didn't see him as an accountant, but surely the rest was up to him, right? I waved at him until I saw him turn around in his seat. Two years. Would it go by quickly or would it feel like forever?

Chapter 19

Futoshi Toba

I experienced another first. My first parent–teacher conference. My elder son, now in middle school, had told me one day that his teacher needed to see me. I immediately assumed the worst. Had he done something wrong? Was he in trouble?

"What happened?" I asked.
"Nothing," my son said, defensiveness in his voice. "You have to go to a parent–teacher meeting."
"Why?" I asked.
"Why? Everybody has to. Mom used to do this all the time," he said and we looked at each other. I suppose I knew that Kumi had gone to these meetings. We must have talked about them over dinner, or she must have told me what the teachers had said when it was just the two of us. Those days seem so long ago now. I was immediately sorry I assumed he'd been in trouble. I was also sorry I just didn't know.

"Sure," I said and tried to smile. "When is it?"
He handed me an envelope. In it was a paper showing the date and time, the number of his classroom. I looked at the paper and saw right away I was booked solid on this particular day.

How I had taken Kumi for granted. It wasn't that I missed her simply because she took care of the boys and made sure everything was always just right. It was the disruption, the intrusion of despair and sadness in our lives that felt inescapable when I was faced with the fact that I didn't even know parent–teacher meetings were a common occurrence. I would go. I would reschedule my meetings in that time slot and I would go to my son's middle school.

My secretaries had been given instructions to keep me on track with my meetings on the day of the parent–teacher conference. Mayor or not, I didn't want to be late to my first meeting with his teacher. Did I even know who the teacher was? Would I recognize him? Or was it a woman? I slapped my cheeks with my hands, hoping to energize myself and get the blood flowing. I had to be sharp for this meeting. Was I supposed to know what was going to be discussed? Did I need to bring anything? My mind raced and I felt anxious as I drove to the school.

I arrived at the middle school perched up on the hill behind where our house used to be. I drove up the winding road to the campus. Rows of silver temporary houses lined what used to be the school sports field. The boxy gymnasium used by hundreds of residents as an evacuation shelter until several months ago was now a gymnasium again. I could hear voices of girls calling out to each other. This had to be the volleyball team practicing.

Walking through the front entryway, I removed my shoes and put on slippers. I had the sheet of paper my son had given me and checking to be sure I knew the number of his homeroom, started to walk down the long hallway reading the classroom numbers on signs. Stopping in front of the sliding door to his room, I knocked and hearing a voice, entered.

The square classroom was lined with desks and chairs resembling all classrooms I'd ever been in. Here was where my son spent his days. His teacher and I exchanged greetings and sitting down on the chair near the teacher's desk we began to talk.

The meeting went well. My son's grades were excellent. He was a good student, had friends, got along well with everyone and seemed overall happy. Reassuring words. My son was now a teenager. I remembered back to my teenage days, serious about wanting to be a rock-and-roll star, my band touring the world. I sensed my elder son wouldn't be a difficult teenager. The younger one, however, was going to be a handful. The boy had an ever-present look of mischief in his eyes.

I felt good as the meeting came to an end. Just as I was about to get up and leave, the teacher said, "One last thing, Mayor." Just the way it was said felt ominous. What now?
"Have you noticed your son's glasses?" he asked. I hadn't.
"No," I said.
"He's missing the left temple," the teacher said. I frowned. The left temple?

"I'm sorry," I said, completely embarrassed. "I don't know what you mean." "This part," he said, taking off his own glasses, and he tapped the long arm that went from the hinge to the ear. "He's missing this whole part. He needs new frames," he said, putting his glasses back on.

That couldn't be. I would have noticed. Surely. I thanked the teacher, bowed, and left, trying to calm my burning red face by breathing in and out as deeply as I could without drawing attention to myself.

I canceled my dinner meeting and went to my uncle's house. I needed to be home more. This was a sign. My sons were at the table doing their homework. I pulled my elder son aside. "Let me see your glasses." He took them off and handed them to me. The left arm was gone. He had jammed the bridge of the glasses onto his nose, and I could see dark pink marks where the glasses were being held in place.
"When did this happen?" I asked. I knew I sounded angry.
"I'm sorry, dad," my son said. "I got hit in the face with a ball during basketball practice," he said.
"When?" I asked.
"A few weeks ago," he said.
"Why didn't you tell me?" I asked.
My son looked at me as if it was the dumbest question he'd heard.
"Dad," he said. "You're busy."

Something had to change. I had to change. Kumi was gone. My sons had needs. I was their father. I didn't know how, but I would have to figure this out. We needed to spend time together as a family, the three of us. Be home more. Build the new house. Get moved in. Be a family. Be dad.

I had to make this work.

Chapter 20

Amya Miller

Life in Rikuzentakata was filled with starts and stops. Every time there was movement forward, something unforeseen would happen and there would be a setback. There was sadness and stoicism in the air, like humidity, unseen but ever-present. Was that why these starts and stops seemed to never cease?

I watched people try to start over or reach for something new, only to be shut down with a click of the tongue by the others in their community. Have you forgotten those who are gone? How dare you try to be happy while the rest of us are grieving? People tried new things and were put down over and over, fueling more grief and making progress more arduous. The city of loss was quickly turning on itself. It was hard to watch.

The combination of city-wide pain and prolonged trauma was taking a toll. Between the stifling sadness in the air and the stop-and-go pace of reconstruction, time started to take on a strange quality. I heard the same sentiment over and over. Every dinner out, every chat over tea and coffee, every get-together with one of the locals, I heard of this strange phenomenon. By the end of the first year, people felt as though the disaster had only happened a few days ago, yet simultaneously felt that it had been ages. The second year, the sentiment was exactly the same. Time had a pace none of us understood. The third year? The same again.

Even as a volunteer I began to experience this strange stretching of time. Although I had been in Rikuzentakata for nearly four years, I felt like I had just arrived a week ago, like no time had passed. Yet, it also felt like I had been here forever.

I tried to process this one night with Mayor Toba. I decided to pick his brain about what had happened to time, asking if he'd experienced the same thing.

"I think I did," he told me. "But things were so different for me. I had so much paperwork to do, appearances to make. I had projects to manage, and then I had to yell in order to get past the red tape that would have stopped us. I guess what I'm saying is I had lots of ways to mark how much time things were taking. But the people didn't have that."

I nodded. "That makes sense. For a long time Rikuzentakata didn't get to see much progress at all. While the projects were stalled, people just had to sit and marinate in their collective sadness."

"It's true," he said. "These people are very tight-knit. Their mood is contagious. If the majority of them are sad, there will be pressure for others not to stand out or break that norm. In a town this rural, everybody reads the room."

Mayor Toba used the Japanese phrase kūki o yomu, which translates directly as "read the air." It's a powerful idiom which most are familiar with, the idea that one should observe the emotional state of any group and change one's behavior to act accordingly. The mayor's point was taken; around here, the sadness was in the air. Don't buck the norm.

The mayor continued. "Apart from the collective trauma, I think the main thing keeping us locked in time was the devastated landscape. There was evidence of the disaster all around. Piles of debris, pieces of houses, new bodies being found every day for weeks."

His point resonated. It was easy to remember how the piles of debris started to constitute landmarks. At first the asphalt roads, the few that had been cleared, were nothing more than two-lane pathways snaking through a valley of sodden futons, crumpled bicycles, splintered wood, and chunks of concrete.

Over time, piles started to form as the debris was separated. Crushed cars over here, telephone poles over there; heap all the plastic in one place and the twisted metal in another. Some of the materials were hazardous, others recyclable or destined for landfill. Over time these piles grew and shifted, sprawling across the landscape as they were added to and pulled from by massive trucks and construction equipment. It all felt so surreal.

"We couldn't move on like that," Mayor Toba told me. "Not until something changed the landscape. The visual was powerful. Once people could see their surroundings changing for the better, they started to breathe a bit easier. People were able to hope again. That said, we're nowhere close to being done."

Rebuilding the city center was key. The residents wanted to move out of their temporary homes and businesses into permanent structures. I wasn't part of the group that met to discuss and hammer out the logistics of just how an entire city center was going to be rebuilt. I didn't have the expertise to help with this level of planning. What I did have were stories.

Mayor Toba was not shy in admitting that he had made mistakes, and the press and the public flocked to hear him and to print his words. Mayor Toba was also adamant discussing the absolute need to reevaluate existing evacuation plans needed to be a part of my storytelling. In his travels he made his case. Already a powerful speaker, when he pushed for a complete overhaul of policy and shared his frustrations at the difficulties he faced in solidifying local buy-in, people listened. Most of the time. I faced similar mixed results. The stories themselves were powerful. Pushing experts to review and overhaul their plans, however, did not go over well.

Mayor Toba began to travel domestically whenever he could. He spoke about the need for disaster preparedness, and about how a lack of it had cost his city countless lives. By now it was publicly known that the city's fire department of 151 full-time and volunteer staff had lost fifty-one of their fellow firefighters. City Hall had lost one quarter, over 100 of its staff. The library and museums, the hospital and preschools, everywhere throughout Rikuzentakata, staff had died in the process of helping others to safety or by thinking they were safe in their buildings. Mayor Toba became vocal about rewriting the city's disaster preparedness manual and encouraged other cities to do the same.

"Not every act can be prepared for," he would say. "You think you're prepared because you've made the plans and you've done the drills. But nature isn't controllable or predictable. You simply can't prepare for everything."

Though his point was difficult for some to accept, his words carried weight. Yet first responders and people in positions of authority took the most issue with his message. He called for a complete review and an overhaul of any organization's disaster preparedness and response manual.

"Throw it out and rewrite the whole thing if you have to," he said. "Allow first responders to abandon their posts and save their own lives if that's what needs to happen." For a country that had dealt with natural disasters throughout its entire history, many Japanese officials were disturbed to hear that their attitudes toward preparedness were flawed. Many local leaders shot back with, "But, we know what we're doing."

Mayor Toba would fire right back at them. "Oh yeah? I did, too. I thought I knew what I was doing when my town designated buildings throughout the city as evacuation sites. People fled to those buildings because the city had said they would be safe there. And because they took shelter there, many of those people died. People died because they went where we said they would be safe. Don't tell me your plan doesn't need reviewing. Every plan needs reviewing."

Over the years, the City of Rikuzentakata had designated sixty-seven locations as evacuation sites. Of these sixty-seven facilities, thirty-eight were damaged by the 2011 tsunami. Of those thirty-eight sites, at nine locations people lost their lives because the structure could not withstand the tsunami. It's impossible to get an exact count of the loss of life in these evacuation sites, but the numbers range easily in the hundreds. What's certain is that these people died because they went where they were supposed to—to places they had been told would be safe. That, according to Mayor Toba, was inexcusable. And the fact that some disaster planners weren't willing to accept that their plans might lead to loss of life was worse than inexcusable—it was grossly negligent.

The designated evacuation sites had been chosen based on scientific data and research, the selection intentional and thoroughly studied. Scientists and specialists from the prefecture weighed in. Proximity to the nearest road, elevation, past tsunami inundation levels nearby, and the city's hazard map had all been taken into consideration.

When I spoke abroad, I echoed Mayor Toba's words. "If, after all that study and planning, our designated evacuation sites still weren't safe, then every expert needs to be humble enough to say their plan also may be flawed as well. We all need to be willing to revise our plans to remove these unintentional deathtraps."

In the course of repeating Mayor Toba's sentiment, I butted heads with people of varying titles and credentials who took these words as a slight against their work and expertise. Many of them had put a considerable amount of time and effort into making their disaster response plans practical and safe. To some, the stories of loss from someone representing disaster survivors made the truth of the matter undeniable. But others stood by their plans, unwilling to budge. Plenty of community disaster management directors and heads of departments for local emergency services had spent their entire careers on disaster preparedness. Just because some city they'd never heard of had a bad experience didn't mean the statistics applied to them. When I was asked to stop disrespecting the experts, I spoke to Mayor Toba for advice. Should I stop or should I keep going?

"How important is it to you that these people like you?" he asked me.
"It's not," I replied.
"Then keep going. These people's plans are based on data, but so is the message you're putting out there. Real deaths. People I know died in those buildings because of a plan I believed and told them was safe. This is personal. If you don't care whether they dislike you for speaking the truth, keep saying it."

So I didn't mince words, pushing every audience to reevaluate their existing plans. Lives depended on plans. There could be no patience for ego. I took seriously the fact I was representing a community with a plan that cost lives and brought on immeasurable pain.

While I spread this message on the international stage, Mayor Toba directed his words to anyone and everyone he could reach domestically. He was dynamic and charismatic, and his sincerity captivated audiences. When he spoke, his voice cracked with emotion and he faced the audience rather than head down with a script in his hands. This made him a truly unusual politician. Listeners would often tell me after his speeches, "I felt like he was speaking to me directly. I could have sworn he even made eye contact."

His honesty, while grating to some, was powerfully comforting to others. Here, too, experts and other municipal leaders pushed back against his call for a review and overhaul of existing disaster manuals. When a landslide hit a community in southwestern Japan, swallowing homes and demolishing roads, the mayor of that city went on record lamenting the fact his manual was insufficient. Mayor Toba lost it.

"Did I say to review your manuals? Yes, I did. I'm not saying that to pick a fight. I lost people too because we all thought our plans were good enough. They weren't."

Publicly he renewed his call for overhauling manuals. Privately he seethed, disgusted at the arrogance and ignorance of leaders who chose protocol over the lives and well-being of their citizens.

One particular message he and I would address in our talks was the history of *tsunami tendenko*. Equal parts axiom and social mandate, the concept of *tsunami tendenko* is simple: if a tsunami comes, focus only on getting yourself to safety. This mandate has been passed from generation to generation in the Tōhoku region, and behind it is a deeper and much harsher implication, one that isn't spoken aloud as it simply sounds too callous. Don't take anything with you and don't help anyone else. Focus only on immediate evacuation, get yourself to higher ground and don't stop—for anything, or anyone.

When I first heard of these two words and had the concept explained to me, I was sure I had misunderstood. Help yourself only? Leave everyone behind? Really? It sounded so heartless. Why wouldn't you help others if you could? But the longer I worked in the region, the more it became clear to me. This system worked precisely because every person was responsible for themselves.

As I asked around, I learned a bit of context for *tsunami tendenko*. This concept had been discussed as a commonplace response to a tsunami for at least 100 years. In the past, rights of the physically disabled were not widely considered. While village elders were respected for their age and knowledge—hierarchy firmly entrenched in those days—they too were responsible for their own safety. If the elders didn't survive, it meant that the era for the next generation to take over had been hastened by nature.

I contemplated *tsunami tendenko* one evening after a particularly large and unsettling aftershock. If I was going to convey this message to others abroad as part of disaster preparedness, I had to come to grips with it myself. I climbed into bed and spent the night doing some brutally honest soul-searching. If a tsunami hit this area again, would I run up the hill behind my room without stopping? I knew the path well because it was where I walked to clear my head at night. Yes, I would. I would run, not walk. I would get myself to safety.

Would I leave behind others who could not save themselves? I hesitated, unsure if I could knowingly look past their safety and their lives just to save myself. Could I do it? Could I leave behind an old woman who couldn't run up the hill with me, knowing if I didn't drag her along she would die? Would

I intentionally put myself in harm's way to save her life? What if that old woman was my mother?

I tossed and turned that night, unable to come to a conclusion. Is it not human nature to help one another? *Tsunami tendenko* seemed to require going against human nature. Did I really agree with this? Did the people in the communities I served really believe this? That seemed to be the consensus. No one will hate you for leaving someone behind, even though it's a painful choice to make. Making that choice is expected of everyone. It's a necessary step in order to get out of a disastrous situation alive. No one said it would be easy or pleasant.

But the mayor was still weighing the pros and cons of the concept. For obvious reasons, *tsunami tendenko* did not resonate well with many—in particular, with first responders. A key part of a first responder's job is the willingness to run into a building to save others, a situation fraught with risk. In light of having lost a third of the firefighting force in the city, Mayor Toba decided to examine the practice of *tsunami tendenko* with a more critical eye. Would young people want to join the police and fire department if they knew losing their life was more likely a possibility living on the coast? Loss of life was the case for fifty-one of the firefighters in the city, so it needed addressing. With the population aging and the birth rate declining throughout Japan, finding the necessary firefighters would be difficult enough. Now that so many had been lost, recruitment seemed an impossible task.

Maybe a century ago when the region first started talking about *tsunami tendenko,* it was acceptable to leave the elderly and disabled behind. But Mayor Toba knew better than to continue projecting that sentiment now, especially when he was trying to rebuild his city into one that would be safe for everyone. If he pushed through the historical and traditional concept of *tsunami tendenko,* he would lose supporters. If he didn't, he would also lose supporters. In the end, he chose to set local lore aside.

"How many chances does one get to rebuild a city from scratch? We're doing it right. There's no excuse for a half-baked plan. This has to get done correctly. For good, this time."

Chapter 21

Futoshi Toba

Not feeling heard is not the same as not being heard. The divide is expansive and fraught with emotion. The tsunami flattened downtown, our city center. Rebuilding at sea level was out of the question. What then? We didn't have enough space in the hills even if we were to shave the tops off and flatten them to make it suitable to build. Then again, rebuilding at sea level was off the table.

Ancestral land is a big deal in town. Many families stayed on the same property, adding to or modifying their houses, generation after generation. There was pride in raising families on the same plot of land our ancestors slept on. Asking families to forsake their land and move elsewhere was going to be met with wild discontent. I knew this, and I could handle the backlash. What I needed was a plan.

How could I keep families living where they were before and keep them from rebuilding at sea level? The only option I could think of was to raise the land. Fill in the city center with soil and rebuild on raised land. Their ancestral plots would be fifteen meters below, but an argument could be made saying it was still the same plot. A long shot, perhaps. I was willing to try.

I started talking about my plan with several key personnel in City Hall. I gradually widened the circle, and as I suspected, soon the city was buzzing with rumors. Someone had leaked the fact I was attempting a major project that wouldn't let people build on their land. The pace at which rumors of my plan spread was surprising and yet impressive. Tempers flared immediately, and I had to manage the disinformation quickly. As is typical of rumors, most of what people were hearing wasn't accurate. The parts that were accurate were missing major facts. Clearly, I wasn't aware of who in my inner circle wasn't completely on board with my plans. Or was this a personal dissatisfaction with me personally? I couldn't be sure. Either way, my plan had been leaked and it was spreading throughout town.

Needing a concrete plan on paper I could share with others to make it official, I called in experts. Engineers who understood seismology, structural integrity, hardening and compacting soil, everything I could think of. I delegated and told the experts to bring in whoever they thought was needed to form a team who could create a science-based plan.

We had already been told by the government that we had to rebuild our seawall and it had to be higher. I wasn't going to get the full height I wanted: the tsunami averaged 15 meters along the coast and Hirota Bay, so I wanted a 15-meter wall. In the end, I was told by the powers that be in the government that it could be 12 meters. That meant if a similar-sized tsunami came, it would clear the seawall and the city center would be inundated with water again. That wasn't happening. Not if I had anything to say about it.

I had a different solution. I lobbied to raise the town above sea level. No building houses at sea level ever again. Ever. We're doing it right this time. This was my message to the residents and City Hall staff alike. This kind of devastation was not going to happen again. No future generation of Rikuzentakata residents would lose their lives, property, or well-being because of mistakes made by previous generations. I and others were going to make sure of that—even if it meant this might be our biggest challenge to date.

If we raised the land in the downtown area, then the city center could be ten to 12 meters higher than sea level. How much soil was needed for that and where would I get that soil? Would people move back to where their land was, even if their ancestral land was 12 meters below? And what about those who had rented? They didn't own their property or land, but many families had lived and operated their business out of the same building for generations. Where were they going to find the money to rebuild? How long would they live in or have a temporary storefront before they gave up and moved into the hills? This had to happen fast.

The experts created an extensive plan. I agreed with it and submitted it to the city council. Their decision was going to take a while as not everyone on city council liked or agreed with me. Some of their dislike was political and for others it was personal. In the end, there was enough support for the proposed plan and next we had to take it to the residents. They needed to be told what was happening.

We held open forum meetings in community centers throughout town. Of course, there was pushback. I knew from the beginning not everyone would be on board and yet a decision had to be made. We soon came across a catch 22. Those who had rented their property as living space or as a business couldn't apply for a loan until they could identify how much space they would need. We couldn't assure them we could guarantee that space until they could tell us how much they needed, which they couldn't do without knowing they would have the money to pay for it. Then there was the fact their buildings weren't destroyed in the earthquake. They were destroyed in the tsunami, and not everyone had tsunami insurance. A loan was necessary but both parties needed the other's information before there could be any agreement. Here again, protocol overruled the real-life needs of the residents in town. It was cruel.

It wasn't my intent to complicate the process or cause hardship. I wanted these obstacles gone as much as these people did, but my hands were tied. There simply wasn't anything I could do. They had to give me their information first, which meant they would have to convince the banks to give them loans. If they couldn't get loans, they had to either find money elsewhere or give up on building on the same spot and try to find land in the hills. Rules are necessary. I understand that. But our culture's complete reliance upon these rules made reconstruction that much more painful.

~~~

Takashi Kubota, my Deputy Mayor, had worked on many projects in the Prime Minister's Cabinet Office before moving to Rikuzentakata. One of his projects would prove extremely useful. Ship for World Youth was a program bringing together the brightest minds of young leaders—politicians, academics, doctors, and so on. The program put them on a giant ship and sailed them around certain parts of the world. The idea was to create a future generation of leaders who have known each other from their twenties and thirties onward. It's much more difficult to go to war with a country when you're friends with leaders of that country. Create peace ahead of time through an intensive and intimate, sometimes difficult cultural program. Keeping them on a ship and strategically stopping at locations that would push them to think creatively was an added bonus.

Takashi had organized this project and now was in a position to bring this ship to us. Ōfunato Bay had a large enough port for the cruise ship to dock. From there, we could bring these leaders from eleven countries to schools, organizations, and companies. They could meet locals, and see for themselves what life in the aftermath of destruction looks like. I was fully on board. This was an excellent idea.

Soon enough, news spread of the arrival of what to the residents of Ōfunato and Rikuzentakata looked like a luxury cruise ship. Was it luxurious? It certainly looked that way. How many of us had ever been on a ship this large? Winding staircases with chandeliers, multiple levels of floors and rooms and a dining room with exquisite silverware and white tablecloths. It certainly looked elegant and expensive.

The program chose young people from all over the world. Kenya, New Zealand, Peru, Saudi Arabia, and more came into Rikuzentakata. There was no point in being subtle about it; these people stood out.

One such group came to Rikuzentakata City Hall for the day. Amya gave a long and moving speech that had people crying. I spoke and more people cried. In the Q&A session that followed, I was asked what I did when there wasn't consensus on a project I wanted to implement.

I thought for a moment. Then, I said, "As a leader, reaching consensus and having buy-in is the ideal outcome. It's also unfortunately not always possible. Whenever we start big projects, I make it a point to take my plans and ideas to the residents. I would love to have the residents of the city approve and agree with everything I want to do. Not everyone does and I have to live with that. In my opinion, a good leader has to know when to just implement a project, to do something that's unpopular because the leader believes it's the right thing to do. It's an unfortunate reality of leadership. It may mean people feel I'm not listening to them, but the truth is, I can't. There are too many differing opinions. I can't do what everyone wants. It may come across as lip service, asking for input and ignoring it, but sometimes that's what a good leader has to do."

Amya interpreted these words for me. Later that night when she and I and others from City Hall were invited to a dinner reception on the ship, she interpreted for me again as I made another speech. We mingled with the sea of foreigners in bright-colored outfits and chatted with various delegates throughout the night.

The evening was a success. As Amya and I walked down the steps toward our cars, she called to me. "I need to ask you something," she said.

"What is it?"

"What you said earlier today, about not listening to what everyone has to say and just doing what you think is right."

"Yeah," I said.

"There were people there in the audience from city council," she said and I could guess where she was going.

"You think I shouldn't have said that," I said, not as a question.

"I think they're going to repeat what you said," Amya said.

I felt my face flush with unwelcome anger. Yes, those city council members in attendance who didn't like me would indeed tell people in town what I said. But I was right. I couldn't listen to everyone.

"Do you think I'm wrong, not to listen?" I asked.

"You do listen," she said. "But you have the final say. I just think you need to be careful how you phrase that. You might be listening to their words, but if you're saying up front that in the end you're going to do what you want, they're not going to feel heard," she said.

"Thanks for that. So, what do you suggest?" I said, and I knew she could hear my sarcasm—as if she had the answer—there was anger in my voice.

"I think there's a decent sized group of residents that don't agree with you," she said and added "or like you." As if that wasn't bad enough, she then said, "And, I think their numbers are growing."

"Again, what do you suggest I do?"

Amya paused. This was uncharacteristic of her. I sensed she was either going to blow up at me or cave and drop the subject.

"I'm not mayor," she finally said. "Still-" before she could continue, I cut her off.

"That's right. You're not. I am."

I could see in her eyes she was angry.

"I was just trying to be helpful," she said.

"Then give me a concrete suggestion," I snapped. She looked straight at me.

"You do what you think is right." With that, she turned around and walked toward her van.

I was tired. She was tired. It had been a long day and a long several years. I would cool off as would she. But tonight I didn't like her tone and I knew she didn't like my response. We needed space.

I didn't see her the next day or the day following. I saw her van driving down a road from a distance so I knew she was in town. I had back-to-back meetings and appointments. She surely did as well. Next thing I knew I saw she was posting on the city's Facebook page from Tokyo. She had left town.

And I had work to do.

The following week, I heard her before I saw her. Someone was laughing in the large room outside my office. Amya's voice rang out and more people laughed. I couldn't hear what she was saying but I was grateful for the laughter. When I came out of my office after a few more meetings, I saw she was at her desk typing away on her laptop. She had headphones on and was staring intently at the screen. I walked up to her, stopped, and she looked up. Taking off her glasses and pulling out her earphones, she smiled.

"You okay?" I asked her. She nodded.

"You?" I nodded, too.

"Good," she said.

"I'm going home," I said.

"Okay. Have a nice evening," she said, and then added "Tell the boys I said hi." I started to walk away but after a few steps I turned back and said, "Don't stay too long!" Still facing the laptop, she waved at me. Got it, Mayor.

We were fine.

Chapter 22

Amya Miller

Cost benefit analysis. In the aftermath of a disaster of this magnitude, it was a loaded topic. Fraught with more questions than answers, someone needed to first decide whether this city was worth saving. It sounds cruel because it is. If a city that was already losing population is essentially wiped out, should it be rebuilt? Who decides that, and how?

The powerful imagery of the women weeping in front of what used to be their homes. The number of white boxes—makeshift coffins—lined up neatly and never-ending. The aerial views of the coastline taken from police, Self Defense Force, and media helicopters and airplanes. All of this indicated the sheer scale of the tsunami disaster. All of this made the idea of abandoning reconstruction a nonstarter. The central government couldn't easily say to these communities, "Sorry, folks, it's simply going to cost too much to rebuild all your cities. Take what you have and move somewhere else."

Declining population was certainly a problem all throughout Japan, and not a new one. The cities and towns along the 500 kilometers of coastline in the region, Aomori Prefecture to Chiba Prefecture, were all steadily declining in population, and after being utterly flattened by this disaster there was no reason to expect they'd start to grow. This left the government with very few options. To expect these cities to reverse the trends wasn't realistic and yet not investing in the region because it was dying even before the disaster wasn't an option. The Government of Japan couldn't very well tell these disaster victims "You're all on your own. We're letting the cities return to the wild. You'll have to find somewhere else to live and work." The national and international public relations disaster that would have ensued would have been catastrophic.

If the Government of Japan was not going to abandon these cities—and it wasn't—then reconstruction needed to be about recreating a city while making it safe for future generations. Both elements were paramount in the planning.

The administration of the third Prime Minister since the disaster, Shinzō Abe,[14] had tasked all cities along the coastline with the non-negotiable stipulation of rebuilding their seawalls. There was an immediate backlash. Every single seawall, including all 15 of those off the coast of Rikuzentakata, had been useless in this most recent disaster. No seawall had protected a city. Every single one had been demolished. Why should they be rebuilt? They hadn't worked before. Why would anyone believe they would work in the future?

To the residents and leaders of the cities and towns and villages, this was both a ridiculous and unnecessary addition to the tasks that lay ahead. Still, the Abe Administration had mandated it, so Mayor Toba had to move forward with the plan. Arguing against the Prime Minister, he knew, would never work. Since the tsunami that squarely hit the areas of Takata and Kesen had been around 15 meters high, Mayor Toba asked for a plan to rebuild a seawall of 15 meters. If this was truly a disaster that came along once every 1000 years, then a 15-meter seawall should be plenty high for the foreseeable future. The reply he received was "No," and instead, the city was told it would receive funds to build a 12-meter seawall.

Here we go again. More bureaucracy. More red tape. More negotiations that take forever and we still don't get our way. In the end, Mayor Toba's arguments for a 15-meter wall didn't sway the decision-makers, and preparations were made for a 12-meter seawall. To the politicians and residents of the city, this was a slap in the face. Mayor Toba was not prepared to accept this. He wasn't going to rebuild on land that's not safe. How would he be able to look future generations in the eye and tell them this was the best he could do?

If rebuilding at sea level was out of the question, then Takata and Kesen—the areas worst hit—had two choices. They could forever abandon erecting new buildings, or the land had to be raised to a height that made rebuilding safe. Mayor Toba chose the latter. Although it would be a massive process, elevating the land above sea level to a height that was safe was the only logical way forward that Mayor Toba could see if the town was going to continue to exist.

So it was decided: the land would be raised. This meant a new committee needed to be formed, comprised of locals as well as experts who understood the science and engineering behind such an endeavor. Academics and urban planning consultants were hired and together with city council members, agricultural and fishery cooperative representatives, local leaders and other City Hall staff, a 50-person team was created to work through the logistics of physically raising the land.

In the areas of Takata and Kesen, there were approximately 2,200 households' worth of land. This meant a large number of landowners needed to be contacted. Eminent domain was not an option in Japan, the laws regarding land transfer being very different in Japan than other parts of the world. The creation of a new airport in Tokyo (Narita) in the 1970s, and the debacle that ensued with riots and protests and violence as the government tried to take over farmland to build the airport, is recent enough history that it dare not be repeated again. There is an intense attachment to land in Japan, especially if it is land passed down through a family for generations. Asking people to abandon the land where their ancestors lived and walked is a tough sell. This is exactly what needed to be done to these 2,200 or so landowners, many of whom were tsunami victims. All of these landowners had to be identified, located, and contacted in person. Almost 60% of these landowners lived near enough that visiting them in person and asking for their cooperation in working out a land swap deal would not be too much of a burden on City Hall staff. The goal was to have the city purchase the land where their home stood and give them either land of equivalent size somewhere else in the city or the cash necessary for them to start over.

City Hall had begun receiving staff from other municipalities across Japan on loan, usually on a one-, or two-year basis. A problematic but humorous situation soon arose. Those who were new to Tōhoku could not understand the thick accent of this region. Locals who were middle aged and younger were accustomed to speaking in standard Japanese—the style spoken by newscasters—and could make themselves understood. Many could switch off the dialect and speak 'normally' when called for. Unfortunately, many of the elderly in town couldn't—and it was they who owned most of this land. Staff who weren't accustomed to this accent simply couldn't be sure they were getting through to these elders or understanding them clearly. This was no way to negotiate anything, much less something as serious as a land swap. Still, Mayor Toba didn't have the headcount he was used to, as City Hall had lost one quarter of its staff. He had to make do with the staff he had, including those on loan. Paperwork was reviewed even more thoroughly, making sure everything was written down: sheets of paper handed over for confirmation that the landowners really did understand what they were agreeing to.

For the remaining 40% of the landowners, the staff had to first identify the owners themselves, and if they had perished, their next of kin. With the computers gone and the databases needing to be restored, this process alone took months. Once the next of kin were found, City Hall then had to send staff to them wherever they were located. Some of those whom the staff visited thought this was suspicious, and accusations of fraud and dishonesty ensued. At other times, the staff visiting the relatives were met with firm "this has nothing to do with me" responses, clearly shocked that someone's land so far away was now theirs and they had to actually make a decision about it. On more than one occasion there were multiple individuals listed as next of kin, making it profoundly more difficult to identify which one or ones had the final say.

The construction to raise the land in Takata and Kesen could not begin until all landowners in those areas had been contacted and approval attained. The approval process became so time-consuming that the city council wanted to pass a new ordinance: four-fifths of the landowners' permission was enough to begin construction. Mayor Toba went to the Ministry of Land, Infrastructure, Transport and Tourism multiple times trying to get them to either expedite the paperwork (again) or allow this exception. The ministry was concerned about legal ramifications on laws relating to property ownership. Without these approvals, city officials couldn't authorize stepping onto someone else's land and digging or building. Mayor Toba pushed Diet members he knew to allow an exception without delay. Finally, permission was granted. All that was needed was for four-fifths of the landowners to approve. Still, the whole process to get this approval took three years. It was ridiculous.

During these negotiations, Mayor Toba was dealing with city council members who had lost family and homes and everything resembling the past. He worked side-by-side every day with people who were still grieving. One city council member would not let go—he openly wept at the memory of his wife and continued to live in temporary housing. Repeated attempts to ask him to move out, to show leadership by example all failed. Public sentiments that showed discord or friction within the leadership of City Hall led to confusion among the locals who were unsure whom to believe. In the end, while Mayor Toba was focused on rebuilding a city, more and more locals became frustrated with the pace, the lack of visual change. Their voices started to turn neighbor against neighbor.

Mayor Toba saw all of this happening and desperately wanted to speed the process. With approval from Tokyo, the change finally began. Again, the discussions with Tokyo had taken far too long and the already-frayed nerves of the residents needed addressing. It was time to speed things up. Understanding and buy-in would be ideal but Mayor Toba had long since learned he couldn't rely on that. He couldn't expect everyone in town to be on board. The grief in town was still palpable, and time was not on his side.

Practically speaking, the goal was to move earth into the former area of downtown, raising the land ten or twelve meters and rebuilding the new downtown area on top of that. This way there was no chance of anyone ever building at sea level again. It would be physically impossible. The Mayor's first hurdle was the sheer amount of soil needed to do this. The committee in charge of the project calculated that the soil needed to raise an area several square kilometers wide ended up being an amount so immense that it would take 4,000 dump trucks hauling 20,000 cubic meters every day for about ten years to complete. This was obviously unfeasible. Japan as a country did not have 4,000 extra dump trucks the city could use, and waiting this long was not an option.

Mayor Toba had to think creatively. After weighing the options, he began entertaining a proposal to build a massive conveyor belt. The calculations done by experts and engineers told him it would take two and a half years to move the soil needed across the river. That was a considerable improvement over the near-decade estimate from the trucks.

The Mayor's plan was to take down the mountain across the Kesen River and haul that soil over to Takata. The mountain was the area closest to Takata, and usable land was already scarce. The construction project started by blasting the side of the mountain in order to install the mouth of the conveyor belt. While that was happening, a bridge to haul the large rocks and soil from the mountain had to be built, with the conveyor traversing its length. Arms would extend out with each new area of town that needed earth. When activated, soil poured out of the spout on the end at 250 meters per minute, creating a mound beneath it and causing a cloud of brown dust to rise up, covering the city in a thin film of grime. In total, the conveyor belt stretched for three kilometers and looked very much like a giant metallic octopus that had invaded the city.

Foreigners flocked to the region to stand and gawk at the scale of the massive conveyor. Soon, news of the conveyor belt was on the CBS Evening News throughout the U.S.[15]

There was some opposition, mainly environmental groups unhappy with the destruction of nature and the habitats of various animals. Mayor Toba didn't keep track of who they were or what cause they represented—they were just one more element that needed dealing with. To them he came up with a one-sentence answer, and he repeated it every time he was cornered in interviews. "Human life is more important than that of a plant or animal right now." The people in town depended on this space being rebuilt, and Mayor Toba wasn't going to explain to a community of elderly why they couldn't rebuild their homes because it was more important to save the eco-system of a mountain across the river.

Mayor Toba focused on the conveyor belt and the possibilities it brought. Here, finally, was a visual sign of rebuilding. The growth of the belt was a concrete and immediate symbol of progress, the tool that convinced all.

It didn't take long for the questions to emerge. In newspaper editorials and in academic settings experts began openly asking whether Rikuzentakata's latest construction project was worth this much money—a figure that came out to approximately 1.1 billion U.S. dollars to build, operate, and ultimately dismantle the conveyor after the job was complete.

Many detractors took issue with the fact that this staggering amount of money was being spent on one city, one that was already decreasing in pop-ulation and luster even before the disaster all but wiped it out. That much money could have been put to a great many other uses—funding public health programs, securing and running educational programs, or financing medical research for the betterment of humankind. Instead that tax money was spent on one city. Was the government really going to pour in hun-dreds of millions of dollars per city, billions at times, all up and down the northeastern coastline of Japan? That might end up in the tens of billions of dollars. Sleepy, quiet cities and towns would be rebuilt, but was rebuilding the same thing as revitalizing? Would this dynamic expenditure result in an increase in population? Would these tired economies boom once again? No one could answer those questions. But the questions kept coming.

It all came back to the larger issue at hand—was this city worth rebuilding? Was Rikuzentakata, a city with a population hovering around 20,000 people, worth spending 1.1 billion U.S. dollars on? The danger was in the question itself. If the answer was 'No' then the Government of Japan made a dramatic error and would have to explain that to its citizens. It also opened up a larger question: would cities that faced future natural disasters also need to be prepared to one day be leveled and ultimately abandoned? Was there a cutoff number for population, or a population-to-cost ratio the government used to make these determinations? Was there a notoriety factor, a certain popularity level that entered in the decision making? Was Rikuzentakata chosen as a city suitable and worthy for rebuilding because Mayor Toba kept making a fuss and attracting so much attention?

Japan is entrenched firmly on the Pacific Ring of Fire. Tokyo and the coastline southwest of Tokyo Bay are said to be long overdue for a mega-quake. It's assumed Tokyo will always be rebuilt; it's government-center after all, financially important nationally and internationally. Letting it return to nature is not an option. But what about the smaller towns along the coast like Rikuzentakata, places that will surely experience a similar disaster?

The impending mega-quake notwithstanding, if the government determined whether Rikuzentakata was worth rebuilding, then they needed to find a way to funnel billions more when it came time to rebuild after the next disaster that occurs in Japan. Where would this money come from? Further, this reconstruction effort was not occurring in a vacuum; the world was watching. If one portion of Rikuzentakata's reconstruction was worth 1.1 billion U.S. dollars, was it safe to assume small cities all over the world could ask the same of their governments? Conversely, if cities and towns the size of Rikuzentakata and smaller were not worth saving, then that also set a precedent. Would that precedent spark a global mass exodus from rural areas into cities?

On World Awareness Tsunami Day in 2018, Mayor Toba spoke at the United Nations in New York City. He reiterated that simply accepting the death toll was not an acceptable outcome to a tsunami. Preparedness was a must. There could be no compromise. With this global stage also came the responsibility to showcase how reconstruction can and must be done.

Reflecting upon the cost of rebuilding the neighborhoods of Takata and Kesen required an acknowledgement that the costs reached 1.1 billion for a reason. If the decision to build the seawall at 15 meters as requested by Rikuzentakata City Hall had been approved, there would not have been a need to raise the land.

This fact makes a powerful statement to those creating and enforcing policies regarding recovery. Perhaps it was one man and perhaps it was a committee. The fact remains, someone outside of Rikuzentakata—someone who didn't fully understand the situation or didn't think through their reply—made a decision to deny City Hall's request. That decision led to the need to raise land to a safe height. The amount of additional and unnecessary hours, sleepless nights, and anxiety this decision cost are all incalculable.

Mayor Toba held accountable those who questioned whether his sleepy town of 20,000 deserved this price tag, or any. This process required him to step forward with a simple retort: "What are you suggesting I do?" Without a concrete, realistic answer that was actually possible to implement, he had to be clear that he wanted no more part of this discussion.

Chapter 23

Amya Miller

The message read, "Hi, my name is Kota Kobayashi. I'm a graphic designer from Brooklyn, New York." A young Japanese man had created a brand of homebrewed beer called Ippon Matsu Beer,[16] had held a fundraiser in Brooklyn, and wanted to donate the money raised to someone in Rikuzentakata.

Ippon Matsu, the name of this beer, commemorates the disaster area's Miracle Pine or Lone Pine, the only tree left out of the 70,000 pine trees that made up *Takata Matsubara*, Rikuzentakata's pine forest, abutting the white sand beach on Hirota Bay. Considered one of Japan's top 100 scenic spots, the photos I've seen show the contrast between the white sand and blue water, framed on one side by the green trees with brown trunks. It had been an elegant grove with walking paths and benches.

Akira, one of the guys who had helped with my preschool holiday events over the years, told me this forest was where he had had his first date in high school. I was sorry I'd never gotten the chance to see it. The pine grove had been planted over 300 years ago by the ancestors of the residents of Rikuzentakata specifically as a tsunami barrier. That it didn't do what the ancestors had hoped it would—save the city—was a bitter reality.

All of the trees, except for the one pine, the Ippon Matsu, were washed away. Tree trunks along the coast remained for the first several years of my stay in Rikuzentakata, looking like toothpicks snapped at various lengths stuck into the sand. Uprooted trees with roots exposed lay here and there. When the piles of debris were sorted by category, the pine trees made up a pile of their own, becoming bleached white from constant exposure to sun and wind. The Ippon Matsu stood all the way over to the right of the pine grove, already taller than the other pine trees surrounding it. Even before the disaster it was seen as a loner, taller and with a unique crown of branches at the top not shared by the others. Its survival was a miracle, a symbol personifying the spirit of strength of the people of Tōhoku. It projected hope: quiet, stoic, stubborn. It wasn't going anywhere. No tsunami would tear it down. It was staying put.

The men in town insisted the tree was male. The women listening to this rolled their eyes. To the men, it was important the tree was male—reflecting the spirit of the *samurai*. The women didn't care what gender it was. To them, it symbolized a miracle—a visual reminder: we're still here.

Though the Ippon Matsu stood tall, the salt water left behind by the tsunami took its toll. Over time its root system began to die, and eventually the tree was officially declared unsalvageable. Not one to call it quits, Mayor Toba launched a fundraising campaign to save the tree. The plan involved cutting it down, dividing it into sections, and then boring a hole through the sections and inserting a steel pole up the middle. The bark would be injected with resin to keep it looking real, and the branches and pine needles would be artificial.

Funds poured in from all over the country and within a few months there was more than enough money to preserve the Miracle Pine. With the help of an expert arborist, the tree was carefully cut down and sent to a woodworking facility to be preserved. The finished product arrived shortly afterwards, and the Ippon Matsu was replaced on the ground where it had once stood. For anyone looking up at its majestic height, it was nearly impossible to tell it was not a real tree.

However, this project was met with outrage from some foreigners in Japan who thought the money used for the tree was siphoned off from other development projects. I was barely polite in quelling rumors and objections raised by some of the locals or members of the press.

"The donated money is specifically for the tree. It's a symbol of what remains," I explained to anyone who pushed back. "It's Tōhoku's version of the Atom Bomb Memorial in Hiroshima. It will be a place where generations can come to learn and mourn. There's plenty of money left for the development projects we have scheduled, and besides, no revenue was taken from existing projects to fund this."

Kota Kobayashi's message to me had been fraught with possible misinterpretation, since anything with the Ippon Matsu label on it had the potential to be seen as another misuse of funds. I carefully asked him about his fundraiser. Certainly, I was grateful for what he had done, but I needed him to elaborate. Back came a video about his brewed craft beer. His design label had won an award, and the beer was getting good press. Kota had raised 100,000 yen (approximately 1100 U.S. dollars) for donation, to be contributed on his behalf to some Rikuzentakata business owners.

In my role in Tōhoku, I found that many projects had a tipping point. There came a point where the decision had to be made to trust and dive in or drop the project altogether. With Kota, the decision was to trust. The money arrived and went to a local business, a gift shop in town, *Iwai*. I had gotten to know the owners and liked the fact they showcased art from local artists—pottery, prints, jewelry, glassware, and fabric all beautifully displayed in their temporary storefront, the artists' names on a card underneath.

I continued to work with Kota and his fundraisers every year in commemoration of the March memorial. He would hold an event in Tokyo with an admission fee, with beer and pizza, where he would auction off art and other items donated by his friends. All of it went to a local business in town of my choice. One year he and a group of friends cycled all the way from Tokyo to Rikuzentakata. The money raised that year was donated to a bicycle shop in town whose owner had died in the tsunami.

Another important Rikuzentakata connection for Kota was his acquaintance with the local *sake* brewery in town, Suisen. I put Kota in touch with Suzuki-*san* and the other members of the brewery. By this point the men who worked at Suisen had gradually become like adopted brothers to me. We would argue like siblings, we would kid each other, and I knew if I ever truly needed something they were there to help. And as fellow professionals in similar industries, I hoped they would make a connection with Kota and get to know each other, brewer to brewer, not just funder to recipient.

More than just a professional connection, however, it was important to me that these two breweries connect over their shared significance to this region. The Ippon Matsu was a symbol of hope to the people of Rikuzentakata—to name something after it carried weight. Likewise, the name Suisen had been coined by a local artist Kagaku Satō, around seventy years ago. He had written a poem about the land of enchantment, a place that was said to be where the magi, wisemen, or hermits lived. According to the poem, it was best to enter the land of enchantment drunk. The term *Suisen* translates as "drunken magi" or "drunken wiseman" or "drunken hermit." The idea was to enjoy this local *sake* enough that when people decided to enter a life of hermithood, they would do so drunk.

Indeed, in the newly rebuilt front entryway of Suisen hangs a large painting of an old man with long white hair and a wild white beard in a white smock walking around the mountains. Is he drunk? Obviously. But he also represented this bit of local pride, the poem written by an artist from their region. The poem was a bit of culture that had come from their community, and they wanted to preserve this lore through their *sake*.

Kota's fundraisers kept pouring money into the local companies as well as into the local economy as he brought people up from Tokyo and spread the word of the needs of those affected by the tsunami. Over a period of six years, Kota and his friends through Ippon Matsu Beer raised and distributed over 1,300,000 yen (approximately 14,000 dollars).[17] He donated to the Orphans' Fund in town through the Board of Education. He got in touch with Iwai-*san*, a gift shop owner who told Kota how every house in his neighborhood, including his own, had been destroyed. Kota met Katsurō-*san*, who ran a local farm-to-table restaurant and made his own craft beer out of local apples. From Katsurō-*san* he heard that, "After five years we just assumed people around the world would have moved on," words Kota took back to Tokyo to share with his friends as they planned another fundraiser for the following year.

Ippon Matsu Beer's slogan is "Brewed with a Purpose." Kota's actions proved the beer brewed with the purpose of helping people out did just that.

Chapter 24

Amya Miller

Eight preschools a month, always in the morning because after lunch was naptime. Meetings had to be planned around this timing, as the preschool visits were a project unrelated to my work at City Hall. I was doing this on my own time. It couldn't conflict with my other work. The workload varied wildly from one preschool to the next. Some schools had only ten students, while others had nearly two hundred. At the schools with few students, I could play with everyone together, all ages represented, babies through five-year-olds.

At one preschool there was a set of twin girls, Rio and Mio, who would always scream in terror when I walked through the door. They were eighteen months old when I first met them and it was heartbreaking each time shoved their faces into the teachers' chests, tears dripping onto their bibs, their screams carrying all the way down the hallway. I looked and smelled so different than anyone else they had seen that my foreignness was threatening. The teachers all assured me the children who cried would get over it.

"Don't change anything you're doing," they said everywhere I went. I took their advice to heart and kept showing up. It took months, but eventually Rio and Mio grew comfortable with me and would even seek me out. We played as if nothing was wrong, as though they had always felt comfortable around me and it was the most normal thing ever to have a foreign auntie show up at their preschool for playtime.

When Rio and Mio were four, a little boy, Naoto, joined the preschool. He had just turned two, and would scream every time I walked through the front door just like the twins had several years back. One day, I saw Rio poke

Mio and pull her over. Rio whispered to Mio as I stood and watched. When Rio was done, they both nodded, marched over to Naoto and told him that they, too, were once scared of Amya-*sensei*. But see, now we are friends and she's not scary at all. He didn't have to cry. Amya-*sensei* was nice. She'll bring us candy for Halloween. Naoto warmed up to me shortly after that. Did those four-year-old twins actually convince two-year-old Naoto that I was safe? Was it really that simple?

The children in the region had heard of Halloween on television, watching commercials featuring people in pumpkin and vampire costumes. They knew of the concept of Halloween, but the holiday wasn't celebrated in these towns. No one was familiar with trick-or-treating, and costumes were nowhere to be found. With the Christmas party the previous year a resounding success, I approached the teachers about doing a similar Halloween party. I would bring more candy, I assured them, firmly believing people would come through with more donations. The teachers were delighted and told me they wanted an excuse to dress up as well. None of them had ever worn a costume before. I asked around for more donations of American candy again, and this time had the donors ship directly to my room in Rikuzentakata. The previous Christmas had featured a long drive in the snow in a giant van filled with boxes. Not a particularly pleasurable experience. This time I would keep it simple.

I dressed up as a witch for the first Halloween party. I had told my friends in both Ōfunato and Rikuzentakata of what I was doing for Halloween. They all wanted to see me as a witch.
Mayor Toba said, "You show up here dressed as a witch, I'll call the police on you."
"Oh yeah?" I replied, hoping my reply would outwit his. "I'm a witch. Witches have powers the police will never have. Go ahead. Call the police. I will unleash a mighty storm, right here." People in the office started to chuckle. I held out my arms and said in a loud voice,
"Behold, the power of the witch!"
To this he simply replied, "Ooooooh", his fingers wiggling in the air in mock fear.
The staff listening into our banter burst into laughter. Mayor Toba seldom joked publicly like this, letting his guard down and showing such vulnerability. They enjoyed seeing a softer and silly side of him and they felt more relaxed witnessing our back-and-forth.

In Ōfunato, I was met with more comments.

"It suits you, being a witch," Kōtarō said, chuckling.

"That's a compliment, yes?" I said, genuinely curious. Kōtarō just rolled his eyes.

"What?" I insisted. "Is it or isn't it?"

"You're a witch," Kazuki said. "Read his mind. Is he telling the truth or not?"

"Fine," I said and squinted my eyes at Kōtarō, pretending to read him.

"Hmmmm," I said. "I don't like what I'm seeing in your brain."

Everyone else around the table laughed. All the intensity that surrounded us in the recovery environment left us collectively exhausted. These moments of genuine and unexpected laughter were treats.

Kōtarō was a local businessman running his own print shop. He was divorced, around my age, and known for his love of beer, so much so that he had to build dry nights into his calendar. He had been seeing a doctor and undergoing bloodwork to check his liver, which showed clear signs that he needed to cut back on alcohol. Every now and then he would show me his small pocket-sized calendar, indicating the dates with red lines through them. "These are my dry days," he said proudly, as if the calendar was a photo of his children.

"That's a lot of red," I said, counting the days. "You've gone almost half the month without alcohol." This was unusual for Kōtarō.

"Yeah, well, my liver numbers were pretty high last month," he said.

"Good," I said. "I'm glad you're cutting back then."

He announced he would be joining me for the Halloween party the next morning over the phone.

"You have to dress up, too," I said, grinning to myself.

"Nah," he said.

"Oh yes you do. It's Halloween. Everyone wears a costume," I insisted. I could imagine him on the other end of the phone, his eyes narrowing, trying to decide whether I was telling the truth or pulling a prank.

"Really," I said.

"I'll think about it," he finally said.

I told him which preschool to be at and gave him a time.

"Don't forget your costume," I said over the phone. "Oh, and can I borrow a broom?"

"A broom?" he asked.

"Yeah. I'm a witch. I need a broom," I said matter-of-factly, and he laughed out loud. I didn't think it was that funny, but then again I was the first and likely the only witch he would ever see. In his world there were no witches. It made sense he didn't know I would need a broom.

The morning of my first Halloween party Kōtarō showed up on time, broom in hand. He was dressed all in black and carried a large plastic trash bag. "Where's your costume?" I asked, once we were inside, hidden away in a side conference room off the teacher's lounge.
"In here," he said, tapping the plastic bag.
"Let's see it," I said. He grinned and opened the bag, pulling out a long black cape followed by a massive black hat. The hat was made with black paper, the staples visible all over. Had he made this himself? It looked like a cross between a pilgrim's hat and something Zorro might wear.

Kōtarō put the hat on and wrapped the cape around his neck with a flourish. I still couldn't figure out what he was supposed to be.
"Um," I started.
"Don't tell me you don't know what I am," he said, visibly upset. I had no idea. Should I guess?
"You're a wizard," I finally said, hoping I was right. The hat was all wrong for a wizard and the all-black outfit wasn't particularly telling, but I guessed this is what he thought a wizard was.
"Of course I'm a wizard!" he said, sounding a bit disgruntled at my lack of enthusiasm. "You're a witch, so I'm a wizard."
"I think that's great," I told him, hoping I sounded sincere. "Really, it works."
He nodded, looking pleased with himself.

Careful not to be seen, we made our way in through a side door so we wouldn't spoil the surprise for the children in the front classroom. I wanted our costumes to be a surprise so we could make a grand entrance. We peeked out of the conference room to see a swarm of children dressed in a variety of handmade costumes moving toward the preschool gymnasium. The excitement was palpable. Children laughed and screeched, trading details about their costumes. "Mine has an orange pumpkin *and* a white pumpkin!" I heard someone brag, pointing at objects pasted onto the paper bags on their heads. There was a lot of surreptitious whispering about the traditions of this unfamiliar holiday. I kept hearing words like "ghosts" and "pumpkins" and "bats" passing from kid to kid. I was witnessing something entirely new. This preschool, teachers and staff and children alike, they were all going through a new experience together. A positive experience. Something fun. I smiled. This is why I did what I did.

The last to show up in costume were the babies. They, too, were to be included in this parade of goblins and ghosts and pumpkins. Kōtarō nudged me, peering out from our hiding place. I glanced over at him.

"That," he said pointing, "is the cutest thing I've seen in a long time." I turned back to look where he was pointing. Four babies sat in a carriage, all of them dressed in adorable costumes. In the front sat a turnip and a dog, and behind them were a pair of siblings dressed as Daisy and Donald Duck. All were completely oblivious to why they were wearing outfits. This was incredible, far more than I had ever hoped for. And Kōtarō was right. It was adorable.

The principal went into the gymnasium. She wore layers of black plastic trash bags covered in orange paper cutouts, had on a wild wig of a mass of curly hair, and she had mismatched fake long nails that looked more like claws— what was she supposed to be? With the door to our hiding place closed, the principal's words were muffled. But when she finished speaking, I heard the children squeal in unison. Whatever she'd said had gotten them excited.

One of the teachers snuck over to us and nodded. This was my cue. I started around the corner with my broom and suitcase full of candy but she held up a hand, stopping me just short of the entrance to the gym.

I heard the principal call out to the kids. "You all remember Amya-*sensei*, yes?"

"*Hai*," the kids said in unison.

"Well, today she's here to play with you again! But," and she lowered her voice conspiratorially, "today she's dressed up as a witch!" The last word was said in a loud voice and I heard the gasps of the kids.

"Let's all call her together. One, two, three, Amya-*sensei*!" The kids raised their voices together, calling to me through the door—their chorus both hilarious and glorious. I made a grand entrance, sweeping my black cape around me as the children shrieked in delight.

I twirled, bowed and introduced myself as Amya the Witch. Producing my suitcase from behind my cloak, I whispered to the kids about a magical treasure I had brought for them. With some faux magic words and a wave of stick I picked up outside for a wand I slowly started to unzip the top of the suitcase. I peeked inside, gasping and feigning surprise. The kids gasped back at me.

"It worked!" I said, looking from the suitcase to the kids and then back at the suitcase. "There's a ton of candy in here!"

The kids erupted in cheers, and I heard the babies start to fuss from all of the din, which had gotten so loud it almost drowned out their wails. Several of the teachers—Minnie Mouse, a snowman, and something that might have been a squid—ran to the babies, picking them up and hushing them.

I told the children I needed an assistant to help with the candy, realizing Kōtarō was nowhere in sight. I said I had brought along a wizard and asked the children to help me call him to us.

"One, two, three, Wizard!" we all screamed, the babies crying harder.

Kōtarō poked his head out from behind the door, his face scarlet. He clearly hadn't known what to expect. Now I wasn't sure why he had insisted he come along. Surely he knew I would put him to work?

"Here's Mr. Wizard!" I said, gesturing with both hands to a very reluctant Kōtarō, who shuffled into the gym. "I need your help, Mr. Wizard," I said, laying on the theatrics. He stood frozen. "Will you help me hand out candy to these wonderful pumpkins and ghosts?" I pointed at the kids. Kōtarō nodded but still didn't say anything. Inwardly, I rolled my eyes. Come on, be a wizard. Do some magic. Something. I dragged Kōtarō over to me by the sleeve and the kids burst out laughing. Kōtarō turned even redder but I shoved the suitcase into his hand and took the pumpkin pail from my belt.

"I need candy in here, please, Mr. Wizard." He quietly put piles of candy into the pumpkin as the children laughed and fidgeted. Two other teachers came forward, and we started to hand out handfuls to the rapidly forming lines of children. They had been taught to say "trick or treat!" in English as loud as they could, and each one grinned and showed off their costume as they accepted the sweets. By the end Kōtarō got into the spirit as well, waving his finger and casting imaginary spells at the kids who giggled and ran away, their pockets and hands full of candy.

Preschool after preschool each outdoing the other, we celebrated and played, orange and black decorations all over the halls and classrooms. The kids were thrilled, the teachers ecstatic. My first Halloween was a grand success.

The second year I was a queen, regal in the mass of fake pearls my mother had bought as a special order for my birthday, a blond wig of curls and a red velvet dress with a high collar. The third year I was Elsa from Frozen trailing glitter off my costume everywhere I went, and the fourth year I was a penguin, my yellow webbed feet sliding off me with every step I took making the kids giggle as I carried a heavy, decorated cardboard box of candy and trying not to trip. The fifth and sixth years I dug out my witch costume again, running out of both ideas and money to spend on costumes.

The seasonal celebrations continued. Subsequent Christmases were no different. Each year the events became grander and more elaborate as more people showed up to help. My husband David was Santa for two years. Another year, staff from the U.S. Embassy in Tokyo came up as reindeer. Akira, the interpreter for Mrs. Claus, showed up to one Christmas as Spiderman.
"What does Spiderman have to do with Christmas?" I asked him, laughing.
"I've had this costume for ages and I've never gotten a chance to wear it," Akira said.
"Why didn't you wear it for Halloween this year?"
"I forgot," he said, giving me a guilty grin. But we couldn't turn back now. So Spiderman was one of my elves for me that year along with Kazuki who actually wore the elf costume I bought for him along with the green tights. Vocal in his complaints why he had to dress up as an elf while his elder brother wasn't, he took it well but there was plenty of post-holiday chiding in the following months.

"Nice legs, Kazuki," I heard often. "Green is your color, especially tights." Kazuki was a good sport and I told him so. No one ever wore the elf costume over the following Christmases, but I was fine letting it remain in the back corner of Kazuki's closet. It had done its job.

Mamoru, now studying to be a Buddhist priest, was the one who started it all, introducing me to his mother. It took two months for word to spread to the other preschool principals. I found out later from Mamoru's mother that the preschool principals met once a month, and she had shared the story of my time at her school. By Christmas, word had spread and I was in demand as Mrs. Claus. I got to know the communities these children lived in, many of their temporary houses smaller than my garage back home. I saw their playgrounds which had been filled in with more rows of these temporary housing. The city needed every available inch, and couldn't afford to leave the space as an area for the kids to play after school or on weekends.

I thought back to my own memories from when I was five years old. Again, I thought about Okuno-*sensei* and how terrifying he had been. I recalled playing on playgrounds that didn't look too different from these. If I could remember this now, forty years later, then these children might remember these years just as easily. They'd been through so much at such a young age. A disaster wiping out their home, months of sadness and a laborious rebuilding process. Many of them would grow up without people they loved. I wanted these children to have at least some memories of happiness from their childhood. I could be one of those memories—the foil to Okuno-*sensei*. That foreign woman who showed up and taught us about fun and exciting new holidays—that was enough.

For these children abnormal was the new normal, something in life was always off. I wanted to give them laughter, hope, and fun. Would they remember me in twenty or thirty years? I hoped some would. I wanted them to know that life wasn't always scary. Bad things happened, but there was also good in the world. Sometimes, there was even chocolate.

~~~

It had been years since I watched *The Lion King*. I remembered the storyline well enough, but when it came to specific quotes, I had none. This is why when a five-year-old girl from one of the preschools in Rikuzentakata came up to me one day and quoted me a line from the *Lion King*, I was profoundly confused.

"Amya-*san*, do you know the big monkey with the blue and red face from *Lion King*?" she asked me, intent and serious. Did I know the what? A monkey from *Lion King* with a blue and red face? Possibly. Vaguely.
"I'm not sure," I said. "Why?"
"The monkey said we needed to learn from our past."

What was she talking about? I looked at the two teachers in the classroom for help. They both shook their heads, confirming they also didn't know what this girl meant. I knelt down to eye-level with this little girl and said, "I promise I'll watch *The Lion King* before the next time I come back to play. Okay?"

"Okay," she said and stuck out her pinky. We pinky-swore.

Later that night in my room I prepared the film on my laptop. I started to watch, and sure enough there was a monkey with a red and blue face. And he did say something similar, something about how the past can hurt but you can either learn from it or run from it. I found it extremely interesting this five-year-old had picked up on this line.

The next morning, I called the preschool principal and told her about what the girl said to me. I had indeed watched *The Lion King* and had a better point of reference. I repeated the line to the principal and asked for her advice.
"Should I bring it up again?" I asked. The principal was silent for a long time. "Hello?" I said, worried I had gotten cut off.

"Just a minute. I'm thinking," the principal replied. Finally, she took a deep breath and let out a long exhale. I had a bad feeling.

"Please don't take this the wrong way," she said and I knew that I would. "There's a lot of emphasis in America and Europe on finding the best out of a bad situation. I've heard you say that to the kids even. 'Try to think of one happy thing that happened to you today as you go to sleep.' Do you remember saying that?" I told her I did.
"Finding reasons to be happy, focusing on the positive in life, it feels..." she trailed off, searching for words. "When you say that, what children hear is that their sadness is bad. That sadness is wrong."

Immediately, I became defensive. "That's not what I meant at all!" I said, horrified.
"I know that's not what you meant," the principal said. "But, there are children here who have lost their homes or family—their parents or their grandparents. Life is not normal for them. Asking them to find something good when there's very little good around them isn't fair. It may work for people in the West, but it doesn't work for these kids. Let them feel their pain. Don't try to force them to be happy when they're not."

I was speechless. As a child in a Japanese classroom I had grown up being taught *gaman*, but as an adult I had replaced those influences to a great degree with a more Western philosophy. It would never occur to me that encouraging the kids to be happy might actually be doing harm. I thanked the principal for being honest and promised I would stop.

I spent the rest of the evening staring at the ceiling thinking about how I approach sadness and death. How different was my perspective from that of the people here? I would never have said "find the silver lining" in reference to a death. But whenever I had to stop and mourn at any point during my own life, I would reflect on the happy memories I had with those whom I lost. I wasn't trying to negate the children's sadness and I was truly upset that's how I had come across.

"Let them feel their pain," the principal had said. But, how did this fit into everything else I was seeing? The poster of the boy on his bicycle insisting to the world he was not the least bit sad. The boys who were told not to cry and the girls not to whine. The spirit of *gaman*, of quiet stoicism and the unspoken understanding that there was something noble and important about not showing emotion or pain. Why were these toddlers allowed to feel their pain when the rest weren't? What was going on?

I remembered having seen a toddler, maybe two years old, throwing a massive temper tantrum in the hallway of one of the preschools as I walked past. A teacher was standing over him, not saying anything. I found the encounter difficult to understand. I asked the principal about the scene I'd witnessed, and I was told the boy had lost his father in the disaster. These temper tantrums were his way of expressing his grief. He wasn't able to articulate in words how sad he felt, but with his body he could release all that was wrong. There was no attempt to comfort, hug, talk to, or touch the boy. After a few minutes of wailing and kicking, he would get up and go back to his seat. This was an important part of healing, I was told.

Let children be sad. Let them feel their pain. It had been a long time since I had raised a toddler, and I found this different approach fascinating and unique. I agreed with letting children feel their pain. Denying it delegitimizes their feelings. But I also felt that comforting them was a crucial part of healing, to let them know they are loved and safe. Surely that wasn't wrong, was it? I didn't sleep well that night. The next day, I called Kōtarō.

I would visit Kōtarō when I needed a reality check, when I had a particularly difficult question, I needed help in understanding or resolving. He would give me a straight answer. He liked telling the truth when he was drunk, but then again, so did others. I found if I got him alone, Kōtarō would tell me honestly what others wouldn't even say when drunk. Today I wanted the truth. I told him everything that happened the day before.

"The principal had said, 'Don't force them to be happy when they're not,'" I told him. "That's not what I was trying to do at all. I just wanted the kids to feel happiness. To know that life isn't all about the sadness around them. Am I wrong? Should I not have said that?"

"You want some tea?" Kōtarō said. No, I didn't want some tea. I wanted an answer. Was he stalling? Kōtarō poured tea into two cups and set one down in front of me. He pulled out a stool from beneath a long table and nodded to it. I sat down and picked up the cup of tea.

"Foreigners," he began, "Westerners in particular, are so focused on happiness. Finding it, having it, sharing it. Don't get me wrong, it's good to be happy. But right now," he paused and looked down at his steaming mug of tea, idly blowing on it. "Right now we're not happy. We're sad and angry and disappointed. We all have our frustrations. None of us want to hear 'gan-batte.' None of us want to be told 'be happy.' Not right now." He sipped his tea and I cupped mine in my hands, feeling the hot mug on my palms.
He looked me in the eye. "Do you understand?"

Did I? Was it truly a Western ideal to focus on happiness? "If we're too happy, it feels like we're disrespecting the dead. This is where *gaman* comes in. Because if one of us breaks, we'll end up breaking each other one by one. When these kids enter first grade, *gaman* will be expected of them, too. So they have to feel their sadness now while it's still okay to cry." His voice was stern and level. "So many died, Amya. So many people died. We're not just going to all get over it and move on with our lives. There's too much death."

There it was. Time may heal all wounds, but whoever coined that saying didn't complete it. Time heals all wounds—eventually. But when exactly? There's no way of knowing when that healing might occur. Until it did, people were still wounded. I needed to let everyone around me mourn in whatever way suited them and believe they, too, might someday be happy again.

Chapter 25

Futoshi Toba

In my early twenties I wanted to be a rock star. My friends and I formed a band in high school and we played together for years. One of the four, the bassist, wanted to go pro. Take it up to the next level, get serious about our practices and focus on our individual skills and instruments. One day the four of us sat down and had a chat, a real soul-searching moment where we reluctantly acknowledged we were good but not great. Certainly not nearly good enough to compete with the real rock-and-roll bands out there. We split up.

I decided it was time for a change. Never one to shy away from adventure, I decided to go to the U.S. I would study English and hang out a bit. I first went to Tampa, Florida, and later on spent time in New Orleans, Louisiana. Back then my English was good enough that I was able to get around every day and do what I wanted. I was still in my early twenties and I didn't have enough life experience to think anything about what I was doing was odd or all that unusual.

This was in the 1980s. The U.S. and Japan were different countries from what they are now. A lot of what I saw in the U.S. was brand new to me. Shocking even. The differences I saw were both about human behavior and societal patterns.

I had spent my youth in a suburb of Tokyo. Although not downtown Metropolitan Tokyo, it was still large enough that it had the added benefit of being big and bustling. My father was born and raised in Rikuzentakata, but I didn't move there until my late twenties. My time in the U.S. was firmly sandwiched between my youth in Tokyo and my adult life in Rikuzentakata.

It never occurred to me that those years in Florida and New Orleans would end up affecting post-disaster reconstruction policy for Rikuzentakata.

Florida and New Orleans were sunny and warm, and people spent a lot of time outside. I did as well. I enjoyed bar-hopping, golfing, hanging out with friends bowling, and in between, taking language classes at a community college. Here, in these communities, I saw for the first time parking spots designated for physically challenged drivers. In the 80s in Japan, no such policy existed. Openly acknowledging the presence of the disabled was taboo. Instead, people with physical, mental, social, or emotional challenges were shunted off into facilities. It was a stain on a family to have someone with special needs, and it was thought to be better for all if they were out of sight and thus out of mind. I don't know that anyone ever said this out loud, as even back then, people knew it was rude and discriminatory. But it didn't change the fact that the presence of the disabled in a family threw the balance of harmony off, and that was neither tolerated nor allowed. The elderly were also a category of people who, while respected for their age, didn't have the kind of rights and lives they do today.

This is why, when I saw an elderly U.S. couple wearing matching polo shirts and walking together hand-in-hand, it blew me away. It wasn't simply about the open display of affection. It was the gall, the fact they dare walk the streets as if it was the most normal thing in the world. I'm not saying the elderly don't walk the streets in Japan. I am saying, instead, back in the 80s there wasn't the kind of public visibility of the elderly there is today.

Even more unusual to me, I saw a guy in a wheelchair drinking in a bar. I went golfing and saw a man on the course with a prosthetic leg. It had never occurred to me that a man missing a partial limb would let others see the fact he was wearing a prosthesis. Going out in public in a wheelchair? How would you get around, in a car, on the sidewalk, much less enter a bar? Were they not embarrassed? Clearly not. Were those with them not embarrassed? Evidently not. The elderly and people with special needs were out in public in the U.S. I saw this all everywhere, repeatedly. Wouldn't it be nice if this type of free expression of self occurred in Japan as well? Wouldn't it be better if those who were categorized as different weren't shunted off into homes, hiding them both from society as well as their families?

Disability rights became topics more often discussed in Japan. The elderly became more active physically, and thus more present in public, partly because they were increasing in numbers. People were living longer and the population was declining annually, the birth rate simply not keeping up with what the politicians wanted.

All these memories and thoughts went through my head, as I looked at how to make Rikuzentakata a city that would increase our population and make it a place that would welcome everyone, much like I was welcomed in the U.S. as a foreigner, and like what I saw in the U.S. What if, in Rikuzentakata, we rebuilt it into a place where those in wheelchairs could go into the barbershops with ease, if all stores and facilities had wide doors and large bathrooms so that people in wheelchairs would go outside in comfort? What if we could say we were going to showcase how we wanted all of Japan to be? That we were breaking new ground? What if we were the role model for how to be inclusive? We had to rebuild the city from the ground up regardless. Why not welcome those who didn't fit the typical nuclear family model— mom, dad, two kids, and a dog? We could be the city who said, "If you need a place that welcomes you regardless of who you are and what might make you unique, that's us." People would move to Rikuzentakata, be part of our community. Our population would grow and we could prove to the world it is absolutely possible to come back stronger and better.

I decided to make it official. I called this new policy—the one where everyone was welcomed—The City That No Longer Needs To Use The Word Normalization. I brought Amya in to get her take on it. I needed a Western perspective, and as an American, outspoken and sharp, she was the perfect person. We sat in my office as I laid out my plan. The first comment out of her mouth threw me.

"What's 'normalization' in this context?" she said.

What did she mean? How, as an American, did she not know this word was used? She pulled out her laptop and typed the word in, presumably looking for a definition. She sat staring at the screen for a few minutes, her brow furrowed.
"Okay," she finally said as she sat back, and then she said, "can we change the name of this policy?" I was confused.
"Normalization," she pointed to her laptop, "I get where you're going, and a general definition does contain the idea you've explained to me. But, it's not the first thing that comes up. And I've never heard it used in the context you mean. That might be just me, I'm not a social worker." I had no idea what to

say. Amya just shrugged and continued. "Others may get it right away, but I'm going to guess not. I think using the word normalization in the name of the policy is confusing. And as far as the name of the policy, in English? It's a non-starter. I can't translate that and make it sound any way other than awkwardly long and unclear." She sat back in her chair.

"We can't change the name," I said, annoyed. "I've already announced it."

"What you're trying to do is be inclusive. That's a word commonly used. I wish you would have discussed this with me…" she trailed off, leaning forward and massaging her temples with her fingers.

Well, I hadn't discussed it with her before I made the announcement. The way she responded was a shock to me, and I wasn't enjoying being told the name of my policy wouldn't be clear in English.
"How about," Amya started, "in English we make it short and easy to understand?"
"Like?"
"Like saying Rikuzentakata will be an intentionally inclusive community. Keep the long name you have now, use a literal translation but then briefly explain it using these words: 'What we're trying to do is rebuild Rikuzentakata into an intentionally inclusive city.'" I considered it for a moment. I told her that was fine, still not completely thrilled with how this conversation was going. But at least we were back on track.

I went through the list of people whom I included: single parents, the elderly, women, children, people with mental/physical/emotional challenges, anyone with special needs, and foreigners.

"You need to add LGBTQ+ individuals to that list, " Amya said.
"Right. Yes," I agreed, and scratched myself a note.

We talked about how we would do this. Clearly, I needed to explain to everyone in town what I was trying to do and why. I would hold town hall meetings and lay out my plan. It might take some time, but I felt strongly that people would agree and cooperate. Our city had been losing population even before the disaster. With Japan's birth rate declining steadily every year and with the elderly living longer, the balance of age demographics was quickly swinging toward many more elderly than youth. Add to that, once our youth got a taste of the big city, many wouldn't want to come back. We didn't have famous brand name stores in town. There were no chain restaurants or coffee shops. While rent might be cheap, our low income reflected that. The city was by no means well off. What would the youth have to look forward to if they returned? What kinds of jobs did we have to offer that would interest them? What was there to do here?

It wasn't just that the main crux of the city, what had been downtown, didn't exist anymore. The truth is that even before the disaster there were plenty of stores with their shutters closed, many permanently. What college graduates would want to come back to Rikuzentakata after experiencing life in a big city? I knew how much fun large cities were; I had grown up in one. Having options to choose from for food and entertainment is a key part of what makes life interesting, and here in town those options are extremely limited. Furthermore, the idea of raising a family here is even less attractive. Schools have to consolidate because we don't have enough students to keep all of them open. We desperately needed some way to bring in new people, and I knew we would have to compete with many other little towns and cities throughout Japan that were also losing population. This is why offering something entirely new, something unseen in Japan, was key.

Amya and I talked about what kinds of resources were available in the U.S. to teach us how to do this, and who on our staff might be good candidates to learn these best practices. She agreed to contact the U.S. Embassy to find out what kinds of programs they knew of, as I combed through the list of personnel who had enough English that they could actually understand what they were being taught. She would look for other similar programs in the public and private and non-profit sectors while looking for grant money to cover travel expenses.

I knew how great a change this would be for the residents of Rikuzentakata. With the population of roughly 20,000 and easily half that at age 55 and over, and especially for the elderly to accept the idea there might be an influx of foreigners, people with special needs, and people who are LGBTQ+—this was both going to be a tough sell and a hard pill for people to swallow. Still, I was determined. We needed to increase the population, and while I had every intention of rebuilding the city into one that was attractive as well as functional, I also believed we needed a new angle, some other way to draw them in. I knew there would be opposition, because it seemed everything I did these days resulted in some sort of push-back from a segment of the population. Of course that mattered, but it didn't matter enough to stop me. This project might take time, but I hoped if I wasn't able to institute the policy completely during my tenure, the future politicians of this city would see it through.

Chapter 26

Amya Miller

Both Mayor Toba and I were experiencing starts and stops. We would make progress on an issue only to get blindsided by an interruption or blockage, then we would bounce back again. This back-and-forth was draining. We were both getting attacked on social media—accusations of Western imperialism, of exaggerating the reality on the ground, and of egregious outspokenness. We constantly had to pick our battles, deciding when to engage and when taking a stand online would only be a time-consuming nuisance.

Not one for throwing in the towel, we instead buckled down and focused on our primary goal of keeping the city relevant in the news. If the media's interest in Rikuzentakata dwindled and the press visits slowed, we would have to find other ways to drum up interest. There was more than one way to make news. This became my new mission.

My travels had garnered a lot of attention among international schools in Japan, universities in Japan and abroad, organizations wanting to learn about disaster preparedness, and others who wanted to form some kind of long-term connection with Rikuzentakata. I was flooded with requests for student exchanges and for civic and educational partnerships. With these requests came a whole new set of challenges, particularly when it came to the infrastructure of the city. No single school or organization in the city had the capacity for handling anything that formal yet. We had to start small. I chose to focus on inviting delegations from several universities to meet with key people in town.

I had found storytelling to be a powerful tool. In my international travels, I saw how the drama, despair, or hope within the stories I shared would capture the attention of listeners. Still, when I was the storyteller merely repeating the experiences of others, the audience was left one step removed from the actual situation.

Now it was time for people to hear the stories directly from the locals. Instead of setting up any arranged and formal partnerships the city didn't seem to be ready for, university and graduate students could be brought to Rikuzentakata and introduced to locals who were willing to tell these stories themselves. The stories were real-life examples of what to do and what not to do in the aftermath of a disaster. Listeners heard firsthand the reality of disaster: what goes on in our brains—fight or flight. How would the university and graduate students incorporate these stories and lessons into their lives and careers? What would they tell their parents and friends upon returning to their hometowns? How would these stories affect the way they would raise their children? These questions were posed to the groups before they heard the stories, hopefully encouraging them to listen more deeply and inspiring them to make change.

Indeed, these students listened with solemn nods and earnest expressions, drawn into the intimacy of the experience. They underwent the bonding possible with in-person contact. They received accounts delivered directly from those who experienced the disaster, saw the consternation on their faces, heard their voices crack, laughed along with the humorous moments, and shed tears during the moments of tragedy. Mutually, the people of Rikuzentakata felt they were being heard, and the visitors experienced various levels of shock, but departed inspired.

One Rikuzentakata resident was the perfect candidate to relate his experiences. Konishi-*san* was an elderly businessman from the community. Outspoken and engaging, here was a man ready to share. Put him in front of an audience and he could go on for hours, holding everyone's attention the entire time. His stories were both funny and moving, and he wore his emotions on his sleeve—a rare Japanese man unashamed of his tears. He said his secret was that he was too old and too powerful a man in the community for the opinions of others to have any effect on him.

One story personified his character perfectly. I had stopped by his office unannounced, hoping he was available to chat. I planned to tell him of a new delegation I was bringing to town and wanted to ask if he could give them two hours of stories. Yes, of course, he told me. Not only that, today he had a surprise for me.

"I never told you how I made it from Tokyo back to town several days after the disaster, did I?" he says.
"No, you certainly haven't!" This sounded promising.
"I haven't told many people, mostly because I didn't want to get my friend in Tokyo into any trouble, but enough time has passed now that I think I can."

I sat back in my chair. This was going to be good. I just knew it.

"On March 11, I was at the shop of a friend and client in Tokyo. All of a sudden, the shaking started. We turned on the television for updates and sat there glued to the screen, he and I both. The announcement said the earthquake was just southeast of Rikuzentakata. My stomach fell. Shortly after that, there was news of a tsunami and I knew we were hit. I just knew it in my bones. I had to get back. I absolutely had to get back. I called my wife and I got a recorded message saying the call wouldn't go through. I tried my son. Same thing. I called my staff. But I couldn't get through to anybody."

Konishi-*san* stroked his chin and I could see him recall the pain and fear that day. I knew plenty of others who had gone through the same thing when the cell service cut out.

"I sat there staring at my client. I had to get back, but what could I do? When I put this to my friend, he thought for a minute and said, 'Give me 48 hours. I'll get you a way back.' I didn't know what he could be talking about. I had no car. I figured I couldn't rent one in Tokyo—there were bound to be thousands of people like me, here on business and desperate to get back home to find out if their families were safe. I figured the trains would have stopped running too. Not having a car was bad enough, but soon enough I heard on the news that gasoline would be rationed in Tokyo. Each person could fill their car with 2,000 yen worth of gasoline at a time, and there were already long lines of cars waiting to fill up. Even if I could get a car, there's no way I could leave Tokyo with a full tank of gas."

I listened to his story intently. This was a whole new perspective for me. I hadn't heard from anyone in Rikuzentakata who was in Tokyo on the day of the disaster. All of the stories I'd heard were from people in town on that day. To be isolated from your home as a disaster strikes, to have no way back—it was a completely different kind of anxiety and trauma.

"I went back to my hotel room that night and barely slept," Konishi-*san* continued. "My client and I had agreed I would come back two days later in the evening, ready to head back. I had no idea what he was talking about and couldn't figure out what he was planning to do. Get me a car, sure, but how? And gasoline? What was he thinking? I kept trying to call my wife and son all the next day and the next day, but I still couldn't get through." He picked up his cell phone, tapped it for effect, then set it down on the desk.

"Finally, two days later, I made my way to my friend's store in the evening. He was closed for business, but I slid his door open and went inside. He came out from behind the counter and handed me a set of car keys. 'The car is out back,' the shop owner said to me. I was stunned. I asked him how he did it, but all he told me was that a guy owed him a favor. This was a borrowed car from some friend, someone I didn't know. I told him that I had no idea when I could return the car to him, and he just shook his head at me."

I sat in silence, nodding appreciatively at the shop owner's resourcefulness. Konishi-*san* continued. "The shop owner said that he would in turn owe this guy if he could manage to find a way to fill up the car with a full tank. 'I don't care how you do it,' the shop owner told the guy. He needed a whole day to drive all over Tokyo to get in line to fill up. So, now my friend owes this guy. Just so he could get a car full of fuel for me. And, they're both fine with me borrowing this car indefinitely."

Here Konishi-*san* choked up. I passed him the box of tissues on the small glass table next to my chair. He had tissues ready. How many people had wept in his office?

"My client then hands me this square laminated sheet of paper and tells me to put it on my dashboard. When I asked why, he said only people with this item were allowed on the expressway to Tōhoku."

"Wait," I said. "I thought the expressway was closed? There were parts that were damaged."

"That's right," he said. "Only people with this pass were allowed through. It basically meant I was a high-ranking government official."

"How did your friend get that?!" I asked.

"I have no idea. But it worked. I started driving that night, and I had the whole highway to myself. I don't know that anyone can picture that, having a whole highway to oneself. I realized I could go as fast as I wanted but I'm also too old to be driving through the night. When was the last time I spent the entire night awake? I decided it was better to be safe. I didn't speed. Well, not too much."

Konishi-*san* looked at me, and I nodded at him.

"Every time I approached a damaged section there was a police barricade. They'd wave me off the highway and then back on up at the next on-ramp. As I passed each checkpoint, the officers saluted me even though they had no idea who I was. They thought I was somebody important, but I was really just some old man not-quite-speeding his way up to Tōhoku. I felt guilty, but not enough to turn around and admit that I wasn't really who this pass said I was."

He paused for a minute, searching my face for any signs of judgment, then took a deep breath and continued.

"I got to Rikuzentakata very early the next morning, around six o'clock. It took me at least nine hours to drive, getting off and on the highway like that. I was exhausted. I had driven all night, and desperately wanted to sleep but, when I got to town I went straight to where my company used to be, and sure enough it was gone. Then I went to where my house was and that was gone, too. The whole town was just this tangled mass of broken concrete and rubble. I didn't know if my wife was alive or dead. My son and his family, my employees. Were any of them alive? I knew nothing." Konishi-*san* dabbed at his eyes with the tissue and I handed him another.

"I drove around a bit and stopped in at schools that were undamaged, wondering if my family had evacuated to one of them. I had decided as I was driving through the night that if my wife was alive, the first thing I was going to do was hug her. I didn't care who saw me. I didn't care if that's not something a man my age does in public. I just didn't care. I was going to hug her and tell her I loved her and I was glad she was alive. I was going to do it."

I smiled. I could just picture him having a pep talk with himself as he's driving, telling himself over and over, 'I'm doing it. I'm doing it. I don't care what anyone thinks.'

"That's beautiful," I said.
"Yeah, well, wait until I tell you what happened next. I think it was the third school I went to, I finally heard from someone in the shelter that my family was there. Next thing I know my grandkids come running out to the entrance. They're bawling and screaming, 'Grandpa! Grandpa!,' and they almost knocked me down, running into my legs and hugging me. I hug them back, crying and not caring who's watching. Then I see my wife coming

toward me and I think to myself, 'Okay. Here I go,' and I stretch my arms out to hug her."

"Did you do it?" I asked.

"I didn't get a chance. The moment she saw me, she started screaming. 'Where *were* you!? I was *worried* about you! I can't *believe* you didn't try to call me!' She just started reading me the riot act, right in the middle of this crowd of people." He broke into a wry grin at the memory, and I could picture this elderly woman berating him in the middle of a nervous crowd.

"'Why didn't you call? Why didn't you *tell* me you were alright? What is *wrong* with you?' And each time she says something, I open my mouth to tell her how I *tried* to get back, about borrowing the car and pretending to be some important government official. I tried to explain how desperate I was to get back, and how I was worried about her too, and how I *did* try to call. But she kept shouting at me like I'd forgotten our anniversary and her birthday and our son's birthday and every important milestone all rolled into one. While she's yelling at me in front of everyone, I just wanted to hug her. My arms were still outstretched the whole time, but when she was finished, she just turned on her heel and stormed off."

"Oh my," I said and I paused for a minute. I wasn't sure how to react. His story was sad, but on another level it was deeply funny. Hilarious, even. I could picture the entire scene in my mind. Finally, I cracked a smile. I imagined the courage it took for him to decide he was going to hug her in public—and instead she gave him a verbal beating, all while he's trying desperately to explain he did all this for her, arms outstretched the whole time.

"It's funny. It's definitely funny," Konishi-*san* grinned.

"Your wife is quite the woman," I said and let my face produce a full smile.

"That she is," he laughed. "I knew right then I married the most perfect woman." We both laughed out loud, and our laughter rang down the hallway of his office for the next several minutes.

I could visualize every step of his trip. I was proud of him for the effort he made. It was everything I could do to keep a straight face the next time I saw his wife.

Chapter 27

Futoshi Toba

There's a rumor I have a female companion; a lover I've had since before the disaster. Some tabloid printed the story and now the city is buzzing with the news. Hushed voices discuss the article, some certain of its accuracy, other vehemently denying I would be so brazen and disloyal. It's a lie, obviously. The same article printed scandalous gossip about my late father. More pettiness. Several people in town have stopped and asked me openly, mostly women. I find this fascinating. Perhaps they are projecting solidarity with Kumi, making sure even in death she has a say, to be certain I was faithful. Amya even called asking.

"You heard about it, too?" I asked.

"I assume it's a lie," she said.

"Of course it's a lie," I snapped.

"I'm sorry. I had to ask."

I sighed. "It's fine."

"Do the boys know?" she asked.

"I don't think so."

"Would they tell you if they did?"

"Probably not," I said, annoyed. She was right, though, and I knew it.

"Is there anything I can do?" she said.

"No," I said. "It'll die down eventually."

It did. During this time, I tried to be more present at home. Over the *Obon* break, the festival of the dead that occurs every year in August, I made sure I was home. The boys had homework assignments they had to complete over summer vacation. My elder son, the studious one and who took grades seriously, was caught up with homework. He got together with friends, played basketball, and was in and out of my uncle's house constantly. My younger son, the one who preferred play over homework, was at the table with papers and textbooks strewn out in front of him. He had left his homework until the last several days before school started back up. When I came over to see how he was doing, I saw he was watching television. I smiled.

"I thought you were doing homework," I said.

"I'm on a break," he said, looking up at me, not bothering to hide his mischievous smile.

"Uh huh," I said, making sure I didn't sound angry. "How long have you been on break?" I asked.

"Since 10:30," he said. I looked at the clock. It was noon.

"It's okay, dad," he said, lowering his voice. "I've got this. I do 30 pages at a time when I do my homework. I deserve a break." Now he looked at the clock. "A long break," he said, his grin genuine and innocent.

"I know you've got this," I said. The look on his face was worth the lie. His face exuded confidence and pride, but there was also an understanding he knew that I knew this wasn't entirely true. It was as if he wanted to say, "I knew you'd understand, dad," and "Oh, and thanks for letting me watch television." He was only thirteen, still just a kid. So what if he didn't finish his homework? He would be fine.

I left the room and went outside for a cigarette. How did Kumi deal with homework? Was my son more cooperative with her? Was she stricter and expected the boys to obey or did they do as they were told with her without complaint? I contemplated this as I inhaled deeply.

My boys weren't the only ones who had lost a parent in the disaster. There were several hundred children in town who had lost both parents and had to be taken in by relatives. Pain comparison is unfair and most of the time it's not discussed. There was a general understanding that we in town don't go around comparing whose life is harder. The only exception would be the orphans. To lose both parents at such a young age and be completely dependent on the generosity of relatives whom they may or may not like, that was no way to grow up. The board of education had set up an Orphans' Fund that funneled money to the families who had taken these children in to help with home and school expenses. The understanding was the Fund would support these families until the children graduated high school. Here was yet another source of fundraising that was an immediate necessity.

Compared to the orphans, my boys at least had me. I wasn't dead, but I wasn't fully present, either. I had relied on my uncle's family to take them in, very much the same way the orphans had been taken in by their relatives. Now I had to work out how to balance being their dad along with running the city. Kumi was gone and we were slowly, reluctantly becoming used to that. I was the one who was here now with the boys, not Kumi, and that meant I needed to start being physically present. Over the *Obon* break I watched the boys eat, argue, and play basketball. After *Obon* I would become busy again, but I would make the time to see them. I would start by freeing up my weekends whenever I could, even if it was just one day.

Our new house would soon be finished. We needed all new furniture. Maybe picking out their own desks and beds would get them excited about moving in and starting over. I mentioned this casually to my aunt one night and she stopped me.
"Start by taking the boys shopping," she said. "They have things they want. Not furniture, but things. They just haven't told you."
I was confused.
"What do you mean? What do they need and why aren't they telling me?" I asked, sensing my voice was rising.
"Think about it," she said. "Buying furniture is something adults do. For the boys, it'll just remind them of the fact their old house is gone. For them, buying a new bed won't be fun." I started to speak but she stopped me by raising her hand.
"Wait," she said. "You're trying, and I get that. But you have to think like a boy. Put yourself in their shoes." She nodded as she said this. "And they're not telling you what they want because it has to do with growing up."

My look of confusion must have shown because my aunt continued, "That one," she said, pointing to my younger son, "Wants to grow taller quickly. He thinks he's not growing. His brother is taller than average, and he's shorter than average. He says it's a disadvantage in playing basketball. He saw this commercial on television about a calcium supplement that helps build bones. He wants that. He just hasn't been able to tell you." I tried to speak again.

"Because," she said, taking a deep breath, "It's not cheap. As in, it's really not cheap."

I wanted to laugh and cry at the same time. My head swirled with a combination of frustration and amusement. I was heartbroken to learn that the boys were keeping secrets from me, yet I couldn't help but chuckle at my son's innocence to think a calcium supplement would make him taller.

"Okay," I finally said. "Thanks for telling me." My aunt nodded, patted my shoulder and walked off. That weekend I took the boys shopping. We went to Ichinoseki, the nearest large town that had sufficient shopping options. An hour inland from the coast, it was a city fully operational. There we were largely anonymous. A few people might recognize me but we could blend in as just another family on a shopping trip. I bought the boys new basketball shoes, and a few items of clothing. We all got haircuts. Toward the end of the day, I asked if there was anything else they wanted. After a silence that felt almost painful, my younger son finally said, "Dad," and then paused."Yeah?" I said.
"There's this thing I want."
"What is it? A PlayStation?"
"You'd buy us a PlayStation?" my elder son asked, his eyes shining. I laughed.
"I'm talking!" the younger one objected.
"Right," I said. "Sorry. What is it that you want?"

He finally told me. My elder son didn't laugh, nor did I. We weren't short. He was. His physique was much more like Kumi's: small-boned, thin, and short. If he wanted to take a calcium supplement, I didn't see why he shouldn't. I wasn't sure it would help him grow taller, but it was calcium. It wouldn't hurt him. We huddled around my cell phone as I looked up the brand name and tried to find a store that sold it. The boys kept shoving their fingers onto the screen trying to scroll, pushing each other's fingers away and arguing over who should get to have a go next.

I laughed as I batted away their fingers. "The more you argue, the longer it's going to take to find." We finally settled on a store, calling ahead to make sure the supplement was in stock. We drove there together, the boys reading directions off my phone in the back seat.

My younger son took that powder almost religiously for years. He did grow, but he's still the shortest of the three of us. What he lacked in height, he made up for in speed. They were both good basketball players, but my younger son was the one who could steal the ball the best.

Chapter 28

Amya Miller

Even in such a small city it's hard to work out who's related to whom. I didn't realize I worked with a certain woman's husband at City Hall—in the same department, until he casually mentioned to me one day how much his wife enjoyed having me in her preschool. I stopped myself just short of asking, "Who's your wife?" realizing they both probably assumed I knew they were a couple. Now I had to figure out which teacher at which preschool the man was married to. The answer presented itself by chance.

I was having lunch with a colleague. It was payday for him, and he offered to treat me. I gladly accepted, needing both food as well as a quick respite from work. Any chance to actually eat, as well as get out of the office was welcomed. We were at a *soba* shop in town, always packed, as the buckwheat noodles were exquisite. When I was taken to the *soba* shop by friends and visitors, I always got the cold noodles with a side of *tempura*. The crispy crunch of the tempura, the shrimp piping hot and the vegetables always a surprise of whatever was in season, perfectly complemented the cold noodles. An old woman walked past our table and bowed. I didn't know her, but bowed back. She walked up to the door to leave and stopped. I watched her turn around and head back toward me. She bowed again and said, "You're Amya-*san*," and I nodded. "You teach my grandchildren English at their preschool."

"Oh!" I said. "I love going to the preschools. Which one do your grandchildren attend?"

She told me the name of the school, and I told her again how much I liked going. She bowed, I bowed, I waved, and this time she left.

My colleague looked at me and said, "That's where Kajiura-*san*'s wife Atsuko-*san* teaches." Out of the blue, I had my answer. And then it hit me. The Kajiuras had lost their two young sons in the disaster along with Atsuko-*san*'s parents. Here she was, teaching and playing with children when hers were gone. How did I not know this? Then again, if I had known this, what would I have done differently?

My mind spinning with these thoughts I didn't realize I had gone quiet. "What's wrong?" my colleague said, and I looked up at him. "I didn't know Atsuko-*san* was Kajiura-*san*'s wife. I know her. I like her. She's an excellent teacher," I said, becoming quiet again.

When people did *gaman*, they knew not to compare their pain with one another. There was never any "I hurt more than you" sentiment, the general consensus being "We're all in pain. This is awful for all of us." And, because everyone had lost someone, people didn't regularly share details. No one ever asked, "How many people do you know who died?" or "Whom did you lose?" It was a subject off limits, and yet everyone somehow seemed to have these various bits of information. "She lost her children," and "He lost his parents" were facts of which people were aware, but were not always obvious to me.

"I know what you're thinking," my colleague said, putting down his chopsticks. I looked up at him. "I know because I wondered the same thing. How can she be around other people's children all day every day when hers are gone. Right?"
"Right," I said. With a start, I realized I was going to cry. I also put down my chopsticks. This new piece of information was too much for me. How did I not know? For this long? He handed me a tissue and said, "We don't have to talk about it. It blew me away when I first heard, too." I quickly wiped my eyes and continued eating in earnest. I had to focus on my health. I needed to eat.

Each subsequent visit to the preschool where Atsuko-*san* taught, I felt my behavior toward her change. I tried not to let it show. I kept telling myself to be normal. But with more visits, I found myself giving her shoulders an extra squeeze as I said goodbye. I smiled at her more than I did the other teachers. I tried to be subtle about it, making sure it didn't come across as favoritism. Who else had stories like hers I didn't know about? Who else hid their pain in such a way I would never know of whom they'd lost?

Some of my friends, my aunt, and my husband had started sharing articles with me about the science of trauma. What I took away from this was the fact that a certain part of the brain—amygdala, the decision-making part—shuts down in a crisis. The brain goes into fight-or-flight mode in order to survive. When amygdala shuts down, we end up making bad decisions. We do things we would otherwise never do. Split-second decisions go horribly wrong. I didn't understand the science behind it— neurology was far beyond my area of expertise—but I did get the gist. I knew because I had made mistakes and poor decisions and only figured it out later, sometimes too late. I wanted to talk about this science with my friends in town but I didn't know how to bring it up. I didn't have the scientific and medical vocabulary to explain neurological patterns of behavior in Japanese. On top of it all, I wondered if this somehow related to the Japanese sentiment of *gaman*. Was that why people around me were hiding their pain so well?

I thought more about the mistakes people around me had made. I thought of Mayor Toba not telling his sons about their mother's death. I thought about Konishi-*san* who had misrepresented himself as a government official and about his wife who blew up at him. I thought about all the complaints hurled at Mayor Toba, completely unreasonable requests and expectations. Was this all somehow related to the brain shutting part of itself down? Was this a survival tactic? I wasn't sure. I would often lay awake at night wonder- ing if *gaman* was tied to a fight or flight response. I felt I was close, that if I just thought about it long enough, I could make a connection. In the end, I would always fall asleep before making that last leap, or finding that magical piece that tied it all together.

I had taken a group of foreign teenagers to Rikuzentakata one summer, a delegation from an international school in Japan where I had spoken earlier. They wanted to do a volunteer project and had asked me for specific input as to where they might be welcomed. I took them to one of the preschools. Atsuko-*san* was there. I hadn't seen her at this preschool before.

"They keep moving me around," she said smiling. "Two years here, two years there. Now I'm here!"

"I'm glad I'll get to keep seeing you," I said, smiling back, and I introduced her to the teenagers. She beamed up at two of the guest boys in particu- lar, and suddenly everything on her face changed from her normal smile to something extraordinary. In a moment I witnessed a metamorphosis, and

I almost couldn't believe I was looking at the same person. Atsuko-*san* wasn't simply excited. It was as if someone turned the light switch on in her eyes, changing her eyes from brown to gold. Warmth I could almost feel cascaded across her features, and she suddenly glowed as if there was a ring of light around her head. I had never seen anything like this.

What was going on? It all happened within seconds. What was this? I looked around at the others. No one showed any sign of witnessing what I'd just seen. Why didn't anyone else see this? Was I seeing things? Her face actually changed. Surely someone else saw this as well.

I kept my eye on her all morning as she helped the two teenagers play with the kids. She spoke no English and the two boys spoke no Japanese but somehow they communicated. She laughed the entire time, tossing her head back and clapping and jumping up and down like a kid herself. Something was definitely up. I didn't know what yet, but something was going on. I wasn't imagining what I was seeing. Something changed in her.

Several hours later as we were getting ready to say goodbye, I started gathering the kids in the playground for a group photo. I herded the kids in groups back toward the teachers standing by the blue elephant slide when I saw her. Atsuko-*san* stood between the two teenage boys, her arms linked through each of theirs, smiling like she was posing for a family photo.

In an instant it hit me. These two boys were the age her sons would be if they were alive. In her mind, she must have seen these boys and knew somewhere inside that with them, with these foreigners, she could emote. She could pretend to be mom, even for just a few hours. She was seeing her two sons in these two teenage boys. They laughed with her; they were there with her all morning in her group of kids. She had made sure of that. When it came to my turn to take the group photo, I saw through my camera lens Atsuko-*san* looking up at the taller of the two boys, her face beaming. She glowed. She actually glowed.

The photo session over, I took a last look at Atsuko-*san* and saw her reach up to hug the taller boy, then quickly turn around to hug the other. When was the last time she had hugged two teenage boys? Never, I guessed. She couldn't very well go up to a Japanese teenage boy and hug him. Even if she had nephews, hugging wasn't a common enough form of expressing emotion. I was secure in my belief. Here, today, she was hugging her two dead sons, who were teenagers in the form of these two foreign boys. I was witnessing a magical act of a private expression of love from mother to son. I had watched the beauty of parental love, even when it was expressed to someone who was not kin. This, I knew, I would remember for the rest of my life.

Chapter 29

Amya Miller

My Tokyo dinners with Mayor Toba were essential to both of us. This was our time to strategize without interruption, to speak without the worry of being overheard. Sometimes our chats were strictly business while at other times we would talk about our families, our health, and our insomnia. Work had left our minds buzzing, and we bonded over the fact that neither of us could sleep. We couldn't turn our brains off, so we tossed and turned for hours. Our mutual acknowledgment of insomnia led to text messages about sleep: "How many hours last night?" "Tonight's another all-nighter." "Try masaging lavender oil onto the soles of your feet."

Speaking freely without the worry of being overheard was rare. The walls of the prefabricated City Hall were thin, and while the staff outside Mayor Toba's office couldn't hear everything word-for-word, enough did spill over so that privacy wasn't guaranteed. We needed to vent, to be able to speak without a filter. Dinners in Tokyo were our refuge.

This particular night in Tokyo, we had met up in an *izakaya* to relax and reflect. After settling in and ordering drinks I had asked him for some hindsight, posing the question of what he would do differently in the weeks and months immediately following the disaster.

"Oh, I've got a list," he said. He rattled off a dozen examples—policy changes that would have helped with preparedness, clearer divisions of labor, focus on family, making others focus on their families, taking better care of our overall health, saying "no" when necessary, changing priorities of various projects, different ways to deploy emergency services or communicate with the Self Defense Forces. He'd clearly thought about this.

Midway through his list, he mentioned changes regarding the role of volunteers. I stopped him. That was a world I knew well. What changes did he mean? Could he be specific? Mayor Toba leaned forward, his index finger pointing upward.

"Japan just passed a law that says volunteer organizations or individuals going into a disaster region must bring their own food and water," he said, pointedly. "It's in direct response to the March 11 disaster." He sat back.

I remembered back to the meeting with the village elders in Ōfunato. How the leader of our volunteer group, intending to be brave about Japanese food, had avowed, "We'll eat what you eat." Inwardly, I cringed again.

"With hindsight," the mayor went on, "I agree with this new law that the immediate aftermath of some dire situation isn't the time to add on a stressful element. Good intentions notwithstanding, my allowing volunteers in so soon after the disaster was a mistake. When people first started to show up, I said yes to everybody. I said yes to everything. It seemed like simple math: the more people to help, the better things would be, and the quicker they would improve. It made sense to me at the time."

He paused, picked up the menu and asked me if I wanted to take a look as well. We both ordered more food. There were days, just several years ago where sitting down and ordering off a menu was a luxury. My first day off from the NPO I couldn't find a restaurant in town that was open. I wanted a bowl of *ramen*, thinking I would be helping a shop-owner get back on their feet—and I loved *ramen*. But at the time I could find nothing open, so I reluctantly went into a convenience store and bought an *onigiri*. I'd been given these rice balls all week, as they were several of the few items that were restocked. I was sick of *onigiri*. I desperately wanted protein and a vegetable. My body craved it. Being able to enter a restaurant and order off a menu was a luxury. Tonight's dinner was a reminder not to take food for granted. Ever.

The mayor continued. "What I didn't realize back then was that when those volunteers arrived, I'd need to free up resources to coordinate them. I didn't have the luxury of giving up those resources. The volunteers needed to be directed, to be assigned tasks. For that I had to commit personnel at a time when I was already shorthanded. I had too many pressing issues—finding food, locating and housing the dead, working with shelters, building temporary housing, creating bathing facilities for hygiene. Coming up with projects for the volunteers to do wasn't a priority for me."

"What did you have them do?" I asked.

"The most obvious was to have them clean up the debris on the roads so vehicles could pass. That was just pure manual labor. Then I also had people go into evacuation shelters and just do whatever was necessary. Be available. Some would play with the toddlers to help young mothers get a break, others would help with cooking or with cleaning out the toilets that weren't flushing. But even then, there were problems. There was the incident of a group of volunteers who went into an evacuation shelter to help prepare meals. The Japanese women who usually cooked only had a small amount of donated food to work with. They had created a meal plan and rationed their ingredients to last the shelter for several days. This volunteer group didn't know about the rationing or the pre-set menu. They saw all this food and just used it all up cooking one big meal. It ended up being a feast that night with a huge amount of food for the evacuees. But when the women came in the next morning and saw the food gone that was supposed to last for days, they were furious. That particular volunteer group was not allowed back."

I sat with this information for a minute. Volunteers had simply shown up, myself included. In hindsight I wanted to believe I had helped, and certainly did more good than harm. But in those first few weeks, I was another foreign volunteer coming over unannounced and uninvited. Did I add to Mayor Toba's headache? If I hadn't shown up when I did, I wouldn't have gotten to do the projects I started and completed later on, but I didn't know that at the time. In trying to be helpful, was I actually a nuisance? In the end, I had to hope my actions, the seeds of positive change I planted, outweighed whatever headache I caused.

~~~

I had become busy bringing in guests to town, running around with delegations showing them sites and having them meet with locals. Mayor Toba's schedule was booked solid all day, every day—so much so that when we did meet in his office, I needed to schedule an appointment. Many times I stockpiled a list of issues to discuss at a dinner next time he was in Tokyo when neither of us were pressed for time.

One topic that came up during a dinner conversation was travel. His and mine. The Mayor's speech at the Foreign Correspondents' Club of Japan had attracted attention from the international media, and Mayor Toba was receiving requests to speak overseas. We were contacted for more press conferences, as well as interviews and fundraisers by organizations looking for a worthy recipient of some kind of grant or stimulus. This was an opportunity we couldn't miss.

Unfortunately, Mayor Toba was needed in Japan to oversee reconstruction. He could afford neither the time nor the cost associated with traveling abroad. While his travel cost might be paid for, it was expected and assumed he would travel with at least one of his staff, and the funds for that kind of travel simply didn't exist. He asked me to go in his place. This way the story still reached an international audience, and Mayor Toba could stay in Rikuzentakata where he was needed most.

I began to travel internationally in earnest, making the rounds to fundraisers and press events throughout Japan, as well as North and South America, Europe, and Southeast Asia. The Japanese were fascinated to hear about the American woman who slept in a sleeping bag and did her laundry in a bucket, and the foreigners wanted details only someone on the ground could provide. After months surrounded by devastation and debris, I found myself standing at podiums and gesturing to slideshows. I had to convey through words and images alone exactly how much work still needed to be done. And many of the people who would hear my words had the funds to make it happen.

Money was one of the most limiting factors we'd encountered in the rebuilding process. Reconstruction funds from the Government of Japan kept arriving steadily—albeit conditionally at times. But donations from private companies and individuals had tapered off. The initial shock of the disaster had worn off months ago, and many news cycles had moved on. The only coverage Tōhoku was receiving anymore was about the nuclear situation in Fukushima, or came in the form of stories we'd fought to get the media to publish. Without international attention, we were in danger of having private relief money dry up altogether. Rikuzentakata desperately needed resources to fund the projects not covered by tax money. And with the red tape we faced in using the resources allocated by the government, running out of money was simply not an option.

So I traveled, and I beseeched. At times I sat among socialites who were born into wealth. Other times I sat with women whose spouses earned more in a year than I'd made in my entire career. I sat among people who had created items sold at local craft bazaars giving what little they could. Sometimes I came back with a donation I could hand over to City Hall, and at other times I was thanked politely but left with nothing.

I found comfort in the small acts of kindness. At the end of my speeches to large audiences, there were usually several people who came forward with cash donations. These I donated to the city's Orphans' Fund. These children often thought of themselves a burden, causing financial hardship on their relatives who had taken them in. I wanted them to feel as good about their lives as they could. Life had already taken enough from them. Anything that would alleviate their pain I was glad to pass on to the Fund.

Sometimes the end of my speech was met with what felt like the passing of a collection basket. While there was no pressure for anyone to give, many who were in a position to do so were generous. This, too, went to the Orphans' Fund. For the most part this system worked. Many private organizations were sympathetic. Most of the time, people just needed to be reminded that the people of Rikuzentakata still existed and needed help even if their stories had stopped appearing in the news.

But the process wasn't without its hurdles. If there was going to be a donation, especially a large one, it was often offered conditionally. Donors presented large sums that came with numerous stipulations—they wanted naming rights over what was being built, they wanted to dictate the use of materials for the project, they wanted thank-you letters from the disaster victims whom the project was meant to benefit.

Some requests could be accommodated, while others had to be turned down no matter how significant the offer was. The conditions stipulated made it too difficult to accept the funds. An organization in Tokyo was offering the equivalent of nearly one million U.S. dollars toward the rebuilding of the city's public library. But they wanted to name the library after their organization. This wouldn't do. It was a public library run by the city. As a city government building, it couldn't have the name of an outside entity. No matter who gave the funding, it had to remain Rikuzentakata Public Library.

In another case, a foreign religious delegation showed up in Rikuzentakata handing out money, only to follow up days later with requests that those who'd received the funds should come to learn about their faith. Understandably, people in town were upset.

"If you want to preach at us, don't do it by buying our time or pressuring us to listen to your sermons." I heard this sentiment over and over. Religious groups offering philanthropic donations had to be banned in town after that.

~~~

In my travels I began to discuss new methods of donating for future calamities. When I talked about philanthropy, Mayor Toba had one major point he wanted me to drive home: give directly to the source, preferably the account set up by the local government to receive disaster relief funds. Local leaders are the ones who know best about the needs of their community. They are the ones with real-time information. Stop picking your favorite groups to give to and instead give to the city.

At every event where I made this point, I brought up a major example of why this was necessary—one that I had to apologize for in advance as for some in attendance, what I was about to share would likely not go down well. I was about to badmouth a well-known organization. I told the assembled donors about how in the initial aftermath of the disaster, the world came together to support Japan. Sports teams all around the world held moments of silence, heads bowed, the Japanese flag drawn on signs held by spectators in the stands. Schools, religious organizations, musicians, and artists from all over the world contributed what they could, each adding their own unique and creative spin.

Organizations all over Japan and globally joined forces to raise money. Some groups knew exactly where they wanted the money to reach, and funded these projects quickly. But many others simply donated large sums of money to the Red Cross, which then gave the money to the Japanese Red Cross. The Japanese Red Cross was trusted to distribute the funds responsibly. This didn't work. Instead of passing the money on to those in need, the Japanese Red Cross sat on the funds for months, effectively withholding tens of millions of dollars of essential relief money while deliberating over how best to utilize the cash.

After an interminable wait, it was decided that the money would be put to use providing essential home goods like rice cookers, refrigerators, and washing machines to victims living in temporary housing. When the installation crews arrived with the appliances, they were met by the press who followed them into the homes of the victims. Much of the resulting footage lingered gratuitously on the Japanese Red Cross stickers emblazoned on each of the appliances. There was another wave of public outcry and accusations of poorly handled public relations. Subsequent disasters in Japan have handled philanthropy much differently—bypassing the Japanese Red Cross and donating straight into a municipal disaster relief bank account.

It is every donor's right to give to their favorite charity. By definition, philanthropy is the act of giving money willingly from one to another with altruistic intent, and donors have every right to decide which projects receive their funds. It's their money. This becomes problematic, however, when the definition of a worthy project is ambiguous. In some cases donors selected their recipients or offered grants based on applications. Other times, the donor had a project in mind and simply handed over the cash. They would come to town asking for a list of the groups doing the particular kind of work they wanted to support, and then they'd march to the addresses on the list given and simply hand out cash.

On the ground, this ambiguity began to cause problems. People in town came forward with complaints about private project funding. Why was that other person more deserving of support? Why was their project seen as more important? What's wrong with my project? To them there was no discernable logic to who was getting chosen, or why. As a result many of the well-funded projects began to lose popularity, and the donors themselves came across as ill-informed and fussy, playing favorites.

I tried to bring these concerns to the attention of the donors. Perhaps I could explain that the citizens needed money equally—that reconstruction affected everyone, and that a scattershot approach to relief funding was breeding jealousy and accusations of favoritism which reflected poorly on the donors as well as the recipients. But most donors were unwilling or unable to see how their contributions were causing these misperceptions.

While I understood that it was the donor's prerogative to choose where their money went, I also understood the frustrations of the locals whose projects were continually overlooked. Many of these smaller projects were the simplest and easiest to fund, and would have made an immediate difference.

"I want to put a giant electronic dart board in my *izakaya*," a pub owner told me one evening. One of the establishments I frequented, a place where I had sat with scores of locals and heard harrowing stories of survival. The owner was concerned that business had slowed down, and wanted something to set him apart from the other *izakaya* in town.

"I learned about this type of dart board that connects to the internet. You can find other people around the world and connect to them by video. It's massive. It lets you share your game live, compete against others virtually." He gestured at the empty stretch of wall where he planned to put the machine, his expression earnest. "Having something like that in here would help connect people to the world. Not only because it's rare and no one else anywhere near here has one, but people could come in here and feel less isolated. And people all over the world could see us as more than just victims. We'd be people who play and enjoy ourselves and want to reach out. It would help us feel more human. We could connect."

After sensing the tone of waning patience of the city and feeling the palpable sadness in the air, anything that helped lift their spirits was a worthwhile investment. I asked him about the price.

The machine cost 200,000 yen, around two thousand U.S. dollars. Okay, expensive but not unreasonable. I'd spoken with people who had been prepared to give much, much more. I just needed to find the right donor.

But when I presented this idea, I was met with blank stares by donors. I was asking for how much? For one man? For a dart board? Was I serious? And this was supposed to accomplish what, exactly? No matter how much the necessity of community and humanization for these people was explained, no donor would accept the proposal. A dart board was not a worthy enough cause, never mind the intent behind it or what it could achieve. Everyone wanted larger-scale and high-profile projects, specifically those whose results were trackable. For donors, projects needed to look impressive. If they gave money for the construction of a building, they could talk about how many families would live there or how many people in the area would benefit from the service it provided. But simply making an unspecified number of people happy by enabling them to connect to the outside world was too nebulous, no matter how reasonable the asking sum was.

When other ideas like the dart board were pitched but were seen as unworthy, I took it personally. I felt I should have done a better job explaining. It was frustrating that the donors didn't get the big picture. I also wished donors could put aside their egos and give to projects that were truly helping.

Gradually, it became clear that local politics on the donors' end was also a determining factor in who was giving to whom. Being able to say and show how worthy recipients' projects were was something of a status symbol. That said, not all donors had the facts of how money was being spent by the recipients, or how their donations were being perceived on the ground. And not all donors cared. This created more confusion and complications. With scope and worthiness becoming more opaque with differing definitions and expectations all around, asking for funds became laborious and unpleasant.

I found over time that Japan experts (sometimes so-called) and those who had contributed large sums to a fund were largely the ones dictating who received what in Tōhoku. Expertise notwithstanding, not everyone had facts. These donors and experts may have visited the disaster region once or twice meeting mayors and community leaders, but they still left understanding only part of the bigger picture. The snapshot they returned home with didn't coincide with the needs on the ground. Fundraising became tricky and receiving donations far more complex than I wished.

One prime example was the disparity between the victims in Fukushima compared to those in other Tōhoku prefectures. The Fukushima region stayed in the international public eye much longer due to the nuclear power plant that was damaged in the tsunami and the ensuing explosion that leaked radioactive material. Headlines overflowed with speculations about the reactor's safety and the potential of another meltdown further endangering the area. With a nuclear disaster in their backyard in addition to the devastation of the tsunami, people there were considered "double-victims," or even "triple-victims" when factoring in the earthquake and aftershocks. More attention meant more donation money, and more projects went to residents of Fukushima. It didn't take long for rumors to start circulating about extravagant shopping sprees, taxis taken to and from nights at *pachinko* parlors, or expensive new cars.

"Why are people in Fukushima being given free trips to Italy?" I was once asked. "We lost our homes, too. But they're treated differently. They're getting special attention because they're from Fukushima. Why does it matter whether our homes were lost in a tsunami or because they were in a nuclear zone? Loss is loss."

The source of this discontent was due to the fact that different prefectures had been destroyed to different degrees, but they all needed immense amounts of support—support that many of them were not receiving. Funding by private organizations was certainly helpful, but it shouldn't have been necessary. They had suffered a collective erasure of their lives. To be forced to watch relief efforts wane with public interest and to see aid distributed unequally and not in accordance with their actual needs—many were justifiably upset.

Life in Tōhoku was becoming intricately more complex. Donations were drying up and requests for assistance were routinely turned down. The decline in the number of organizations leading projects was noticed and commented upon. With every non-profit organization that came and went, hearts were broken. Lack of donations meant fewer projects. The familiar tickle of despair was becoming more and more present and I saw people around me struggling. Little in life was fun. Gratitude for life became harder and harder to express. I saw pain in the faces of people around me. I saw fatigue. I saw resentment. On top of it all, I was running out of energy and ideas.

Chapter 30

Amya Miller

It's not called *Mah-jong* when played with kids. Real *Mah-jong* is played in smokey rooms on the fifth or sixth floors of office and apartment buildings all over Japan, middle-aged men and sometimes a few women here or there shuffling plastic tiles, table after table of foursomes betting and passing time. Once long ago I knew how to play, but I've since forgotten.

And so when Chiaki and Akina, Kazuki's daughters, told me they wanted to play donjara, a game with a name I didn't recognize, I had to ask what they were talking about. Kazuki mouthed to me, "*Mah-jong*" and I nodded. Got it. We can't as adults very well encourage gambling. This was not technically *Mah-jong*. At least, we weren't going to call it that. I told the girls I would play and I sat down on the floor as they set up the pieces.

Chiaki is one year older than Akina, and this year they're ten and nine. Chiaki was five and Akina four when the tsunami hit. For them, post-disaster life was all they remember. They were accustomed to seeing the bulldozers and dump trucks kicking up dust and multiple sections of town always being under some degree of construction.

Athletics ran in this family, and these two girls were no exception. Throw them in a pool and they swim like a fish. Put them on a track course and they're two gazelles outrunning everyone. If it wasn't for Kazuki's father forbidding his granddaughters from playing baseball (because girls don't play baseball, according to the grandfather), they would have gladly played on the team formed for local boys. And excelled. Instead, they played tennis and won trophies at every competition.

Both girls insisted they would win at this game that was not *Mah-jong*, and since I hadn't played for so many years, I was afraid they would. But not to be beaten before we even start, I decided to talk a big game.

"If this game was a sport, you two might have a chance. But since it's not, I'm going to win. Prepare to lose!"

Kazuki's high-pitched laughter cut through the room as the girls objected to my statement with some nine- and ten-year-old trash-talking. Keiko, Kazuki's wife, popped her head out from the kitchen and asked what's going on, and why was there so much of a racket? The girls talked over each other trying to explain my audacity as their father Kazuki looked on, grinning and shaking his head.

Chiaki, Akina, Keiko, and I were seated around the low table that doubled as a dinner table and a homework desk. Instructions for fake *Mah-jong* given, within five minutes Akina had won. Two more games, and I had yet to win. I told them I was adamant, and that the next game would be mine, when suddenly we all heard it. The gong of the fire truck as it rolled down the street stopped the game.

The local fire trucks didn't have sirens. Instead, they rang gongs which sounded very much like a cross between a temple bell and a church bell. I hated it. It was haunting, forlorn, almost morbid. Normally, I loved the calm and serenity offered by Buddhist temple bells and church bells. This was neither. A sad sound, it projected doom. The ringing bell offered no sense of urgency. It was completely wrong for an emergency vehicle. Year after year, the toll of these gongs gave me goosebumps. Both girls froze. Kazuki's back straightened. Keiko went over to the window and opened it. The girls perked up and listened as well. The city-wide PA system announced something, but with the echo that rang through the hills I couldn't make out what was being said. Keiko looked down at the girls and said, "It's okay. Daddy doesn't have to go." Kazuki's brigade wasn't called up.

Kazuki was a volunteer firefighter. If it was a fire large enough to need the volunteer firefighter brigades in town, a city-wide announcement would have informed us which brigades had to report for duty over the loudspeakers strategically placed throughout the city limits. Tonight, Kazuki's brigade wasn't needed.

Chiaki and Akina, even at their young age, could remember Kazuki having to go out day after day in the aftermath of the tsunami. They didn't understand what he was doing, but they knew it was serious and dangerous. Kazuki had never talked about his role in having to recover bodies. He was one of the few who did not want to discuss any part of the disaster. Every time the disaster came up as a subject on a night out with others, he would get up and say that he had to go buy cigarettes. No one objected. Everyone knew what he had done and that he needed to walk away from these stories.

I finally caught my stride and won a game—then another, and another. Unaccustomed to losing, both girls soon told me and Keiko that they were done. Keiko reminded the girls to go take their bath before they ran off to play and the girls quickly departed, leaving the three adults to sit and relax with cups of coffee and slices of apples.

In all the time I had known Keiko and Kazuki, I had sensed that she was careful not to push him to talk about the disaster or his role. I took her cue. She was also less open to sharing how she felt about the disaster. If she wanted to talk, she did. I didn't push.

Kazuki was still watching television, mumbling English sentences as the actors on the screen said things to each other. Keiko scooted herself over to me and said in a voice slightly above a whisper, "My mother told me something the other day," she said. "I haven't told anyone yet. Not even Kazuki."
"Is everything okay?" I asked.
"Yes," she said. "Sort of. Well, yes. Do you want to hear a story?"
I nodded.
"Okay," she said, "It's funny but it's not."
My confusion must have shown, because Keiko patted my hand and said, "It's okay. Really." I nodded again, and she began. "My mother and grandmother knew a tsunami would come on the day of the disaster. It shook too much and for too long. They just knew it." Keiko looked at me and I nodded again. Keiko giggled. That threw me off.
"They knew they had enough time to gather things that were important to them, so they went around the house looking for all the cash they could find. They grabbed bottles of water and tea and some crackers. I think my grandmother even found her handbag and grabbed that."
She giggled again. "They didn't want to lose everything in the tsunami, assuming it hit the house of course, so they decided to take the most important appliance."

Keiko took a deep breath, "So they took the refrigerator."
"They took the fridge?" I asked, almost shouting.
"My parents aren't rich," Keiko said. "And refrigerators aren't cheap. At least, my mother didn't think they were."
"Yeah, but still. How were they going to carry a fridge up a hill?" I asked.
"They just took everything out of the fridge and left all the food behind on the kitchen floor. My grandmother grabbed one end and my mother grabbed the other, and they just started tilting and lifting and scooting it across the floor to get it out of the house."
Still shocked, I was beginning to picture the scene in my mind.
"Then," Keiko said, suppressing a fit of laughter, "they were trying to move it along but they realized they were stuck. It was still plugged into the wall. So, my mother grabbed the first thing she found—a pair of scissors—and cut the cord."
"No!" I said.
"Instead of just pulling the plug out of the wall socket, she cut the cord!"
Keiko burst out laughing. I sat stunned.
"Of all people, my mother and grandmother knew to escape. They knew how and they knew where to go. They should have known better than to take an appliance, a refrigerator of all things, but they just weren't thinking. It's like suddenly all logic escaped them."

My mind wandered and I wondered how this was possible. What's the point of the Tōhoku area having raised generation after generation to believe in *tsunami tendenko*, conducting drills and making evacuation plans and practicing both. Why bother with all of that if, when the day comes and there's actually time to escape and get to safety—on a whim, logic fails and an entirely wrong decision is made?

Lost in my own thoughts, I heard in the background as Keiko went on with the story, explaining how angry her father was that he had to pay for a new refrigerator when there was nothing wrong with the old one. But my mind was still wandering, confused. What does this say about disaster preparedness? Where does the idea to take the most important appliance fit into the fight-or-flight response? How can two seemingly contradictory sentiments coexist in an emergency situation? Totally rattled and frustrated, I couldn't make sense of this story. As I tuned back in, I found myself joining in on Keiko's laughter, but I suddenly tasted bile. My body was reacting to the utter chaos in my brain. This story was wrong and I knew it. It was funny, except it was real, and that made it profoundly unfunny.

The same sentence repeated itself on a loop in my head: what's the point of preparing at all? Why fool ourselves into thinking we can be ready if, when the time comes, our fear and panic will trick us into making stupid mistakes?

Chapter 31

Futoshi Toba

Outside Rikuzentakata and the disaster region, most of the world has moved on. There are events every year marking the memorial, but aside from that news coverage is practically nonexistent. Time has passed on for others. Their lives are back to normal.

The year of 2016 was a marker year. This would be the fifth memorial. There's something about the number five; half of ten, a halfway point to what, none of us knew. There would be another marker at year ten, but five years after the disaster we knew was a milestone. The fifth memorial, I decided, would be particularly noteworthy. The sixth through the ninth year, there would be little or no press. These were just numbers with no particular significance attached. Five felt different. Ten would be different. This was our chance to make a statement. The next one wouldn't come for another five years. Go big now.

I wanted to use this event as a way of bringing people back to our reality here in town, to my reality, and that of many of my colleagues and friends. The media showed up again in droves, foreign and Japanese, and I was inundated with requests for comments and interviews. Here was my chance.

Amya and I discussed the idea of having a message read in English for the foreign audience who would be attending. This would help us make a point in the media coverage about the gratitude felt by the people of Rikuzentakata for what people had done, and were still doing, for the city. Having a script we could share would help us prepare for the foreign media and get the word out globally: we're still here, we're trying, don't forget us. We needed to be remembered for what we went through, and if there was still help to be offered, we were willing to accept it. As ever, I was battling the government in Tokyo, and the pace of reconstruction was still not at all what I had hoped it would be.

I asked Amya to draft a statement to read at the memorial. I told her she should write in the voice of the people here in town, and I told her I wanted to see it when she was finished. A month or so before the memorial service, she brought me a sheet of paper.

"What do you think?" she said, sliding the paper over to me. I read it through twice.
"Keep it just like this," I said, looking up at her.
"Good," she said. "I'm glad you like it."
"I do," I told her. "It's perfect."

~~~

We had a dais placed on the stage, decorated with a symbolic and elegant display of hundreds of white chrysanthemums. At the center of the dais, its base surrounded by a wall of flowers, stood a tall rectangular pillar painted a glowing white and covered in black calligraphy letters. In elegant *kanji*, the inscription read, "To Honor the Souls of those who left us in the Great East Tōhoku Disaster." A veil of solemnity hung in the air, and the mood was clear. We were here because too many had died. We were here to honor their memories and grieve along with everyone else whose pain still ran through their bodies.

On a massive screen we broadcasted the National Memorial Service taking place in Tokyo where the Emperor and Empress sat stage left of an even bigger display of chrysanthemums. The Emperor and the Prime Minister each read a statement, and we held a national moment of silence at 2:46 pm for one minute. Foreign dignitaries in the audience bowed their heads in unison, an international recognition of the ever-present pain.

After the two speeches and the moment of silence, we turned off the screen and began our own service. I gave a speech, followed by an address delivered by Kawamura-*san*,[18] the Mayor of Nagoya who had signed a friendship city agreement in the fall of 2014.

Amya was meant to follow him with a statement in English. I knew that many of the foreign dignitaries in attendance would understand Amya's words, but

I didn't know how many of the Japanese politicians would. The point was to reach a wide audience by providing an official statement in English as well as Japanese. This disaster hit Japan, but the aftermath was a global event. The aid alone received from abroad needed to be publicly recognized, and here was the way to express our gratitude.

Amya stepped up to the podium and began to speak.

"On this day five years ago, we woke up thinking it would be just another day. We sent our children to school, went to work, stayed home. We ate lunch, queued in City Hall to file our taxes, and sat down for tea. Then everything changed.

We never imagined ourselves sitting here five years out, our city gone, all of our lives different. Today we mourn: our spouses, children, parents; our aunts, uncles, cousins; our neighbors and friends and colleagues. We miss you. We wish you were here with us.

Our loss is collective and deep. The cloud of sadness hanging over our city affects us all. Some days we function well. Other days it's a struggle to move on with life. Each day is different; each day is the same. It's been five years and many of us are still lost. We will likely never get over our losses but will instead learn to live with the pain. We will heal ourselves, rebuilding our lives around the losses we have suffered. We will someday be whole again, but we will never be the same.

But today must mark a shift. As we mourn, we must also find ways to heal, love again, and appreciate moments of joy. While we will not forget you, we ask that you let us go on, move forward, recover, and learn to live each day with an appreciation for the past and hope for the future. Stay with us in our hearts and let us feel your presence. Help us see what it means to have the gift of life.

We mark on this day our collective memories of those we lost, and also new beginnings. As we learn to appreciate each day, week, month, quarter, and year, we commit to live for you as well. Here, today, we start a new chapter of our lives.

Our collective memory of the past five years is not all about loss. We are keenly aware that our lives would not be what they are today if it weren't for the incredible outpouring of support we received from those throughout Japan and the world. You gave us water when we needed to drink. You gave us food when we needed to eat. The clothing, bedding, medicine, daily essentials, expertise, volunteers, cash, and goodwill we received from people from afar will affect us forever. We are here because of the kindness of strangers. We will never forget these acts. You sustained us then, kept us living, and your interest in our lives continues to be fuel and sustenance for us.

For your generosity, support, affection, comfort, assistance and more, we say thank you. Most of you we will never know or meet. Even without a face to go with the aid and kindness we received, the depth of our gratitude does not change. We are so incredibly grateful, and we want you to know how much it all means to us. On this day of remembrance, please accept our thanks and know we will cherish forever what your kindness has done for us as individuals, families, and a city.

We will remember, and we will move on. Stay with us as we create a new city, one that is vibrant, beautiful, welcoming, and whole."

She looked up at the monument on the dias, bowed, and walked back to her seat. Later she told me that when she sat down next to her husband, David, also sitting in the front row with her, she saw he was crying. Wondering if he was ill or hurt, she whispered to him, asking what was wrong, and he only shook his head and replied, "That was beautiful."

It was. Moving and graceful, she captured what I wanted the world to know. We were grateful. We were trying.

~~~

Japan had been buzzing with anticipation in the several years before the 2020 Olympic Games. The announcement of the bid itself was old news. Would Tokyo get it? A convincing speech had been made in French by Christel Takigawa, a half-Japanese, half-French celebrity. Her speech promoted and promised Japan's *omotenashi*—superior customer service, displays of exquisite manners, and hospitality that goes above and beyond. Come to Japan and we will blow you away with the elegant spirit of Japan. It worked. Tokyo would be filled with foreigners in a few years. Some would surely come up to visit us in Rikuzentakata, curious to see what reconstruction looked like almost a decade after the disaster. But until then, we were officially old news here in Tōhoku.

While we assumed and hoped the years leading up to 2020 would mean a new influx of foreign visitors, that meant there was much to do to prepare the city as a worthy destination. I wanted us to be a showcase for what recovery looks like. I wanted visitors to arrive and explore and see what we went through. I wanted my city to be the northern version of the Hiroshima and Nagasaki Memorial Parks. We were on track to create a memorial park here as well. A place for remembrance, prayer, and learning.

Grateful for the anticipated increase in foot traffic, I faced an unexpected hurdle. By five years after the disaster, the construction companies that had been working in cities and towns throughout the Tōhoku region had started bidding on contracts relating to the Olympics. Cities along the coast started feeling like ghost towns all over again. We had plenty of work for contractors and we had the money, but we simply could not get the bids. Construction of public housing and large apartment complexes to replace temporary housing units, as well as the completion of the electrical wiring, plumbing, and carpeting—all were delayed as contractors left Tōhoku and flocked en masse to the more prestigious Olympics-related projects.

It was a ridiculous scenario. By securing this international mega-project, politicians in Tokyo had inadvertently slowed our recovery yet again. Had they simply not considered the scarcity, this would cause for contractors and construction crews? While I watched the rest of the nation celebrate the great honor we'd received, I was inwardly livid at the inability of those making the decisions to see how this would affect us.

I had spent years taking two steps forward, only to regress by three and five and ten steps. Just when I thought we would have forward movement, we were stuck all over again.

Chapter 32

Amya Miller

I had fainted. I woke up, unsure of where I was, only to realize I was on the floor of my room in Rikuzentakata. How long had I been out? My head hurt. Did I hit it on my way down or did I hit it on the floor? Did it matter? Not really. Fainting wasn't good, and I knew it. I also knew I wasn't sick. Nor did I have the flu. There was nothing wrong with me except for being immensely hungry and weak.

My agreement with David when I moved to Japan had been that I was responsible for earning my own living expenses. I had long since blown through my savings and had reneged on my promise to David that I wouldn't tap our joint bank accounts back home. I was on an unrealistically tight budget. I had to pay rent and utilities for my apartment. My cell phone was needed for work. What could I live without? Having long ago given up buying clothes or shoes or items fun and perky, there were no extra expenses to cut except food. Food was the easiest to go without. I could feel incredibly full after drinking a liter of water. Thirty minutes later, drink another liter. A full stomach was a full stomach, whether it was water or a seven-course meal.

Over the years, thanks to various people, I was the guest at many meals. Rarely did I pay for food the first several years of my work, but gradually when finding myself alone at night, I had to fend for myself. I had long since given up breakfast, usually buying a can of coffee (one can't go without caffeine) out of a vending machine. If I was at City Hall, there was often a box of donated cakes or cookies, and with two cups of coffee from the communal coffee machine for free, I could have a meal, albeit with no nutritional value. Still, on these days, breakfast, if it could be called that, was free, and I was less hungry than the times I paid for my one can of coffee on my own.

When we were at our dinners in Tokyo, whether he knew I wasn't eating or he was trying to be kind, Mayor Toba never let me pay. I would offer, more as a gesture than anything, but he always grabbed the tab saying, "No you don't."

While not starving, I still had no extra cash. My friends were generous, especially in Tokyo, people who had high-paying jobs and could easily afford taking me out to their newest favorite restaurant. If I was flat out of food, there were a few people I could go to without hesitation. I didn't abuse requests for food, reserving calling on these people when I had no other option.

But in the interim, I had found a 100-yen shop that sold food, and this was where I went most nights to stock up: two cucumbers for 100 yen; two packets of rice for 100 yen; yogurt and fruit for 100 yen each; one premade packet of curry for 100 yen—this would last two nights. For 500 yen (or around 5 dollars at the time) there could be two meals. It wasn't a lot of food, and surely lacked protein, iron, and all kinds of vitamins, but except for this one fainting episode, I was fine. Hungry, but fine.

I didn't want to abuse David's generosity. Being apart was tough. We missed each other. He would have paid for whatever I needed. I knew this. But this hadn't been part of our original deal. I reasoned to myself that if my time in Japan was going to grow to become longer-term—and clearly it was—then it needed to be sustainable. That would only be fair.

Naturally it was highly embarrassing to think of asking for help. The work done in Rikuzentakata was important and affirmed by the mayor, and I was making a difference. I was getting so much done and knew my role was desperately needed. There had to be some way to get through this.

On several occasions, I asked U.S. contributors about covering living expenses, the consensus was "City Hall should be paying you, not us." The funds these groups raised had already been largely distributed, and the amount that was left, most organizations were hanging onto for just the right project. Paying for a volunteer's food didn't make the cut. If City Hall could have paid a volunteer, they already would have, but that fact didn't seem to resonate with people in the States.

On one occasion, I was told to go to the Mormons or the Republicans for money. "Both those groups have a lot of extra cash," the old man had said, chuckling. That he found my hunger funny was infuriating, his dismissal a cruel and cutting brush-off.

City Hall did pay for my transportation to and from Tokyo but the rest was up to me. They were sorry. Truly sorry. But with half the city's population over fifty and almost one third of the population over sixty-five, the amount of tax revenue the city was bringing in was minimal. Government assistance for reconstruction was key to getting the city up and running, but technically there wasn't a budget category for "the foreigner whom we asked for help."

Once, I was the keynote speaker at a dinner in Tokyo, giving an update on Tōhoku recovery. It was largely attended by spouses of foreign businessmen. I had been tactfully blunt about the fact I was skipping meals to make ends meet because City Hall wasn't in a position to pay me. I saw several women exchanging looks but couldn't read their expressions.

The emcee made a comment about making funds the group had available to me to help with my expenses. This was met with resistance when one woman stood up and said, "I've been volunteering for thirty years and no one has ever paid me." I felt like snapping back. "You live in a 10,000-dollar-a-month high rise apartment paid for by your husband's company, a life of luxury. When was the last time you went without a meal?" But I didn't say that, of course. I was absolutely not going to beg. In the end, I left the dinner full of delicious food, my remuneration for the night.

I continued to skip meals or find ways of stretching my money, buying in bulk when I could or buying from the discount rack, which usually meant expired food. I forced myself not to feel humiliated when everyone but me at the dinner table pulled their wallet out to pay for some group get-together. I also learned not to show frustration when people didn't offer to pay for my meals. Not everyone was generous. I soon learned to keep my distance from them. I got used to eating less, and except for the days following a large meal paid for by a friend, I didn't find myself too uncomfortable. When David offered to send me 500 dollars here and there, I didn't say no. I also didn't tell him I had fainted. I was sure it was an isolated incident. I would buy vitamins the next time he offered cash. Surely additional iron and a mixture of vitamins would be good.

This thinking worked until I fainted again. Walking to a subway entrance that would take me to Tokyo Station to head back to Rikuzentakata, I felt my legs give way and blacked out suddenly. When I came to, seeing strangers staring down at me, I wasn't sure where I was or what had happened. There was concern on their faces—this foreign woman lying on the sidewalk—did she speak Japanese? Should someone call an ambulance? I heard them murmur but couldn't make out clearly what was being said. My head hurt again when I finally sat up. I asked someone to get a taxi. When one stopped, I was helped in and headed to the train station, putting the cab fare on my credit card for David to pay. I would also buy food at the station and put that on the credit card, too. I would come up with a way to explain this to him later. I knew I needed to start eating better. These fainting spells had to stop.

They did stop, and in a most unusual way. Two men from Rikuzentakata City Hall and I traveled to Tokyo to make a pitch to representatives from the Government of Qatar for funds[19] for a shelter for women and children. After our presentation, we parted, and I went out with a friend for dinner. After a hearty meal of pasta and salad and wine, all of which went on his tab, I made my way to the station to catch the bullet train. Recalling the last trip to this station, I willed myself not to faint. I was full and satisfied. Surely I was fine.

City Hall was paying for my bullet train ticket, so I paid in cash at the kiosk and made sure to get the receipt. I put the receipt in my wallet, put my wallet in my purse and headed inside the station to treat myself to a snack. I bought one small packet of caramels—my favorite—went to take my wallet out of my purse and found it missing. I pulled out everything from inside my purse. The wallet was gone. I looked throughout the store, retracing my steps. I checked where I had entered the station through the turnstile, right there, not fifty meters away. I looked everywhere. It was definitely gone. I had been pickpocketed. Beautifully. I had no idea how it had happened, but it had to have been in the last ninety seconds. What skill.

My wallet contained all of my credit cards, my Japanese driver's license, my Japan Residence Card, which I was legally required to carry, and what little cash I had on me. With it gone, I couldn't return to Rikuzentakata. In a total panic, I called a friend.

"What do I do?" I said, almost in tears.
"Calm down," he said. "I'll help you. I'll walk you through it. Where are you? Tell me exactly where you are in the station." I told him.
"Okay. Look to your left. Up about 100 meters. There should be a police box." He was right. How did he know this?

"Tell the station attendant you have to go to the police box and to let you back through the turnstile," he said and I obeyed. I went to the police, my friend still on the line for support, and filed a report. The police officer could not guarantee I would see my wallet again, but he took down all of my information.

Still on the line, my friend helped me get a refund for the train ticket after showing more station attendants my police report, and with that cash I hopped in a taxi. My friend offered to loan me money until I could get a new ATM card issued and have new credit cards sent by my husband. He spread the word among our mutual friends, all of whom loaned me cash to get through the next several weeks. I would need a new residency card and license issued, and all of this would take time. I wasn't going back to Rikuzentakata any time soon.

During this pickpocket-induced time off, I contemplated my cashlessness. I had asked for help from donors and was turned down. While I was grateful for what my sponsor Mr. Kanamaru was paying me, it was a sum so small I was embarrassed to say it out loud. I'd asked for a raise and it had never come through. Why didn't I tell David I needed more cash? Was it because I thought he would say, "maybe you should come home then" and I wasn't ready? I had other family members and friends I could have asked for help, but something about my age, pride, temperament, and stubbornness all had led me to convince myself I could and would manage.

With this most recent obvious and blatant loss of cash thanks to having credit cards, ATM cards and cash all gone in an instant, my friends had come through and both fed me and loaned me money. Eventually with new credit cards necessary identification in hand and with David offering to refund everyone, I was able to get back to Rikuzentakata and back to work.

But when I returned, I thought of the times I had advised people to improve their situation—all the advice I had given to others up north, but I hadn't taken my own needs very seriously. Why had I thought that skipping meals was an actual long-term plan? What sense did that make?

I knew I was getting better when I finally did return to Rikuzentakata several weeks later and ran into the Deputy Mayor, on entering City Hall.
He looked at me and said, "You've put on some weight in your cheeks."
"I know," I said, "I've been eating."
I laughed but he didn't.

"You were looking pretty gaunt there for a while," he said.

"I'm okay now," I said. "Really?"

"Yes, really."

After this conversation, I decided it was time to approach City Hall with the fact that if I was to go on doing this work, I had to receive something in the form of pay. They would have to figure out how to get the money. I didn't enjoy fainting.

Chapter 33

Amya Miller

"He's going away. Three months at sea," Keiko, whom I now considered a good friend, had invited me to see her brother's fishing vessel take off for a three-month voyage. "It's a big deal," she said. She told me about the streamers, banners, flags, and music, about how the family and friends stay on land waving until the boat is out of sight. "You tell stories," she said. "You should see this."

I agreed it sounded like a must-see event, and a week later I drove down to one of the local fishing ports first thing in the morning. I found Keiko and Kazuki, their two daughters running around with their cousins who would soon be seeing off their father. Keiko introduced me to her extended family—starting with *oppi*.

"This is my *oppi*," Keiko told me, pointing at an old woman who looked at me with a combination of mischief and resignation. I stared at Keiko.
"Your what?" I asked.
"*Oppi*," she said.
I looked over to Kazuki, who stood next to me and whispered, "What's an *oppi*?"
Everyone laughed.
"*Oppi* is Keiko's word for grandmother," *oppi* said as she shuffled over to me and patted my arm.
"There's no reason you would know this word. It doesn't exist except for Keiko's vocabulary."
Oppi half-snorted and half-laughed, sending more ripples of laughter through the crowd.

"There's nothing wrong with my word," Keiko said, as she came up on the other side of the old woman. She linked arms with *oppi*, not expecting to be the center of attention for the pet name only she used. "Is there now, *oppi*?"

Oppi rolled her eyes, but grinned. And so for the rest of the morning, I was welcomed into Keiko's extended family, accepted in this meaningful moment where one of them was about to go off to sea. I thanked them for inviting me to this event, telling them I knew how important and private this must be.

Suddenly, *oppi* produced a bottle of green tea and a homemade rice ball. She tried to hand them to me but I declined, afraid this was her own breakfast she was offering out of obligation or excessive politeness. But *oppi* chided me and pushed the *onigiri* and tea into my hands. Once I accepted the meal, *oppi* just stood there waving her hands over the food. Her gesture could have been anything from a wordless blessing of the meal to an admonishment of my resistance—a silent command to shut up and eat. I had no idea what was going on, but I accepted graciously and thanked her with a big smile. I bowed. *Oppi* smiled back and then shuffled off. It was a sincere gesture of friendship, letting me be part of this family moment as well as giving me her food. I didn't want to take this lightly.

Soon Keiko pulled me aside and said, "It's about to begin." Music started to play, a lot of minor notes and melancholy tones rang through the air. I wondered idly if the music is meant to produce such sadness. If this event is meant as a celebration and send-off to these sailors, why was the music this painful? I even saw the daughter of the man heading out to sea, maybe eight or nine years old, burying her head into her mother's hands and crying. Her shoulders shook, her sobs becoming louder and louder. On the boat I noticed a man who I thought was her father waving to her, calling something out as he cupped his hands around his mouth, but the song lyrics drowned out his voice.

I felt a lump in my throat. The melancholy was contagious. I realized I was about to cry. The tears welled up, and in a matter of seconds they started to flow. This was embarrassing. Why was I crying? I didn't know Keiko's brother or his family. She and her daughters, Chiaki and Akina, were running up and down the concrete deck throwing balls of paper string to the ship. They weren't sad. The little girls giggled and smiled, and my friend looked bright and energetic. So why was I crying? Where was this coming from?

Slowly, I backed up toward my minivan and ducked out of sight to let the tears flow in earnest. I didn't want people to think I was leaving early, but I also didn't want to be seen like this. Luckily, I parked far enough away that no one could see this outburst. I leaned my head onto the steering wheel, careful not to honk the horn, and let myself go. I don't know how long I sat there sobbing, but I knew I needed it. I couldn't understand where this sudden explosion of sadness had come from. I quickly texted Keiko an apology, saying something came up, that I had to leave, and drove off before she had a chance to stop me.

Back in my room I paced back and forth across the carpet, still crying. This was not like me. I wasn't a fan of tears, mine especially. Uncontrollable tears bothered me, but for the life of me I couldn't figure out what started this. Was it the send-off for the fishermen? It couldn't be that, I didn't know them. Was it the music that set me off? Why would that even happen? Something was going on inside of me that I didn't recognize and I didn't like it. Was it the little girl saying goodbye to her father? Was it the contrast of emotions I'd seen in the crowd? Seeing one person happy and another weeping? Here again, women and girls were allowed to cry but boys and men weren't. I spent the day in my room, only leaving to visit the convenience store at night to buy dinner.

My release of emotions, unexpected as it was, led me to two more days of off-and-on crying. I decided I needed a break from everything around me. I had to get out of town. I headed out without a destination and spent a few days not seeing anyone and not answering calls or emails. I needed quiet contemplation and reflection to sort this out. I sat by the ocean. I drove to a city I'd never been to before, appreciating a change of scenery. I deliberately got myself lost, forcing myself to take the time and find my way back to somewhere familiar.

After days of crying and soul-searching, I was finally able to admit to myself I was overwhelmed. The stress around me was too much. It felt like I was carrying everyone's burden, all the while keeping up a facade of composure without complaining or releasing any of this pent-up turmoil. A break would help, but what I really needed was to let it out. I had spent so much time giving advice to others about finding creative and healthy ways of releasing their emotions and letting off steam, but I wasn't doing it myself. I was knotted up and bottling everything inside. I was lonely. I was sad. I was deeply, profoundly exhausted. I was completely beaten down.

Driven by my successes and the almost addictive feeling of accomplishment and the high of making a difference, I had pushed myself on pure grit and adrenaline. I had long since run out of money. I was trying to make what little money I had last as long as it would. I was both physically and emotionally exhausted. Something about the bittersweet moment of watching a daughter and mother see off their father and husband as he went to sea for three months had triggered a release. I needed to cry, to tell someone just how exhausted I was, how beaten down by the pervasive grief and harrowing conditions around me. Is grief contagious? Was that why I was so sad? Was I taking on the emotions of the locals when they confided in me? Was my never-ending hunger causing my tears? Either way, the time had come for me to seek professional help.

I asked around and found a counseling service in Tokyo that had bilingual staff providing the freedom to weave between Japanese and English, as some of what I had to say could only be expressed in one or the other and wouldn't translate well.

The first session I had was via video. I spoke with a woman who asked me question after question, ending with "are you suicidal?"

"No! I'm not suicidal," I blurted out. "I'm just overwhelmed and exhausted in a way I've never experienced before. The grief around me is starting to become mine, and I need a way to let it out. I'm always hungry and always tired. I haven't had breakfast in years. There's destruction all around me. I'm living with the grieving. It's too much. It's all too much." It was good to get it out. To say it out loud. I sobbed for the remainder of the first session, signing off only as I scheduled the next appointment.

I stayed in therapy for six months and found enough of a release in just telling someone other than family and friends of my struggles and woes. I had good friends in Tokyo, those from my international boarding school days to new ones I'd made over the years. These friendships kept me laughing and enjoying life when I was in Tokyo. With several of them, but only on occasion, I would say I needed to vent.

"Just give me ten minutes," I would say. "I need to let things out."

They would listen, and I would feel better. If I needed to eat, they paid for my meals. Still, this pattern of short bursts of release hadn't been enough, and I didn't realize how exhausted I was and how deep and intense my grief was until I saw Keiko's niece cry as her father left for sea.

Many times my therapy sessions just consisted of me crying as my therapist sat there patiently. Sometimes she would prod me with questions like, "Why are you crying?" but I found these more annoying than helpful. On some days I knew why I cried; other days I didn't. It didn't matter to me why I was sad. I just was, and I had for so long put on a brave face, fought so hard with the media, made pitch after pitch for money, had dealt with ugly accusations and comments aimed at me by people who were jealous of my visibility and success, and I was just tired. The more stories I heard, the more I felt a responsibility to convey those stories, but donor fatigue had long since set in and the media were reporting on Fukushima and Fukushima only.

After six months I felt cried out. Not better or whole but like I had gotten the sadness out of my system, at least for a time.

I approached Mayor Toba with an idea.

"If I say I'm in therapy, and you say you are seeing a counselor, then maybe people in town would be more receptive to getting help with their mental health care. Would you be willing to see a therapist?" I asked.

"No. It doesn't work like that," he said immediately. "I can't see a therapist. It just won't work."

I trusted his reply. He knew the local politics of his constituents. He was an anomaly in the region, a big picture man who did bold things. But, even with this maverick reputation, Mayor Toba getting therapy? That was crossing a line. He wasn't mentally ill. Why would he need therapy? Even if he said, "I just need to let some things out," they could come back with, "Well, let's go have a drink then," since the stigma of his getting therapy implied mental illness, and if he wasn't mentally ill then surely letting off steam by getting drunk would be enough. This was too big of a social issue for him to tackle. He and I saying we were getting therapy would not be enough to change anyone's mind.

Understanding, albeit disappointed about the reasons Mayor Toba would not see a therapist, I decided I would try the same approach with others but on my own. I sat my friends down, one after another and posed the question.

"I'm seen as a strong woman, right?" I would ask.
"Right."
"So, if I say I'm in therapy, then will others in town be willing, do you think? Maybe people will think 'if she's going then maybe I can too.'"

The answers all led to an adamant refusal, though the reasons varied from friend to friend.

"You're foreign," one friend said. "The rules are different for you."
Another said, "Going to a therapist just makes you look like you don't have friends you can confide in."
Yet another said, "Just go shopping. That always makes me feel better."

I was getting nowhere.

Over drinks and small plates of food at a local *izakaya* one night, I decided to probe deeper. Alcohol releases inhibitions and offers more freedom to be honest.
"There's really no chance any of you would be willing to see a therapist?" I asked. "Tell me honestly."
"First, real men don't need that kind of help," one friend started. "Alcohol, cigarettes, women, and maybe *pachinko*. These are all the distractions we need."
"But, therapy isn't a distraction," I pressed.
"There's this guy I know," my friend said. "He's a retired teacher. Men who use their heads too much don't know how to release their stress. He's on antidepressants now. If he would just find a way to release his frustrations through physical activity, he'd feel so much better. You don't see athletes and people who work outside, like all these construction workers, taking antidepressants do you?"
"Hang on," I said. "How do you know athletes don't take antidepressants?" I asked.
"Have you ever heard of an athlete taking pills to treat mental illness?" he said. "No. And if they did, it would get leaked to the press."

Men who use their heads too much need to take pills, but men who work outside don't. That was my friend's argument, and it was good enough for him. Sure, he was drunk, but I also sensed from him a level of honesty I knew I wouldn't otherwise be privy to. I started to wonder about the role of alcohol and also *pachinko*, Japan's quasi-legal gambling industry. I was seeing more and more *pachinko* parlors being built, and I noticed how packed the parking lots were everytime I drove by one.

It was a notable cultural difference. I knew I could be more blunt and critical of the role alcohol and *pachinko* played in keeping people's emotions under control. But doing so felt wrong. I couldn't bring myself to endorse or criticize the role of alcohol and gambling as an emotional panacea. Maybe this is what was working. The issue felt profoundly complex and I was uncomfortable with what I was seeing around me.

I felt the cultural taboo weigh heavily on everyone around me—between hearing my friends' comments about my decision to see a therapist and remembering back to the campground manager who had given me a firm "no tears allowed." The stigma against mental illness ran too deep, I decided. I couldn't tackle this on my own. The sentiment of my friends and colleagues was that only those diagnosed with mental illness should see a therapist, or that shutting down their thoughts and getting physically active was an acceptable alternative to antidepressants. That meant there was nothing I could do on my own to change their minds. Or so I feared. Announcing that I was getting help from a therapist would only serve to confuse people around me.

I alone couldn't address Japan's understanding of mental health, and I had neither the tools nor the time to go on a one-woman crusade to get people to open up. All I could do was focus on myself and get to a point where being in this debris-riddled city didn't drive me into depression. I needed to start taking my own advice, beginning with days off and better sleep. I called Mayor Toba and told him I was taking a break for a bit and going back to the U.S. to visit David. I wanted real cheese that didn't break the bank. I wanted to hear my child's laughter. I craved a pizza that was delicious and didn't cost 60 dollars. I needed to be around my family, my husband. I needed to earn money. It was slowly starting to dawn on me that I needed a change.

~~~

I found myself using the word "loneliness" in my therapy sessions more and more frequently. In between bouts of crying, I would talk about my need to vent. On Skype, David listened. He always listened. But I also felt the more I complained the more I burdened him. I didn't want to come across as miserable. I was sad, I was hungry, and I was lonely. I was burnt out as well, but I was also getting things done at a pace and rate that even impressed me. I wasn't ready to call it quits. A change, yes. Quitting, no.

David and I soon both came to realize the saying "absence makes the heart grow fonder" is very real. We also realized we were both getting sick of being alone. As I told David of these sessions over our Skype chats, he would turn that report of loneliness or sadness or hunger from me into action.

"I'll come over," he would say.

David would fly to Japan for two to three months at a time several times a year. This continued until one day an immigration official at the airport in Tokyo told him that one of these days he would have to get a visa. He was getting dangerously close to the cutoff on how long a foreigner was allowed to stay in Japan. The frequency at which he made the trips didn't make the immigration officials any happier.

I was coming to a point where my loneliness, hunger, and lack of funds needed a permanent solution. During one of David's visits to see me, we walked around my neighborhood at midnight, me snuggling up to him for warmth, him chiding me for not wearing socks in winter. Was it time for me to return home? I didn't feel anywhere close to being done with my work. Then again, how would I know when I was done? There would always be more work. Most of all, we were both sick of being apart.

One of the stipulations we had first agreed upon when we decided I would stay on in Japan was that when one of us was done being alone, that was that. We had to make a change: I either had to come home or David would move to Japan. As he was the one earning, he would have to work out an arrangement that would let him telecommute. We talked about how realistic that would be. He wanted to give it a go. See what his clients would say. It took time. We went back and forth discussing the pros and cons. I wasn't done in Tōhoku; we both knew that. We were certain we were sick of the time apart. Logistical issues remained. We both had to work through how we felt about David being in Japan, dependent on me for language. Did we dare try? We decided we should. We were both middle-aged. If we didn't do this now, David would never have the chance to live in Japan. David moved in with me almost four years to the date after I had moved to Japan to help with recovery efforts full-time.

We sold our house in the U.S., and put our furniture in storage. We had waited long enough and we were now back together. I told him repeatedly during the first several days we shared an apartment far too tiny for two people that I felt like I was falling in love all over again.

Chapter 34

Amya Miller

We were having poisonous blowfish for dinner. There were four of us: Mayor Toba, myself, the Mayor's chief of staff Kenta, and Koga-*san*, the head of PR. We were in Tokyo for a series of meetings, traveling on a per diem that covered our hotel and food. The men decided on a cheap business hotel with no frills and a set price. Food was a much different story. If we pooled our funds and got serious about our online searches ahead of time, we could apply the rest of our per diem to cover quite a bit of food. Mayor Toba decided on *fugu*, the notoriously poisonous blowfish.

"Have you had it before?" Koga-*san* asked me.

"Nope." I replied.

"Will you try it?" Mayor Toba said.

"Once," I said, hesitant. I reminded myself that the statistical probability I would die was extremely low. The chefs were professionals. They prepared this delicacy all the time. They had special training to know just exactly where and how to cut out the poisonous area in the fish. Highly unlikely that I'd end up eating the one piece that the chef accidentally failed to slice away properly. Surely.

"Yes, fine. I'll try it." I reiterated. Let's do this.

Our restaurant was an old wooden building that used to be a residence, now converted into a restaurant. We went inside and were led upstairs. With its wooden beams across the ceiling, white walls, and wooden tables and chairs, the place was delicately decorated and quaint. I felt like I was stepping back in time, like visiting a friend in elementary school in a home from forty years ago.

Kenta and I sat next to each other, the Mayor across from me and Koga-*san* in front of Kenta. Beers were ordered as a starter but Kenta asked the waiter to follow right away with a bottle of *shōchū* made from potatoes. Kenta was known to love his *shōchū*. I don't touch it. Soon, we toasted to a successful series of meetings and the chatting began in earnest. We all talked over each other, blurring the lines of boss and employee, outsider and insider. The *shōchū* was brought as requested and Kenta's face lit up.

"Want a glass?" he asked me.
"No, I'll pass thanks," I said.
"Not a problem. I'll drink your share!" he said, and he poured three glasses. Drinks were raised again, and the talking resumed.

It felt good to get out of town every now and then. While Mayor Toba and I traveled all the time, the others at City Hall rarely got a chance to leave. This was just as much pleasure as business for them—an opportunity to surround themselves with scenery other than destruction. Kenta was especially happy, and I saw he was quick to refill his glass.

The *fugu* arrived and Kenta and Koga-*san* dug in. Uncertain, I craned my neck over the plate. The *fugu* was laid out in a circle, slim yet somehow fluffy slices of white cotton-like fish. Nicely done, chef. I reached for a slice of exquisitely sliced white meat and gently picked it up with my chopsticks. I held it up to the light. It was like paper, so thin I could see through it. This chef had impressive knife skills. I looked at Mayor Toba. He had been watching me the whole time. He burst into laughter.

"Sometimes I forget you're an American," he said. "You don't have to eat it if you don't want to," he assured me, but there was a twinkle of a dare in his eye. This was a challenge, and I knew it. I dipped the fish in just a bit of sauce and popped the delicate slice into my mouth, mentally telling the gods of fish that they'd better not let this piece be poisonous. I chewed and savored for a moment, waiting for something to happen. It tasted like all other white *sashimi*. That's it? Well, that was disappointing. I didn't understand what the big deal was, but I raised my eyebrows and looked back at Mayor Toba regardless.
"It's good!"
"Really?" Mayor Toba wasn't convinced.
"Hm-mmm," I mumbled. "It's good."
"Want more?" he said, grinning.

"Nope," I said, and he tossed his head back and laughed again. The other two joined in.

"Go ahead. Order something else then. I'll pay for it."

I looked at him and this time it was my turn to grin. Excellent. I'm going to order whatever I want, I decided. The more expensive, the better. I scanned the menu and pushed the button to call back the server. I rattled off a list of dishes and sat back, pleased with myself. I had ordered a huge plate of *sashimi*. Everything I liked. Everything but *fugu*.

We'd been here less than an hour but Kenta was already drunk. Suddenly, he turned to me, his eyes not quite in focus and asked me an ominous question.

"You know about me and the *bāchan*?"

I stared back at him, trying not to betray my complete disbelief and discomfort. A *bāchan* was a grandmother or old woman around the age of my friend, Mitsu-*san*. I took a deep breath. We were getting into a *bureikō* situation. Intoxicated, bosses and employees who usually maintain a strict professional demeanor could break down their walls a little and relax. Alcohol and a casual atmosphere bring down the usual social barriers of hierarchy, the lines of boss and employee are blurred, and conversation is allowed to flow freely. There are limits, and it's uncouth to push this too far. But in general, *bureikō* makes it acceptable to share things that should otherwise be kept to oneself.

Kenta was diving headfirst into the *bureikō* mentality. I did know this story of the *bāchan*—and I knew he would never have talked about this sober.

On March 11, 2011 Kenta fled with Mayor Toba to the roof of City Hall immediately after the earthquake hit. Kenta saw a group of elderly outside City Hall and ran down the stairs trying to rescue them, ignoring the Mayor's order to stay put. A group of other young aides followed Kenta down the stairs, intent on helping him rescue the elderly group before the water reached them. While they were gone, the tsunami hit and the waters started to rise, but none of the young men had returned. Eventually, when the water had almost swallowed the building, Kenta re-emerged onto the roof—alone.

He hadn't shared with many people what happened while he was down inside the building, though he didn't need to say aloud what had happened to the other aides. What Kenta had only shared with a select few was that he had made it to the sidewalk and encountered a grandmother, a *bāchan*, on the sidewalk. He told her to climb onto his back and quickly brought her inside, running up the stairs to take her up to safety on the roof.

Kenta was strong, a former athlete and a fast runner, but carrying the weight of another person slowed him down considerably. He climbed the stairs with *bāchan* on his back, but Kenta could not outpace the tsunami, the water level rising too quickly. By the second floor landing they were both soaked, Kenta slogging through water up to his chest. They were moving too slowly to make it to the roof in time. *Bāchan* told Kenta to leave her behind.

"You'll die if I leave you!" he protested.

"If you don't leave me," she said to him, "we'll both die." With regret, guilt, and horror, Kenta left her in the stairwell.

I didn't know and I didn't ask him how he knew that I was already aware of this story. But his question hung in the air. Did I know about *bāchan*? Slowly, I nodded my head.

He leaned in. "Do you know about my son?"

I didn't see this coming. I hadn't expected his first question, let alone this follow-up. Kenta's son was only six years old on the day of the tsunami. He was still missing. I did know about his son. I also knew Kenta had lost his mother and grandmother that day. Chatting while drunk is one thing, but this is way too personal for comfort. Still, this question also required an answer.

"I do," I said.

Kenta edged his chair over to mine just enough so he could tilt his head and whisper, "I'm being punished by God."

Without a body to cremate there was no ash. Without ash, there was no funeral. Kenta and his family had not been able to enter mourning for the first forty-nine days as stipulated by the Buddhist funeral calendar. Nor would they mourn together at the temple on the 1st, 3rd, 5th, 7th, 13th, 39th, and 50th memorials of the boy's death. Not being able to perform these rituals carried an immense spiritual weight in Japan. It left a person's soul stranded somewhere between heaven and earth, unquiet and roaming indefinitely. Aside from the death itself, not recovering the body was the worst-case scenario.

I was stunned. I had no reply. Two simple questions followed by a statement was all it took. Kenta let someone die, so God punished him by taking away his son in a way that would never give him closure. No body, no bones, no ash, no burial, no way to properly mourn. No finality. Forever. This was Kenta's burden for life. I wanted to tell him that God doesn't punish, but then again how do I know? Should I have said it's not his fault? Should I have said he did the right thing by leaving *bāchan* behind? If he hadn't done that, he wouldn't be here today. But again, how do I know he did the right thing? Can anyone know? I wasn't prepared for this. Nothing I could think to say felt right.

Mercifully, my *sashimi* arrived. The plate was so large that it took up most of the table, eliciting a loud "Whoa!" from all three men in unison.

"Did I order all of this?" I feigned surprise, desperately wanting to change the subject. "Well, I clearly can't eat all of it so dig in." I wanted to distract Kenta with food and drink, discuss the weather. Anything. They went for the *sashimi*, and Kenta and I didn't resume talking about *bāchan* or his son.

I was on edge the rest of the night, fake-laughing and desperately hoping Kenta didn't bring up our earlier conversation. He didn't. I'd been saved by the arrival of a giant plate of elegantly sliced raw fish.

By the time we left, the three men were all drunk and wobbling back to their hotel. I told them I'd catch up, that I needed to stretch my legs. I walked around for a while, mentally replaying what Kenta had said and how I should have responded. I wandered for nearly an hour mulling it over, trying to think of anything to say that would offer him some closure or absolution. But how could I know what he was feeling? What was there to say?

In the years following, Kenta and I never returned to the topic of what he said that night. I don't know if he even remembers, or if that was just a drunken statement meant to be forgotten. Another unspoken tenet of *bureikō* is that it provides confidentiality. You're not supposed to ask about things shared in that environment.

Perhaps there was nothing for me to say anyway. Maybe my role was just to serve as an outlet for his confession. Kenta's story has stayed with me as a quintessential example of survivor's guilt. I so want to tell him that the absence of his son's body is not his fault. But I realize there are no right words. He has to reach that conclusion on his own, and I hope with everything I hold dear that one day he does.

Chapter 35

Futoshi Toba

The obviousness of this reality hits me every now and then: my boys are growing up. One has left for university. Living in a small apartment in Tokyo by himself, he's officially moved on. Watching him pack and move was difficult but I accepted it as a life-transition we all had to make. My younger son still had several years at home. I would be spared being an empty nester living alone for another couple of years.

I tried not to think about living in this house by myself. The reality of coming home to absolute silence bothered me. I would cope; I always do. The transition from married to widower and single father and now from being an active parent with kids at home to living alone, this was yet another life-transition. Why didn't they become easier? Weren't we supposed to mature and become wiser as we aged? I put aside my worry. My younger son was still at home. My focus would be on him now and until he left. We would enjoy our time together.

A new experience was waiting for me around the corner. My reaction to this unexpected event surprised even me. I had become accustomed to parent–teacher conferences. My elder son, the one who took study seriously and didn't seem to think homework was a punishment, was never a concern for worry. My younger son simply didn't enjoy books as much and preferred to play basketball or hang out with his friends. Both boys were well-liked at school and I was proud of them. Perhaps this pride I felt, having raised them with the help of my uncle and aunt but also largely alone for the past couple of years, this pride was what made me defend my son in this moment of unanticipated harshness.

Parent–teacher conferences were not the only school events Kumi had attended representing our family. Every year elementary and middle schools had a parental visitation day where parents lined the back of the classroom observing a lesson. The kids were to go on as if nothing was different; ignore the parents in the back, answer questions like they normally did. I had learned about these visitation days as well and attended whenever I could. These parental visitation days weren't mandatory. The conferences, however, I couldn't miss. Which is why when my younger son, in his second year of high school, came home and told me there was a 3-party conference I was confused.

"You mean a parent–teacher conference," I said, correcting him.

"No, dad," he said. "This is the three of us. You, me, and my teacher. We're all going to talk together."

"Is this a new thing?" I asked.

"I dunno," he said, shrugging his shoulders. Interesting. My elder son never had this in high school. Something was off.

"Are you the only one who's having a 3-party conference?" I carefully asked, looking up again and making sure my voice wasn't accusatory. It didn't work.

"Dad! No way," he said, defensive. "All second-year students are doing this."

"So it is a new thing," I asked.

"Well, new since nī-chan was in high school," he said, referring to his elder brother.

"Okay," I said. "When is it?"

My son handed me the envelope I had become familiar with, having seen similar envelopes over the years. I opened it and noted the date and time.

"Got it," I said. "I'll be there."

Again, making sure my secretaries held me to my schedule, when the day arrived, I left for my son's high school. Finding the classroom, I knocked and entered and found the two of them already seated. We made small talk and then the teacher brought out a notebook.

"It's time we start talking about what happens after high school," the teacher said. "What are your plans?" he asked my son.

"Well," my son started, "probably go to university somewhere," he said, completely nonchalant. University exams in Japan were notoriously difficult; the better the university, the tougher the exam. My son wasn't keen on studying. Which university did he have in mind, I wondered. He and I hadn't discussed this.

"Mayor?" the teacher asked me.

"Yes?" I said.

"What do you think?"

"If he wants to go to university, he should," I said. "It's just a matter of which one." Why were we having this meeting? Why wasn't this something my son and I decided together? What did his homeroom teacher have to do with this?

"I see," the teacher said, opening the notebook in front of him. "Well, here's the thing," he continued. "Your grades," he looked at my son, "probably aren't good enough to get you into a decent university."

Excuse me? I looked at my son and saw in his face a mixture of pain and embarrassment. You asshole teacher, I thought. How dare you talk to my son that way. The teacher continued, this time speaking to me.

"Your son is better suited to a trade school than a university."

That was the last straw.

"Well," I said, loudly, slapping my knees hard with my hands. My son jumped in his chair and looked at me.

"Thank you for that information," I said sarcastically, hoping the teacher picked up on it. "We'll take it from here," I said, and then said to my son, "Let's go. I'll drive you home."

In the hallway I put my hand on his shoulder. My face burned with rage and I felt my hand tighten on his shoulder. I didn't say anything until we got to the car. With him in the passenger seat, I started the car but let it idle. I looked at him.

"Don't worry about what he said," I told my son. "If you want to go to university, do. You'll be fine."

"Yeah," my son said.

We drove home in silence and we went inside. My son went up to his room and I started to make dinner. I called him down when I finished putting the food on the table. He filled his bowl and took it over to the chair in front of the television. He didn't say anything to me, nor did I stop him and insist he eat with me at the table. He had been given a rude shock by his teacher. I was still fuming at the teacher's insensitivity and crassness at which he put my son down. As I ate at the table by myself, I decided to give my son a few months before I brought up the subject of university. He wasn't a bad student. He just didn't have the motivation or desire to focus his free time on studying. He did fine on the tests. Sure, my elder son's grades were better, but that wasn't the point.

It turned out I didn't have to bring up the subject. My son came home after basketball practice one day and said, "I think I've figured it out, dad."
"Figured what out?" I asked.
"University," he said. Surprised, I looked at him. "Oh, yeah?"
"Yeah," he said, his mischief ever present.
"I'm going to trade school," he said. My heart sank.
"To become what?" I asked. "What are you going to study?"
"I'm going to be a preschool teacher," he said, beaming. Of course he was. This was perfect for him. I smiled.
"Good," I said. "That suits you."
"I know," he said, grinning. We both laughed.

For the years my sons spent at my uncle and aunt's house–Kumi gone and me at work–my extended family became their extended family as well. My cousin's children, babies and toddlers, were often cared for by my younger son. He was good with children. He showed genuine love for his little cousins and grew up caring for them. Here was a reprieve from grief. With the children, there was play and laughter, all because elder-cousin (my son) was taking care of them. He was responsible for their joy. He was the one comforting them when they cried. It made perfect sense he would grow up wanting to become a preschool teacher. Care for the next generation, raising them to be strong and smart, kind and clever. He could do that.

My son had taken the slap-in-the-face offered so callously by his teacher– in front of me no less–and spun it into a positive experience. He took the feedback, the implication that he wasn't smart enough to get into a "proper" school, and turned it on its head. He knew what made him happy. He knew what had carried him and sustained him throughout his childhood, in a time of grief and sadness. I was proud of him for working this out on his own. My son wasn't stupid as the teacher implied. He would be a great preschool teacher. Perhaps even one day he'd become a father. He was a kind teenager. Ornery, but kind. I smiled. He would be just fine.

Chapter 36

Amya Miller

I was hungry. Like usual, meetings had consumed my time, and I hadn't had a chance to eat. The biggest appointment on my calendar was the upcoming dinner with Mayor Toba that evening. We hadn't caught up in a while, and these talks over dinner were the times where we got the most done. I was hungry enough that I got out of my van and walked across the street to the newly built Seven-Eleven convenience store. I just needed a quick bite. Something with sugar. My favorite caramels. That's what I would get.

I stared out into space as I sat in my minivan in the parking lot in front of City Hall and ate my caramels. I was tired, all talked out. Meetings had gone on all day. I had spent the previous evening with friends in Ōfunato who had told me of a rumor that the U.S. Military had actually caused the earthquake on purpose by driving steel spikes into the ocean floor.
"What exactly would the U.S. Military do that for? What reason would there be? Seriously? You really believe this?" I was offended and wanted that known.
"I knew we shouldn't have told her," Tatsuo said to his wife, Miki.
"We just wanted to be sure," Miki said to me.
"And now me telling you how stupid that is makes you believe it's a lie?" It was that simple? Miki was now convinced? Confused, disgusted, and in disbelief these rumors were being tossed around I hadn't slept well last night.

Still, tonight's dinner was important. Mayor Toba and my conversation on this particular evening would be different. We had agreed our personal stories needed telling and this required a series of Q&A sessions, long chats, and frank discussions. Very likely he would have to dredge up some painful memories. Events and conversations long since forgotten would have to come into mind. After all the dinner conversations we've had, all the meetings in his office, all of our telephone conversations, and text messages back and forth, details of his life not discussed before would come out. Our stories held power and we wanted them known. Tonight it was his turn to talk. My pages of questions for him were all prepared.

I knew some scattered details about his life. Our pasts weren't topics we usually covered, as there was too much else on our plates that required immediate consideration and resolution. I knew he had wanted to play guitar in a band professionally, but somehow ended up in politics. He'd been mayor for only a month when the tsunami hit, and it changed his understanding of what it meant to be a leader. Then there were his teenage sons, and some of his stories about what they had to go through post-disaster. At the time, they were just ten and twelve. I can't imagine what that was like. And I wanted to hear more about Mayor Toba's wife, Kumi. But most of all, after a long day, I was hungry.

We hadn't seen each other in several months. Mayor Toba and I knew our bodies were failing us as we had both started experiencing odd ailments, some mysterious and undiagnosed while others brutally unfair.

One thing at a time. Tonight we were scheduled to discuss the beginning of Mayor Toba's political career. I got out my notebook and glanced at my pages of questions. This could take hours. I retrieved my phone from my purse and reviewed our text message log of the evening's plans. Had I forgotten anything? No. How much time did I have before he expected me? Plenty. I needed to be there at 7:00 pm.

"Chinese, Japanese, or Western food for dinner?" he had asked in a text message the day before.
"I'll bring something," I said, not answering his question hoping he wouldn't go to a lot of trouble to put out a feast.
"No you won't," he said. I could picture him chuckling.
"Fine," I wrote, half-exasperated, half-amused knowing I was not going to win. "Then Chinese."

Wondering what exactly to expect, I started my old beat-up minivan and began to drive.

The full moon, a large peach tonight, was hanging just above the hills surrounding Hirota Bay, lighting the sky in a yellowish gray. The color washed out the walls of the new buildings that constituted downtown, and all was quiet as my minivan traversed the main road that wound across this newly raised stretch of land. I'd driven these streets for the past eight years.

I was driving on autopilot. My headlights revealed a brand-new road on top of orange dirt, some corners still marked by the treads of heavy machines. It took me back to when I first arrived. The same headlights were little orbs of amber on a black road. The city was gone, and I might as well have been driving through an enormous graveyard. Outside was quiet except for the sounds of the ocean. I had dreaded those drives at night. I knew there were still bodies nearby, and I felt I was disturbing their rest.

Tonight was different. The city had been built up. Temporary barbershops, souvenir shops, restaurants, pubs, cafes, and other businesses had reopened as permanent storefronts. There was a new supermarket and a mall and a library. There was a playground across the street from the library. Soon more permanent structures would be built. After eight years, the city wasn't whole, but it was well on its way. My mind wandered as I drove. I peered at each tall rectangular box covered in blue plastic sheets, half-constructed but rapidly growing. What would that building be? Or that one?

The path I drive tonight should take me to the hill on the north side of town, toward the Mayor's house. It's an easy drive and I knew the route well. But as I drove on, new stop signs popped up out of nowhere. I didn't remember those. I ultimately ended up onto unfamiliar roads. Next thing I knew I had entered a new stretch of freshly packed road I'd never seen before. I came to a stop in front of an unfamiliar landscape of darkness and undeveloped open space. A new neighborhood. This wasn't right at all. I was lost. What had happened?

I retraced my path and looped back around until I found a familiar street. I was definitely going to be late for dinner. I took a different route this time—a right past the new *izakaya*, straight through the intersection with the supermarket, then left toward the high school and up the hill. A right and a left and I should be at his house. Again, I ended up in front of a building I didn't recognize. I was definitely lost.

In the past two years new roads had appeared. One Christmas morning I drove past a construction crew installing telephone poles next to the sidewalk. A permanent road. Merry Christmas, Rikuzentakata. I committed these poles to memory as one of the only landmarks in a town where reconstruction was constantly changing the topography, nearly a decade after the whole landscape changed very suddenly, all at once. I relied on markers like these new telephone poles, since my GPS lacked updates for the area, still showing roads and buildings from before the tsunami.

The old roads that used to criss-cross the town of Takata, one of Rikuzentakata's eight smaller enclaves, were buried under the soil brought over by a conveyor belt from the mountain across the Kesen River. Mayor Toba ordered that the city be rebuilt much farther above sea level. Where downtown once stood were now a series mounds ten or twelve meters high, resembling pyramids with the top half sheared off—a monument to the ongoing work, as these mounds still needed connecting. The city that used to lie proudly at sea level had climbed onto raised land, hardened into miniature mountains. The soil-compacting rollers that swept over these mounds reminded me of giant lawnmowers.

"I remember lawns," replied one of the locals when I shared the thought. "Someday we'll have lawns again. Not big American ones like you're thinking of, but still. Our own lawns."

It took a series of more wrong turns before I finally lucked out and found the narrow drive leading up to the Mayor's rebuilt house. Somehow I was right on time, and when I pulled up he was already opening the door.

"Why is your house so hard to find?" I asked as I opened my car door. "Hi to you, too." He laughed. He motioned inside. "Stop complaining and come on in," he chided, grinning.

In the *genkan*, the front entrance of the house, I removed my shoes. I set them down among the weathered sneakers belonging to the mayor's two sons. Both were away at university now, but with the nonstop pace of rebuilding the city, he hadn't found time to clear away the pile of long-disused shoes.

He walked into the living room to the right of the *genkan* and I followed. I'd been in his house many times before for meetings, private chats, and even occasional parties over the years. The living room looked the same with its stucco walls and white wallpaper, and a large window looking down the hill over the town, watching the slow spread of progress. The dining room was much the same. The mayor and his sons had been living here for five years, and with his sons away, there was even less evidence that the place is inhabited. No art on the walls, just a clock and a calendar looking down at the table in the center of the room.

The table was already set with small plates of spicy shrimp with mayonnaise, sweet and sour pork, green peppers and beef in black pepper sauce. He cracked open a beer and sat at the head of the table. I sat to his right and opened my laptop, setting out recording devices in front of each of us. I spent a few moments arranging the cables among the various plates of food.

"You really went all out," I said, looking over the spread.
"I figured we might be here awhile," he said. I nodded in agreement, mentally going over the many questions I'm hoping to ask him. He took a sip of his beer and looked down at the spread. "We'll keep warming up the food as we go. Okay?"
"Okay."

I asked about his boys. He told me the elder one has a girlfriend, the younger studies when he feels like it, but in general they're well and happy. He asked me if my twenty-year-old minivan had broken down yet, and he laughed when I told him that it drives perfectly but I got lost.
"How many years have you been here now? How can you still not find your way around?" he chided.
"Yeah, well, I don't recognize half the roads, do I? You keep adding new ones and I'm back and forth between here and Tokyo so much," I replied.
"It's called progress, Amya," he said. "Eat. You'll feel better."
"Here's to progress and good food," I said. We both raised our drinks.

Mayor Toba gave me a few updates about the process of filling in the old downtown to raise up the city. "Earth-moving is laborious work," he said. I wasn't surprised. He told me about the various new mounds that they're working on, and described how they'll eventually connect. It was a long way out, and until then the roads on the half-pyramids kept residents of the city and frequent visitors like me all on our toes. Exciting and tedious, learning new routes to familiar places would have to become my norm with every visit.

I thought back to late 2011, not long after I'd begun to work as a liaison in earnest. At the time, the plan to raise the land and rebuild above sea level was still a long way off. Instead, the Prime Minister's Administration was more focused on building another series of seawalls out in the ocean to protect the city from further tsunamis. Many local leaders opposed the seawalls, and one particularly outspoken man was a city council member for a fishing community along the southern coast. One day after a particularly long meeting, the councilman stopped me on the way out.

"I want to show you something," he said. "Bring your coat."

He got in his car and beckoned for me to follow. We headed toward the coast, my minivan tailing him down a road that quickly became surrounded by tall pines. We wound along the hills and through the back country for a while until he slowed, signaling for me to pull over on a roadside overlook. We both got out, and I immediately had to pull my coat tight and hunch my shoulders against the freezing wind.

The councilman led the way down a steep hill that dropped off the side of the road. We half-walked, half-slid, taking small steps down a narrow path that was barely there until we reached a ledge. Laid out before me were a row of white stone pillars with rounded tops and stark faces. From the toll that the weather had taken on them I had to guess they were centuries old. At first I thought they were gravestones. But when I asked who was buried here, he shook his head.

"These were placed by our ancestors generations ago to mark the height of a tsunami." I look down the hill leading to the ocean. How high up are we? Twenty meters? More? Certainly high enough that anyone would consider themself safe. "Our ancestors placed these white stones as markers to tell us not to build below this point. But see?" He points at a neighborhood at the bottom of the hill.

I could see the remains of dozens of homes built near the sea. Square foundations stood in rows next to overgrown driveways, scoured by the wave. Several of the cracked asphalt roads still cut across the land, now overgrown. Months ago this place would have been marked with rubble, but it had long since been cleared away.

"We don't listen. We forget. We keep building down to the ocean, and we keep getting destroyed."

Of course, Mayor Toba had a different solution. His work to raise the town above sea level took years. But thinking back to what the councilman said, I knew that Mayor Toba was taking the words of his ancestors to heart.

"No building houses at sea level ever again. Ever. We're doing it right this time," Mayor Toba had told the residents and City Hall staff alike. This kind of devastation was not going to happen again. No future generation of Rikuz-entakata residents would lose their lives, property, or well-being because of mistakes made by previous generations. Mayor Toba was going to make sure of that—even if it meant moving tens of thousands of tons of earth.

As dinner moved on, the Mayor filled me in on the latest at City Hall and I told him about my meetings earlier in the day. We commiserated over the shared workload. I realized this could go on all night.

"I have questions for you," I finally said.

"Yeah, we should get to those," he agreed.

I nudged the microphones closer to him and hit the button on my recording software. "So, tell me about your career. Did you grow up wanting to go into politics?" I asked.

He finished a sip of his beer and shook his head. "Not at all. I was into music. I was part of a rock band, and I wanted to make it big in the music industry." He mimed strumming a guitar.

I try to imagine him up onstage, surrounded by garish rock stars and blinding strobe lights. In my head he was wailing away on a guitar, still dressed in his rumpled navy suit jacket. The image made me laugh.

"How do you go from rock to politics?"

He turned back to me. "My dad was from Rikuzentakata. His family were pig farmers. Things were run by the merchants in town, those with wealth. Dad didn't like that, nor did I. Politics was the only way to get things done. To make change."

The Mayor gestured vaguely. "My dad was a prefectural assembly member. Then one year he unexpectedly lost the election. With him gone, suddenly there was no one in the assembly who represented the poor. Lots of his constituents saw him as a man of the people. So the community got together and talked my parents into using me as a candidate for the upcoming city council election instead. At least, that way they'd have somebody representing them at city level."

"What did your parents have to do with this?" I asked.

"I don't really know. A lot of it was over my head at the time. I suppose they thought dad would still pull the strings behind the scene or something. I didn't want to run, and even my parents didn't want me to run. I'm not a politician. I knew that. My parents knew that. But this group was adamant about needing someone to represent them. So, it became official. To keep the Toba name in politics, I was to run for city council."

"Okay, so you ran for city council." I said, shifting my plate of shrimp aside so I can lean an elbow on the table. "But that's still a long way to Mayor, especially for a reluctant politician."

Mayor Toba just shrugged. "I won the first election, the one my name got added to, with such a landslide that it became harder and harder for me to back out. There are twenty city council positions, and usually around twenty-five or more people run each election. Among all the candidates, I got the most votes. I won by around fifteen hundred too, which is a huge majority in a town this size. And by this time, I saw what had kept my dad in politics for so long."

I was about to respond when we were interrupted by a phone ringing. I moved to answer it but the mayor waved me off. "Just let it ring. It's probably the press. I don't have time for them right now." He rubbed his eyes. "Alright," he smacked his face a few times and looked up at me. "Where were we?"

"You won by a landslide."
"Right." Mayor Toba leaned back in his chair. "So I got to know another city council member, Nakazato-*san*.[20] He was nearly twenty years older than me. A local guy. A member of the Japanese Communist Party. Really sharp. Eloquent speaker, and a hard man to ignore. At that time, I was running as a member of the Liberal Democratic Party so I couldn't be seen associating with a communist. But I found myself measuring my questions and actions against his. Both of us grew more and more dissatisfied with the mayor at that time. One night, I found myself sitting at a bar with him, and we hatched a plan: one of us would run against the current mayor. I said that I was too young and he should run with me as his campaign manager. So we went forward with the plan, and he won! A complete coup for a communist to win like that. Everyone was surprised but he won. I became his deputy and then when he decided not to run again because of his health, I ran for mayor."

"And won," I said.
He nodded. "And won."
"You were how old?"
"Forty-six."
"So, you went from wanting to be a rock star to becoming Mayor of a city that got destroyed by a tsunami."

We were both silent for a moment. I meant to keep the spirit of the evening light by ribbing him about his ambitions to be a rock star but it flopped. My joke just hung in the air.

"I'm sorry," I said. "I take it back."

He shook his head, grinning in mock defeat. "All because my band wasn't good enough to go pro."

We sat in silence for a few minutes, both of us picking at our food. I knew I had to bring up one other topic and I was dreading it. I wondered if Mayor Toba could sense my hesitation.

"I need to ask you about the last election," I finally said.

"I know," he replied and sighed. "I know."

"Some other night?" I tried to give him an out.

"No," he said, "Let's talk about it now."

In February of 2019 Mayor Toba had won his third term. He won by five votes. I had been monitoring the election results online, refreshing the page over and over hoping to see the outcome, but when the votes were tallied and the results finally made official all I could do was stare at the screen. That couldn't be right. I was so incredulous that I got out a calculator and did the math myself. Five votes. Half of those who voted wanted him out. This was personal.

"What happened?" I asked.

"What happened," he echoed, flatly. "Politics. Politics happened." He sat back in his chair, suddenly looking exhausted. I decided to back down. We had spent almost three hours talking. It was time to call it a night.

"Let's do this some other time," I said.

"Why?" he asked.

"You look tired."

"No, I'm fine. I'm always tired," he said and laughed. His fatigue wasn't funny. I couldn't bring myself to join in his laughter.

"When I say politics," he said, "I mean half of the people in this town truly believe I'm at fault for how long the reconstruction has taken. My opponent did a good job in cultivating doubt. He said I wasn't a true local, so I would never understand. I wasn't born here, so I wasn't 'from here.' I wasn't supportive enough of local projects. I'm too visible. I'm too outspoken. I'm too opinionated. I have too many big ideas. I'm too many things I shouldn't be and not enough things I should be."

I didn't know what to say. I knew people who were openly outspoken against Mayor Toba. I even considered some of them my friends, but refused to let them badmouth him in front of me, always offering a cutting line, "What do you think should be done then? Be specific." It became a joke that no one liked, because no one could answer my question. Complaining was cathartic. Blaming someone was easy. Trying to fix a problem this difficult was neither.

"So I won by five votes. That's the short version," he said, "but that's about the gist of it. It was an ugly race. I just have to focus on the fact that half the people in town did vote for me. I'm going to do everything I can in the next four years. But then I'm done. I won't run again."

There was a recount and a lawsuit filed by his opponent. The suit was lost, and the recount confirmed the results. Nonetheless, they stung. This would be Mayor Toba's last stint as mayor.

Chapter 37

Amya Miller

Every quarter I would have blood drawn at the doctor's office across the street from my apartment. My doctor would always tell me I needed to lose weight and I ignored her because no other doctor had ever said that to me, and I had long since decided she was categorically wrong. My weight was a topic of constant discussion among people around me. I hated this. I was significantly larger than most of the Japanese women around me. I was taller than them. I had breasts and hips they didn't. Still, my doctor's words as well as the chiding from the men and out-of-the-blue comments like, "Oh, your breasts!" from the women in my surroundings took a toll. These "fat American" jokes were getting old. I ignored those body shaming me just as I ignored my doctor. Making it a point to compare myself with other women I saw in airports and on the sidewalks with every trip to a European or North American country I tried to love my curves. In the U.S. and in Europe I was shorter than average and average in weight. I knew I wasn't fat. Still, the comments kept haunting me so much so on one trip back to Boston I even asked my doctor if I should lose weight. He confirmed I was fine. "Ignore, ignore, ignore the comments from the Japanese," I told myself.

Midway through my ten years in Japan my liver numbers started to rise. The doctor drawing my blood asked about my alcohol consumption to which I always replied, "I simply don't drink enough alcohol for my liver numbers to be off. Several glasses of wine several nights a week shouldn't do this to me." She agreed and blamed my so-called weight problem. "We'll keep an eye on it," she said, and we did. For years.

One day as we were reviewing my ever-increasing liver numbers, exasper-
ated with my lack of progress in the weight loss she expected of me she
lashed out.
"Don't you *want* to lose weight? Don't you *want* to be 20kg thinner?"

I laughed out loud and she glared back at me.

No, I didn't want to lose 20kg! She might be skin and bones with no curva-
ture anywhere to speak of but that didn't mean I had to or should look like
her. That day I decided I would switch doctors. Enough was enough. This
was getting ridiculous. And, what *was* going on with my liver? Why weren't
we dealing with that? If she had thought my liver numbers indicated a problem, she'd say something, yes? I was right to trust her in this, was I not?

I had given up on her, but I also didn't do anything about finding a new doctor. I would find one, some day when I had the time. That time wasn't now. I
continued to run back and forth between Rikuzentakata and Tokyo, Tokyo
and the U.S., Tokyo and Europe, Tokyo to Kyūshū and back. I was busy. I
was overworked and I was invigorated. I was making a difference and I had
pride in my successes. Was I burnt out? Yes. Was I ready to quit? No. I had
too much to do.

In all of my accomplishments, it was the failures that nagged at me; the
reality that few around me in Ōfunato and Rikuzentakata were truly happy.
Increasingly I resented the Japanese sentiment of *gaman*. Plod along. Someday we'll be fine. There's pride in this suffering of ours. Don't complain. This,
too, shall pass. We are Japanese; we've been through worse.

Throughout this adherence to *gaman*, I could see it was taking a toll on people.
Mana collapsed and stayed in bed for a week, her husband and children utterly
baffled as to why she wouldn't rise from her futon. All this time, she had made
life look easy but the facade had cracked. Her burden of fake-smiling through
life had caught up. With a vengeance.

"I was tired of smiling all the time," she said. "Inside, here," she touched her
heart, "I was screaming. We're all screaming. We're just pretending everything is alright. That everything will be alright. Will it? When? Will we even
recognize it when we see it, this new 'now life is good' feeling?"

And if Mana can collapse, then so can other women–as if Mana's collapse
was a gift of unexpected permission–and soon they did. One by one they,
too, ended up in bed, their husbands and boyfriends utterly confused as to

what was going on. The women stayed in bed, knowing the burden of house-work and childrearing was being placed without explanation to the men in their lives. The women, collectively, didn't care. *Gaman* was starting to erode peoples' psyches.

Cracks were emerging. I didn't need to look far to find them. Mayor Toba had unexplainable aches and pains, his trips to hospitals becoming increasingly frequent. They never found anything specifically wrong which was comfort-ing only until some other pain flared up out of nowhere. Influenza would hit every winter and spread like wildfire. Two U.S. delegations missed their annual visit with Mayor Toba because he had the flu both times they were in town. We were all running on fumes. Our energy long since depleted, we kept going on remnants of adrenaline, bits and pieces of strength we could find from deep within, and an occasional burst of spontaneous exertion. We all felt it: We were tired. Exhaustion–mental, physical, and emotional–swirled within us.

Gaman kept us going because we had to. Tap those reserves of energy and get up and go one more day. Then another. Then another. I had been hearing all around me the power of positive thinking, the unexpected joy and strength that comes from focusing on gratitude. I understood and agreed with the gist of it but I felt the need for this positivity adding to my stress. I asked it of others–try to find one thing you can be grateful for every day–only to ignore this advice for myself. Forced positivity and the need to find the silver lining and the best in everything in everyday life was quickly becoming toxic for me. I needed to say bad was bad, the situation I was in stunk and wasn't improving, that the lives of people around me were in limbo at best, chronically debilitating at worst. At the root of it all was *gaman*. Just suffer through it.

The key word here was "through." All of this will someday come to an end. Someday we'll look back on this and be proud of our ability to do *gaman*. To have done *gaman*. We will have persevered.

There came a day when I decided to stop complaining. I still rejected the core tenant behind *gaman*, the root definition of the expectation of patience and perseverance at all cost. I still felt I was exempt as a foreigner, a Westerner to boot. But I increasingly felt complaining did no good. It had long since felt like a release; my complaints were always the same. Nothing improved with complaining. I didn't feel any better. It became pointless and banal. I had taken on pain that wasn't mine and intentionally shut down my release valve. Feeling another's pain is a stunningly beautiful gift of compassion until it starts to eat away at the one empathizing. I was empathizing at a level that was dangerous to my own psyche. I had little left to give but I kept on. Deep down I knew no good would come of my decision to stop complaining, but what could I do? What should I do? I took in more of their pain and shut down my emotions even more. I was strong. I was exhausted but I was strong. Handle it, I would.

Mayor Toba developed a kidney stone and sat through three weeks of city council meetings, all day for fifteen days in excruciating pain, because that's what was expected of him. He knew enough to get medication, but blasting the stone away wasn't an option and it simply wasn't moving. I told myself if Mayor Toba can handle three weeks of intense and immense pain, I could do a lot more. I told him so.

"Don't do that," he said.
"I'll be fine," I replied.
"Everyone knows you're tired," he said, then added, "you look it."
"Thanks," I said, not hiding my sarcasm.
"Take a break. Get some rest and come back after you've had some time off."
"I'll be fine," I insisted. "You're the one that needs help. I hear pain from a kidney stone is pretty brutal."
"This is ridiculous," he said.
"What is?" I asked.
"Me working like this and you being this exhausted."

He was right, of course, and we knew it then as we know it now. Still, we kept going.

Until I collapsed.

I had gone to Kyūshū on assignment and came back with a monster flu strain. I stayed in bed, dousing myself in liquids and ibuprofen with no relief in sight. Finally, I dragged myself across the street to my doctor, assuming she would blame this flu on my weight as well. Oddly, she was sympathetic and gave me medication there in her office through an intravenous drip. I went home, fell asleep and when I woke up three hours later, felt remarkably improved. I continued to feel better through the week although I worked from my bed and canceled all my in-person meetings. I needed to fly to Paris for a conference in a few days and decided to go back to the doctor to see if I was well enough to fly. She gave me her approval. "You're fine," she said.

So I flew to Paris. Upon arriving at my hotel in time for breakfast, I realized I had no appetite and decided to take a nap instead. I slept all day and all night. The next morning I knew something was wrong. I could barely move. I spent the week in bed in my hotel room, the conference the furthest from my mind. I thought the flu had come back, this time with a vengeance. I flew back to Tokyo after six days in bed and passed out on the flight only to wake up covered in my own vomit.

Upon arrival, barely aware of my surroundings I decided to call my doctor. She listened, and then told me to go to an emergency room.
"Something clearly isn't right," she said.
"Well, obviously," I thought.
"Go to this hospital," she said, and gave me the name of a major hospital in Tokyo.
"I know one of the emergency room doctors there. I'll call ahead and tell them you're coming."

I took a taxi into central Tokyo, a staggeringly expensive fare, but I saw no other way as I wasn't strong enough to handle the bus ride. Two hours later, I was in an emergency room being told they needed to admit me right away and that next of kin needed to be notified as they weren't sure I was going to make it through the night. Losing focus, jet-lagged, my mind not keeping up with the words I obeyed and was taken up to a room where I slept until doctors and nurses came in and drew blood, tried to find a vein for another intravenous drip, and spoke in hushed voices around my bed. Confused and scared I remember little of the first several days.

The doctors couldn't figure out what was wrong with me. One diagnosis after another ruled out, I was transferred to an even bigger hospital where finally a biopsy confirmed I had a serious chronic liver disease. The reason for the illness? Prolonged stress caused antibodies to attack the liver, resulting in increased liver numbers for years. The flu medication given because I was in so much pain should never have been administered to someone with high liver numbers. My liver shut down in Paris and I had been dangerously close to dying.

Now I am a proponent against *gaman*. I still understand it, and its rootedness in Japanese culture. I know why it's touted as a proud cultural trait. I also know prolonged *gaman* can kill.

If *gaman* has a silver lining, it's the manifestation shown in people like Mana who has now learned the limits of what our bodies and minds can tolerate. One of Mana's children was having difficulty in school and was refusing to attend.

"I told her 'You don't have to do *gaman* anymore,' and just like that, she started to smile and relax," Mana said of her daughter. "I'm not sure the younger generation is cut out to do *gaman*," Mana said. "I think Japan is changing," she said, looking up at me over the straw in her drink. I nodded.

"I hope so," I said.

"I don't like *gaman*," she said.

"Me, either," I said. "Me, either."

Chapter 38

Amya Miller

Two words gave me a lot of difficulty as I tried to interpret: empathy and resilience. As a Westerner and native English speaker, I understood the intention behind commenting on empathy and resilience. I saw why Westerners thought both words were positive. Saying "the Japanese are so resilient" was meant as a compliment, and talking about the importance of showing empathy toward disaster victims was meant to project solidarity. I also heard and saw the frustration and confusion of the Japanese when those words were thrown at them.

The word for empathy in Japanese, *kyōkan,* is defined as "being able to understand another's feelings." But the word could, depending on context, also mean "in total agreement with" or "sharing the same emotion." It is also, again in some contexts, interchangeable with the word sympathy, which complicates interpretation. Context alone is often not enough to determine which definition is intended. There is also another word for sympathy, *dōjō,* which means everything from feeling pity for another, commiserating with another, thoughtfulness toward another, or understanding how someone feels. One could argue the words empathy and sympathy have multiple meanings in Japanese, and one could also argue there's no exact one-to-one translation.

In English, there's a bit of a gray area between the ideas of empathy and sympathy. People say one word when they mean the other, and very often the two ideas are conflated or used interchangeably. But by and large, the difference in definition boils down to feeling sadness or pity regarding someone else's situation (sympathy) versus the ability to feel another person's emotions by putting themselves in the shoes of the other (empathy). It's a very fine distinction, and it's bred the need for clarification.

But those contextual gray areas aren't the same in Japanese. The sentiment of *kyōkan* stems from understanding based on a shared experience—understanding how it feels to get divorced or lose a child because you've been through that pain yourself. It's not just a matter of imagining oneself in the shoes of another.

In Japanese, saying, "I understand how you feel" is a privilege reserved for those who can identify with someone else's pain because they have experienced it. Hearing Westerners say "we empathize with you" implies that the speaker has been through something comparable to what the people of Rikuzentakata experienced. For *kyōkan* to apply, they would have had to also lose a city and loved ones to a horrific event. It meant they, too, had watched helplessly as people were swept away in a flood or a mudslide, or had to outrun a tornado to reach safety. Offering an expression of empathy while not having experienced something similar comes across as fake. To those in pain, it's disingenuous. Asking for people to have more empathy in Japanese is like suggesting that someone should go through the same painful losses in order to be able to relate to one another, and that's neither healthy nor realistic.

Many times I saw this difference in expectation lead to disappointment and anger. Visitors offering empathy had not gone through anything remotely resembling the experiences of the residents of Rikuzentakata. No one who said they could empathize, who openly encouraged their foreign colleagues to cultivate empathy, had any context in which they could say they understood. They were trying to say the experiences of those in Rikuzentakata were important—but in Japanese, that's not empathy. It looked and sounded as if Westerners were lying for the sake of bonding. People in Rikuzentakata weren't having it.

Just as frustrating and confusing to the locals was the complement of resiliency. The idea of resilience—*re-ji-li-en-su*, written in Anglicized Japanese called *rōmaji*—has no exact equivalent in Japanese. As a result, well-meaning English speakers who comment on "the resilience of the Japanese" ended up offering an ambiguous compliment that needed explaining. The word came up more and more frequently as natural disasters occurred all over the world, and visitors started to use the word to describe disaster victims.

Though visitors and the foreign press seemed to believe their use of "resilience" paid a compliment to the Japanese, it became evident that it fell short of good intention. As one city council member said, "I read that a COO of a large American company said something about the importance of being resilient after a disaster. She said that resiliency was about reaching out to one another and encouraging one another and supporting each other. Isn't that rather obvious? I mean, who wouldn't support someone going through a hard time? Why wouldn't people encourage each other after a disaster? Doesn't she get that people whose lives have been turned upside down in a disaster already know how important connections are? Does she not get that we need far more than encouragement? Is that really what Americans mean by resilience? How is what she said helpful?"

I had read the same article and was disgusted by the oversimplification of this COO's advice. I agreed with this city council member. "It's not helpful," I said. "She was just trying to get press coverage for her company. It's bad advice. She doesn't get it."

Another person asked me, "What's a silver lining? I keep hearing that English word."

I tried to explain. "It's from an idiom, 'every cloud has a silver lining.' The idea is that even if things are bad, like a cloud hiding the sun, the glow around the edge of the cloud is still beautiful. It means you're supposed to look for the best in a bad situation. To try to find something positive."

I could already tell where this was going, and the words felt patronizing as I explained the definition. "It means that when something bad happens to you, you're supposed to look for any positive results that came out of the bad thing, no matter how small they are. Focus on the positive. It's about being grateful." I gave the definition but decided not to add, "And, I know that's hard for people here sometimes" because I still wasn't sure if it was entirely a bad idea. Even on days when I was in a foul mood, I tried to find something to be grateful for, something that had gone well. If nothing else, to be grateful I was alive. Surely that was a good idea, yes? At least for a while I believed this. I found myself agreeing with my friend more and more. All this happiness talk was overrated, I thought to myself. It's not that easy.

But the friend challenged, "Is 'a silver lining' the same thing as *re-ji-li-en-su*? I hear that a lot, too."

I had to think. Was it? Perhaps. I told her that I wasn't sure. "Why do you ask?"

"I hate it," she said.

"You hate what?"

"Being told to find the good in the bad. Sometimes bad is just bad. There's nothing good about it. Trying to pretend that bad isn't all bad just feels like lying to myself. It's like I'm being told to ignore it or pretend it's not real. Sometimes it's just okay to have a bad day or accept that you're sad and angry. You Americans like to always be happy. Life's not always happy."

She essentially gave me the adult version of what the preschool principal had told me several years earlier. I was glad I'd kept my mouth shut earlier in the conversation. I was also secretly happy she was saying happiness wasn't all it was cracked up to be.

"Are you okay?" I asked and smiled. She smiled back.

"Yeah, I guess. I'm just tired of having to pretend I'm happy all the time."

Nearly a decade working in the disaster region in Japan has led me to my own definition of resiliency: it is the ability to accept the fact that bad things happen, life can be unfair, and that's just how things are. It's not personal, it's just part of being alive. Those who are truly resilient focus on what they can change about the situation they're in and inject their energy into that change.

There was a flipside to resiliency that was not so obvious. As much as Japan and the Japanese may be more accustomed to working through natural disasters due to their geographic location (perched atop the Pacific Ring of Fire) a blanket statement such as "the Japanese are so resilient" didn't take into account those who had exhausted their will to keep going. There was a collective exhaustion settling in. That wasn't resiliency, was it? No, I decided. It wasn't. And for some, running out of resiliency meant losing the will to live. Certainly, the bravery of many who experienced disaster in Japan deserved commendation. It was true many had initially kept plodding onward, even though they couldn't see their way through to the other side. What wasn't discussed openly in public or with the media post-2011 was the number of people who couldn't hang on any longer. The number of suicides in Tōhoku had been a taboo topic.

~~~

I was on a food quest, shopping for my lunch at a local supermarket, when I ran into Kōtarō.

"I saw you walk in," he said. "Don't tell me this is your lunch." I was hovering at the paltry cheese section, actually considering whether or not to splurge on real cheese.
"I'll buy you lunch. Come on," he said, gesturing.
"Really? Thanks! Where are we going?"
"Have you ever had curry soup?"
"No. What's that?"
"Just as it sounds. Curry soup," he said, unclear why I didn't understand.
"I've never heard of it," I said.
"Seriously? Well, you've missed out. You'll love it."

Glad he was paying and excited to try something new, I joined Kōtarō at a little cafe I'd never been to before. Tucked in a row of houses and shops right next to the supermarket, I'd driven past it hundreds of times but never noticed it.
Kōtarō ordered, "Five red peppers. Extra spicy," he told the server. The server looked at me and I said, "One red pepper, please." Kōtarō laughed. "That always surprises me. You seem like someone who could handle spicy food." Defensively, I said, "I like spice, I just don't like hot and spicy." The server nodded her head.
"I recommend the dish with one red pepper," she said.
"See," I told Kōtarō who laughed again.

The food arrived and I was surprised to find the soup was truly as good as described. My bowl held a yellow-gold liquid loaded with okra, a thick slice of lotus root, a piece of baby corn, and one red pepper. I took the rice and poured it in, creating a curry risotto. It was phenomenal. I would have to make this at home.

Over Kōtarō's shoulder, I noticed the server talking to a tall man who had come out of the kitchen. The tall man suddenly glanced in our direction and started toward our table with a determined look on his face, his walk firm and deliberate.

He reached us and extended his hands to offer a business card. "Excuse me. I know you, but you don't know me," he said. Then he looked at Kōtarō.

"Oh, hello. I didn't know it was you she was with. Mind if I sit?"

Before either of us could answer, the tall man pulled a chair over from the next table and sat down. "You don't know me," he said again, "but I know you. I know you share stories from our town with the foreign media. I have a story I want you to tell." Without waiting for us to respond, he began.

"There was a man in this town," he said, offering a name that sounded familiar. Someone I'd heard of but not met. "This man lost everyone but his teenage son in the tsunami—his wife, his other children, his parents. A good guy, and determined to do something positive with his life. He taught himself enough English to go abroad and learn how to become a helicopter pilot. He came back and set up an organization that would help deliver relief goods to areas damaged by natural disasters. He thought he might also be able to rescue people from rooftops in the future, the way people in town were taken to safety by the Self Defense Force helicopters. He was a good guy. Doing good things. Amazing that he did all this when he was so deep in his grief. *Gaman*, you know. Well-liked and respected, he was a local hero."

The tall man bowed his head a little and continued.

"This man recently ended his life. He is leaving behind a 21-year-old son, and many people in town are heartbroken to have lost such a good man. Many of us are having trouble dealing with his decision to leave this town and us behind." He paused and looked at me. "I hear that you have connections to the foreign media. Would you give them this man's story? Have someone write an article about him?"

This man's directness was off-putting. No one in town had been this obvious or forward in a request, especially someone I didn't know. Moreover, I was bewildered by his request. Did I miss a key part of the story? Local guy lost his family, all but one son, learned English and got his helicopter pilot's license so he could help others. He was considered a hero, but he took his life. I was supposed to get the foreign media to tell his story? What story?

The man's presence at our table was jarring, and I had no idea how to respond. Not sure what was going on, I looked at Kōtarō for some clue or reassurance, but all I saw in his face was shock and thinly veiled anger. I could see the irritation on his face, to have this man use his acquaintance with Kōtarō as an excuse to invite himself up and interrupt our meal just to ask a favor of a stranger.

At last, Kōtarō spoke up, his anger now unhidden. He was embarrassed and frustrated that a person, known to him but not to me, would just sit down uninvited and so tactlessly blurt out a story like this.

"She has your business card," he said curtly. "She'll call you back."
The tall man sat back in his chair, his face showing sudden defeat. "I'm sorry," he said, bowing his head toward the edge of the table. "That was rude of me." He stood up and left.

Kōtarō and I looked at each other. I didn't know what to say.
"Just forget it," Kōtarō said.
"I don't think I can," I said.
"Then call him in a few days, and tell him you can't help him." Kōtarō accented his points—can't, help, him—by jabbing his finger into the table with each word.

We spent the rest of our lunch trying to break the awkward silence by making small talk about anything other than what had just happened. The curry soup was delicious, but I ended up leaving half of it behind. I had no appetite anymore, and I resented the way the man had barged his way into our lunch and tasked me with the impossible.

As I drove back to my room later that night, I thought about my dilemma. The helicopter pilot's story was certainly moving, and it sounded like he had been a man worth celebrating. The man from the cafe wanted me to see the pilot's final act as a noble act, a graceful exit from a painful life. But there was no way that a bureau chief of any foreign news outlet would take this story and make it into anything other than a story focused on suicide. The narrative would be about despair, depression, and the cold decision to leave a 21-year-old son behind.

I can spin stories with the best, but this one I couldn't touch. Owing this man a call, two days later I dug out his business card I had thrown in my purse and dialed his number. He had to be politely told what the foreign media would likely do with the story, something I regretfully could not control.

But the man came back with, "I did a poor job of explaining the significance of the story." He insisted. "Please allow me one more chance. Would you meet with the editor-in-chief of our local newspaper? He's a man of words. He'll do a much better job explaining why this story is so important to share with the world."

Good grief.

There is an art to saying a direct no in Japan. I knew how to politely but firmly shut down a request. Although we weren't especially close, I had previously met the editor-in-chief of the local newspaper. He would understand better why the primarily Western media should never have access to this story. Saying no through the editor should solve this highly unique problem.

"Fine," I said, and silently exhaled.

We met at the headquarters of the local newspaper a few days later. I was ushered into the editor-in-chief's office by one of my journalist friends who looked at me and said, "I didn't know you were coming over today." "Just a quick chat with your editor," I assured.

The tall man from the cafe was already seated. Determined to be the first to speak, I would lay out why this idea was going nowhere, and why it wouldn't go to the foreign media.

I dove right in, politely enough, essentially repeating verbatim the story from the cafe. Yes, grief is terrifying, ugly, and uncontrollable—those of us who did not experience the tsunami can't imagine what must have been going through this man's head. But the press would latch onto the suicide aspect of the story. They would likely portray this pilot as an individual who wanted to help others yet was unable to overcome his own pain. That *gaman* had failed. Worse, they might paint him as selfish or cowardly since the man had left behind a son. Did the town want the story to be told regardless of how this man would likely be portrayed? Obviously not. I knew the editor understood, and told him as much. Once submitted, there would be no control over the story's trajectory in the hands of the foreign journalists in Tokyo.

The two men listened all the way through without commenting. Finally, the editor-in-chief said to the man sitting across from him, "She's right."

There was a knock on the door and a woman started to enter with three cups of tea and three plates of a Japanese confectionery. The editor waved her away. She bowed, surprised at this refusal, and backed out of the doorway.

"Do you understand why she's right?" the editor asked the tall man. He didn't answer. I quickly snuck a glance and saw he was sitting with his head bowed, his shoulders shaking. Oh, God. This is not what I wanted.

"You and I know, and the people that matter know how good of a guy your pilot friend was. Let's just leave it at that, shall we?" I saw the man next to me nod. "Amya-*san*, thank you for your time today. I know you're busy. We appreciate your coming here and explaining it so clearly the way you did."

Having no words that felt appropriate or comforting, I simply bowed and left the editor's office. The meeting had lasted no longer than five minutes.

I went back to my room and turned off my cell phone. Had I done the right thing? I still had time to call and offer help. What was it about this story that had me so riled?

The man had taken his own life. He was seen as a local hero and this suicide wasn't seen as a cowardice act. It was seen as a sacrifice. Was that it? We were going back to the feudal days where *seppuku*—ritual disembowelment—was seen as the ultimate act of self-sacrifice? A noble way out? This man chose to end his life instead of embarrassing his son by revealing his personal trauma and grief and depression. Whatever pain he was going through, he had resolved not to shift his burden to others and instead chose to take accountability—the historically rich act of suicide, an exit that spared those around him by removing himself from their presence—the ultimate act of taking responsibility. Attitudes toward suicide were different in the West. I had not wanted to take this story to the Western media because I was afraid they would see it as a man who hadn't gotten the help he needed and was "driven to suicide."

For those of us who know someone who has taken their own life, the blanket statement "the Japanese are so resilient" rings hollow and false. It's a gross simplification of the complexity of Japanese history as well as of life in this disaster region. Too many of my friends in the disaster region lead lives filled with longing, pain, anguish, and desperation for a semblance of normalcy. For them, resiliency is a concept reserved for those who have the privilege of being pain-free. For the rest, life in a disaster region is about prolonged *gaman*. No one I knew was talking or writing about how unrealistic this expectation was. *Gaman* had its limits, surely. As this man clearly was, many in the disaster region are exhausted—mentally, emotionally, and physically. Years after the disaster, life was still a mess. I decided I was comfortable with what I told the editor and the man who came to me with the story.

Mayor Toba was the first person I knew to openly object to being told he was resilient.

"Why is it a compliment to be exhausted?" he had asked me once, after snapping at a Westerner offering a comment on the resiliency of the Japanese. He had pointed out he was only doing his job, he had no choice, and as a result he was chronically tired. Exhausted. He couldn't sleep. He was getting sick. What was so noble about that? If it was said as a compliment, were they implying there was something good about being this exhausted? I considered assuring him that the comment was offered with good intentions, but thought better of it. Focusing on good intentions behind a thoughtless compliment felt like looking for a silver lining.

"It's a superficial label," he said. "They want to see us as *samurai* or something. Tough and stoic and mysterious, with endless patience. But we're not somehow wired to be able to withstand more emotional turmoil than anybody else. We're just trained from birth not to speak up or complain. *Gaman* is *gaman*, but not complaining isn't the same thing as being resilient. I wish you Westerners would stop with all this resiliency talk."

After hearing his words, I wondered if it was likely there would ever be a true connection made between those who were offering these well-meaning words and those who were hearing them. To locals in the area I worked with, encouraging people to have empathy toward the people in the disaster region made no sense. But what if I could find someone outside of Japan who could actually relate to all that happened on and after the tsunami hit? What if their empathy could be sincere?

I wanted to find a partner for people in Rikuzentakata. Someone who wasn't Japanese, but could nonetheless offer *kyōkan* with honesty. There had to be Westerners who understood how exhausting resilience was—who knew that what people saw on the surface and what was happening underneath were two very different stories. That those who spoke so freely about the virtues of resiliency seldom knew the depths people had to crawl out of just to live, to breathe. How does one go about finding this type of partner? Where does one look? Where does one even start?

Chapter 39

Amya Miller

City Hall staff had created social media accounts for the city as part of the effort to connect Rikuzentakata to the rest of the world—to control our narrative and keep people updated.[21] We posted a profile for Rikuzentakata, and within days of hitting the internet we had over 20,000 followers, mostly in Japan, but an impressive presence of readers from abroad. I was to post information in English and find translators that would be willing to write updates in other languages pro bono. For a while, I was busy posting in English, French, Spanish, German, Arabic, Cantonese, and Korean.

One day the city's social media page received a message in English that read something like, "A boat washed up on the shores of our city and we're wondering if it's yours. See attached photos." Though I'd spent a lot of time monitoring our social media profile, I'd never used the page much for actual correspondence. The message was sent by Professor Lori Dengler, a Geology Professor at Humboldt State University in northern California. I looked at the photos and could see the four characters for Takata High School written in magic marker on the side of the boat. Also, there was part of an inspection sticker indicating the boat was from Iwate Prefecture. The more I examined the pictures, the clearer it became that this vessel truly might be the property of Takata High School. What were the chances?

Takata High School abutted a hill prior to the disaster. The school was dominated by a large complex of gymnasiums and wide-ranging school grounds. It was completely destroyed in the tsunami, and one teacher and twelve students lost their lives.[22] The school was known in the region as an education center for boys who wanted to become fishermen, for girls who wanted to work in the local companies processing or canning fish. Being a coastal region, fishing is one of Rikuzentakata's most critical exports. The school's marine science division prepared students to help sustain their community—and of course, this meant they had quite a few boats for the students' use.

I dialed up a man I'd been in touch with some years before, during a project arranging week-long homestays with Canadian families in Tokyo. Daikoku-*sensei* was a tall man with a deep tan and hair longer than I would have thought a high school teacher would be allowed. I told him I was sending him an email with a few photos. "Tell me what you think."

"Okay," he replied. "That's cryptic."
"I just want to know what you think," I said, and I hit send.
Moments later he called me back, breathless. "That's my boat! Where is it? What's going on?"

By now I had done my homework on the exact California location and could quickly relate that the boat had landed on the shores of Crescent City in the northernmost part of the state.

Crescent City, also known as Tsunami City USA, was the only American city to have suffered a death as a result of the tsunami that hit their coast on March 11, 2011. The earthquake in Japan on that date also destroyed the harbor in Crescent City; they, too, were victims of this particular disaster.

With an extensive history of suffering tsunami damage, the city was eerily similar to Rikuzentakata. Both were perched on a crescent-shaped bay. Both had mountains jutting up right to the coast. Between the demographics—population, income, industry, city footprint—along with the photos of Crescent City, I realized I was practically looking at Rikuzentakata's American cousin or twin.

I explained to Daikoku-*sensei* all I knew. The boat had been swept out to sea along with the rest of the tsunami debris and had crossed the Pacific, taking approximately two years to travel 10,000 miles. If this boat could talk, it would have an endless series of stories to tell: the sea creatures it encountered, the storms it endured, the shipping vessels that passed it in the distance, the extreme heat and cold, the constant tumbling and tossing, wondering where it would end up. The photos received from Lori Dengler showed long, translucent noodle-like barnacles that had grown on the boat's underside. Now it was flipped upside down, its blue bottom topside, the marine creatures having attached themselves underneath.

"You're telling me, that boat of mine I used two years ago has crossed the Pacific Ocean? All the way to America?" he asked.

"Yup," I said. "You're sure it's your boat, right?"

"Yeah, I'm sure it's my boat!" he said, his voice rising. "It says *Kamome* on the side. That's the boat's name."

I looked at the photos. He was right. It said that. Three letters *ka, mo, me* か も め were clearly visible.

"It's unbelievable," Daikoku-*sensei* said. "It's just incredible. Wow."

I could see him in my mind, his hand pushing back his long hair, his face close to the desktop scanning the photos I sent for more clues, more proof this was definitely his boat.

"Okay," I said. "I'm going to write back to the people in California and say it's Takata High School's boat. Give me some time. Let me see what else I can do with this."

A million ideas rushed through my head as I penned a letter to Lori Dengler confirming that the boat belonged to Takata High School. We started to talk. Our correspondence soon grew to include the Japanese Consulate in San Francisco as well as members of the National Oceanic and Atmospheric Administration (NOAA), the two federal entities that would officially confirm and classify the boat as tsunami debris, connecting it to the March 11 Tōhoku disaster. Soon the media got a hold of the story and began hounding me for interviews. There had been plenty of items that had washed up along the western coastline of North America, from Alaska through western Canada and down the west coast of the United States. Some items had been returned, and others destroyed. Very few items had made it this intact, and in one piece. I thought again about the city where the boat had chosen to land.

The word *goen* was perfect in describing this phenomenon. While in English one might use miracle, fate, luck, or synchronicity to describe the boat's journey, anthropomorphic in its choice to land where it did, *goen* beautifully encompassed all of those ideas. I was good at elaborating, sometimes to the point where I pushed the truth just enough to not outright lie but make a story much more interesting, adding my favorite descriptive words one after another. With this boat, with *Kamome*, I didn't have to reach. It was all right there, a ridiculous stroke of *goen* that came out of nowhere.

I had to get the boat back. After all it had been through, this boat could be a symbol of hope and tenacity. This boat personified resilience. Right there we had the definition: to everyone in town who asked what resilience was, I could just point to the boat.

"That," I would say. "That's resilience." Heads would begin to nod. "Ah," they would say. "We get it now." I wrote a quick text message to Mayor Toba saying I had news, promising him to fill him when we spoke. He was busy. We communicated by text for quick messages. For now, this would suffice.

This boat had reached out across thousands of miles and made an international connection with a city on the American West Coast—a city that could actually understand what Rikuzentakata had been through. Attempting to connect the rest of the world with the disaster in Rikuzentakata had been my entire assignment for years, and this boat had accomplished it just by surviving. In a matter of minutes, I had gone from being frustrated over interpreting and explaining empathy and resiliency in Japanese, to having the perfect vessel that would explain it to everyone.

While I was running around Rikuzentakata sharing the news about "the miracle boat," a video arrived from a group of American teenagers from Del Norte High School in Crescent City who had banded together to clean and restore *Kamome*. It showed how they carefully chipped away at the hardened barnacles and mopped and sponged at the hull with soapy water, laughing and acting as if this was the most normal thing in the world. Through communication with Del Norte High school principal, Coleen Parker, it became clear they wanted to return the boat to its home.

This was perfect. Rikuzentakata was a community that so desperately needed a random act of kindness from complete strangers. If a bridge between these two cities could be built, it might be the start of a connection that could last for generations. Here was a reason to have hope.

I rang the secretaries who controlled Mayor Toba's schedule. I wanted a five-minute meeting to tell him about my idea, and that I was going to get it back. The secretaries told me he was away, called out of town. Fine, there were other people to approach. With a few more phone calls, I sat in front of another high-ranking City Hall official and started to outline a plan.

"The miracle boat," I started, "I'm getting it back."

"No," he said, cutting me off bluntly.

Caught off guard, I sat dumbfounded. I didn't actually need his permission to get the boat back. That much I knew. This was a courtesy conversation. Why would he want to turn down an opportunity like this? Building international connections and fostering goodwill was exactly what I'd been brought on to do. This development was perfect—what reason could he possibly have for turning this down?

"Why not?" I asked.

He considered his response for a moment, massaging his forehead in consternation. There were dark circles under his eyes.

"We don't have space for it," he finally said.

It was not only untrue, it made no sense. Downtown was flattened. For the moment, all the city had was space. If he wasn't going to help, I needed to approach someone else. I made small talk for a while longer, then found a way to excuse myself and headed to Takata High School.

After the school buildings that made up the Takata High School campus were destroyed in the tsunami, there was an immediate and desperate need to find a facility large enough to house the 500 or so high school students who had been displaced. Fortunately, forty-five minutes north of Rikuentakata there was an old high school that had been closed down, and the decision was made to bus the students there for classes until the new Takata High School campus could be built. I got into my beaten-up old minivan and headed north.

I made my way to see the principal and was quickly ushered into his office. He showed me his new coffee-brewing machine.

"It's very fancy," he said. "It was a gift. I don't know how to use it yet. Do you?"

"I do," I replied. "You take these little pods and pop them in here." I demonstrated by making a matcha latte for myself and a black coffee for him.

I repeated the same words I had used at City Hall—we were getting the boat back. The principal stared at me for a moment, his demeanor turning suddenly stiff and formal. He gave the same reply, verbatim. "No," followed by "we don't have the space."

I sipped my matcha latte to keep from blurting out something I would surely regret later.

After the meeting, I sat outside the high school in my minivan, scowling and replaying both conversations in my head. Was there something here I wasn't seeing? Maybe the boat had some kind of deeper cultural connotation that I hadn't been told? I considered the name of the boat, *Kamome*. Seagull. It was cute and appropriate for such a small boat. A universally recognizable bird, something that California knew as much as Rikuzentakata and no doubt saw exactly the same way. Not only that, the seagull was Rikuzentakata's official bird. It was rife with symbolism. No, it couldn't be the name. Maybe it was something about California? But no, this city didn't have any connotation different from any region in the United States. So why try to turn this opportunity down?

Then, there were the words the two men had used. "We don't have the space." In my head, I mulled over another word, "*yoyū.*" Though they hadn't used the word itself, the attitudes of these men conjured a clear parallel. I glanced up and saw my face in the van's rear-view mirror and saw circles under my own eyes, just like those of the official. He'd taken time out of an otherwise busy day to meet with me about this.

As for the high school principal, he daily had to make the 45-minute drive I'd just taken to get here, twice a day. This, in addition to time spent administering the school and balancing a budget and dealing with teachers and politics and personalities, all to support 500 students. The boat was one more thing to pile on these men, and a project that would require a lot more work. The town might have plenty of space. But the men I'd spoken with didn't have the "*yoyū,*" the emotional space to carry this project through. I nodded to myself.

At the same time, the boat project just couldn't be given up. I thought back to the TOMODACHI Initiative. Mayor Toba had asked Ambassador Roos for a way to give his people hope, and the answer had come in the form of international connections for youth. That's where hope had to come from, and with this boat, here was an opportunity for hope to reach out and come to us. How often did something like this happen?

Frustrating as these rejections were, there needed to be a new strategy, some kind of regrouping, a new approach with teeth. The boat had to come back. Somehow, others needed to be made to visualize the possibilities it offered and in a scenario in which they couldn't refuse to cooperate. At the same time, this project needed to be accomplished in a way that didn't cause extra work for people whose time was already stretched thin and whose schedules were booked solid every day. Most of the grunt work would have to fall on me.

I started to work out a specific plan. I asked Coleen Parker, the Principal of Del Norte High School, to put me in touch with the Crescent City mayor and with others in a position of authority in Del Norte County. Emails went back and forth stating that Rikuzentakata was very interested in getting its boat back. We had heard that the Del Norte High School students, in cleaning it up, had wanted to return the boat. Great news, for which we were thankful—thanks, by the way–and yes, we absolutely wanted the boat back.

Technically, this was untrue. Apart from myself, no one I knew of in Rikuzentakata had expressed interest in getting the boat back, much less agreed to receive it. Mayor Toba, out of town, still didn't know of my plan. But I was positive he would see the benefits of having the boat returned—the symbolism and the practical exchanges that could take place as a result. Further, both the high school principal and the City Hall official had merely said they didn't have the "space" for this boat. If they had said there was no "*yoyū*," this project would have been an even harder sell. But they hadn't, which meant I still had room to work around their refusal.

Several days later, with an appointment with Mayor Toba already secured, I marched into his office and sat down in my usual seat. He came out from behind his desk and sat at the head of the long conference room table with me to his right.

"I have an idea," I started. I told him the story of the boat from the beginning, its fortuitous landing on the shores of a small northern California city and dove in. "I'm going to get the boat back. And I'm going to start an exchange program between the two high schools. I'm going to turn that into a sister school partnership, and then I'm going to turn that into a sister city partnership."

Earlier, in approaching the City Hall official and the principal, I had stopped after the first sentence. I decided that had been a mistake. This time, leaving no room for interruption, I sailed on. "Oh, and the people in Crescent City want to send it back to us, so we need to be prepared to accept it. It would be rude to say no."

This wasn't a lie. I didn't say who in Crescent City wanted to return it, because it was true.

There were people who had said they wanted to return the boat—these people just happened to be high school students.

Mayor Toba considered for a moment, then nodded.

"One stipulation," he said. He couldn't convince anyone in town that now was the time for a sister city partnership. There were too many other immediate issues that needed to be attended to. In the future he could see it happening, but not now. Stick to the school exchange.

I agreed. That, I could work with.

"If you start by connecting the two high schools, the adults will follow," he said.

Thanking him, trying not to gloat too much over what I considered an absolute victory, I decided there was no need to linger. Mayor Toba was a busy man, and now I had a new, massive project on my hands. Walking out of his office, I had to restrain the urge to do a triumphant little dance.

Emails flew back and forth across the Pacific Ocean, planning and strategizing. Logistically, there were holes that needed filling. How would the boat get across the ocean? Who would pay for it? It was time to fly to Crescent City to lay the foundation more securely.

I arrived in California with several meetings already lined up. I sat down with City Hall and county officials, outlining what happened in Rikuzentakata and suggesting that a sister city partnership based on common experiences and history—tsunamis—could be a mutual foundation for growth, hope, and support. The arrival of "our" boat on "your" shores seemed too beautiful a coincidence to pass up.

I spoke at Rotary Clubs, assuring them this was not my first trip to Crescent City. In the summer of 2001 when our chil turned ten years old, we took a summer family trip all along the western coastline from San Diego to Seattle. My ex-business partner from San Francisco had told me of "the world's best cookie" she stumbled upon in a bakery in Crescent City. We didn't know the name or address of the shop where they were sold, but because the city is small and we were persistent, we eventually came across the bakery. The cookies were indeed the best I'd ever had, peanut butter and chocolate and nuts and butter, and just the perfect amount of saltiness and sugar. It was truly a superb experience, as I told the Rotary members. Here, again, was *goen*.

I went to Del Norte High School to meet the teenagers who had cleaned up the boat. I wanted to acknowledge their kindness and humanity publicly, in front of their teachers to say how impressed I was by their actions. I also decided to frame this in the form of an apology, from my generation to theirs.

"My generation tends to think of your generation as entitled, obnoxious, spoiled brats who don't know the meaning of work and who want everything handed to them. You've proven me wrong. I owe you an apology. I'm sorry. I assumed and I was wrong."

Perhaps they weren't accustomed to adults apologizing to them, or perhaps they weren't used to hearing that people thought of them as entitled. They just sat there, their mouths partially open as if to say, "Who exactly are you?" I reiterated how impressive of an act it was that they had undertaken, and how the ripple effects of their actions were starting to create waves.

"Your actions made this whole project possible," I told them. "Thank you."

Over the next several days, I introduced Rikuzentakata and Takata High School to the Del Norte High School students, and told them of the impact this boat could have on both cities and communities. Would they be willing to make a trip to Japan, if I could find the money to pay their way?

As the mutual acquaintance grew, the officials and residents of Crescent City and Del Norte County shared stories about life in their region. Photos of their city portrayed the devastation of the 1964 tsunami that wiped out 29 blocks. That memory still stung for some in the town. The similarities between these two communities were amazing. The populations were nearly identical. There were wide stretches of farms throughout each community. The ocean was of paramount importance to both communities, with major fishing industries—crabs in Crescent City and oysters in Rikuzentakata— sustaining day-to-day life.

What struck me most was the visual, the landscape, sure to powerfully connect these two cities. How the ocean curved around hills, the beaches pushed up directly against a cliff, exactly like the drive along the coast of Rikuzentakata. The river that ran through both cities. The tall pines—redwood in Crescent City, cedar in Rikuzentakata—it was as if I was back in Japan. These two cities really were twins. If this wasn't *goen* I didn't know what was. Was it luck or fate or synchronicity or an accident of the heavens that led this boat here? What a fortuitous landing the boat had made. What were the chances?

Little by little, companies on both sides of the Pacific stepped up and offered to transport the boat from Crescent City to Rikuzentakata. I was ecstatic, seeing large and small companies come around to the idea of being involved in the unfolding of a beautiful story.

CSR, or Corporate Social Responsibility, had been a buzzword used in Japan since the disaster of 2011. In the U.S., it was not an especially new phenomenon. The idea was for corporations to step up and give something back to the community whether through funds or volunteers or sending expertise or goods. If volunteering was relatively new in Japan, then CSR was definitely unique. It quickly took hold in Japan with foreign companies and embassies leading the way, showing their Japanese staff as well as the country as a whole they took contributing to society seriously as a mandate. It was simply the right thing to do.

Companies were eager to play a role in expressing support for Tōhoku. The complying ones just needed to be found and to be asked politely. With assistance from Recology in Crescent City, the boat was transported to San Francisco Bay free of charge. Nippon Yūsen, a Japanese shipping magnate, took the boat across the Pacific in one of its freighters, then on to Rikuzentakata—again free of charge. This was not a public relations stunt. No one was tricked into helping. The offers to transport the boat without charge were genuine. Companies that were in a position to help simply stepped up.

Kamome arrived back in Rikuzentakata six months after it was discovered on the shores of northern California. The Takata High School principal, Yokota-*sensei*, and students from the school's marine sciences division lined up to greet the miracle boat when it was unloaded ceremoniously at the Rikuzentakata Museum temporary facility.

One Japanese student came up to me and said, "This is like a Hollywood movie, only real." Another said, "I thought our city was bad luck. Good things like this just don't happen here. Maybe I was wrong." What was lost in the tsunami had been considered gone forever. A few items that had washed up on the shores of western Canada and the U.S. had been returned, but these were all isolated cases, anything but the norm. Nothing this big or this significant had come back. There was joy and shock and confusion—how did this happen? There was beauty in this disbelief, jubilance, and awe.

With the return of the boat, it was time to initiate the first aspect of the project, to push toward unifying these two cities. Mayor Toba had said it was too soon to build up a sister city program. Fine, that could come later. I had to start small. First things first.

It wanted to approach the Del Norte High School students who had cleaned the boat, telling them I planned to find a way for Rikuzentakata to invite them to Takata High School. I got in touch with the high school students and staff in Crescent City. I set up meetings where I asked the same question. How did everyone feel about connecting the teenagers from both sides of the ocean, letting them hang out together, and getting to know each other's cultures? Then they could also see for themselves how similar their cities really were.

Were students and staff willing to make the journey to Japan? Some were hesitant and scared, others willing and excited—but they all agreed. If they came, this could be the first step in a formal sister school partnership with annual exchanges of students going back and forth. Of course, grant money to cover expenses for this trip had to be tracked down.

And so, six high school students, the school's principal, the city's disaster management director, a sheriff's deputy, and several chaperones all landed in Rikuzentakata eight weeks later. This was the first delegation from Crescent City and Del Norte County to Rikuzentakata. It would not be the last.

~~~

Teachers and administrators wrung their hands furiously. I stood at the sidelines and watched as adults from both high schools gathered in the corner of the Takata High School gymnasium. They surveyed the American and Japanese teenagers, all with barely controlled looks of worry on their faces. The adults watched as one group of students played volleyball, another group table tennis, and another badminton. While the adults fretted and worried about how the students would communicate, the teenagers laughed and acted as if they had known each other their whole lives, oblivious to the worry they were causing.

Two girls from Crescent City taught the Japanese girls a cheer. Connor showed the others how he could walk on his hands. Halle did a cartwheel without using her hands, causing a massive and collective gasp from the Japanese boys, followed by a loud roar of approval. She did it again, and the gasps and roar got even louder. A girl could do something the boys couldn't. Who knew? All was caught on camera by two videographers from San Francisco who had been commissioned by Facebook to do a short documentary. The Japanese press showed up in droves.

I prepped the Del Norte High School students on how to respond to the press. I told them what a soundbite was. They needed to know they had no control over what part of their answer to press questions would be quoted in print or shown on television.

"Make sure you know exactly what you want to say. Keep your answers short, so they can't edit you." I had learned over the years how to pick my words carefully to make sure they conveyed my intent. Short and sweet, so short there's nothing to cut.

"You'll be asked why you came on this trip," I said. "What's your answer?" This brought forth some answers that clearly could not be shared on camera or in print. The students needed to focus on the reasons why they gave of their time generously to complete strangers they had been unlikely to ever meet.

"They'd been through so much that we thought it would be a nice gesture," Halle responded. I told the students I wasn't worried about the journalists who would interview them, trying to trip them up. I was more concerned about their lack of experience being on camera—it's intimidating for some people to have a giant camera shoved in their face. If they all gave out great answers, then the press would choose whichever one they wanted, and everyone would be happy. We practiced, and when the time came for them to give their answers on camera, they were spot on.

I took another group of Del Norte High School students to Fūmon Temple nestled up in the hills in Rikuzentakata. The head monk, Kumagai-*san*, was a kind man, mild-mannered, his voice soft yet commanding. Being in his presence alone was calming.

I had visited him over the years, quietly walking the gardens around the temple by myself, or taking others with me, showing them what peace there was in being surrounded by tall cedars and pine trees. This was the temple that housed the hundreds of urns of ashes of the dead, waiting for families far away to come and claim their relatives' remains. There were several urns that had never been claimed, that still remained on the premises of the temple grounds. The assumption was these ashes belonged to the last of the line, people with no family, or were the ashes of an entire family that had perished together. These remains were buried in the cemetery behind the temple, the stones marked with numbers instead of names. I cried every time I saw those unmarked graves.

Kumagai-*san*, as usual, spoke eloquently about what he had done over the years and the students and teachers present took in every word. Their attention was a sign of respect not only for the man and his mission but also for the dead. I had held back my tears and focused on repeating Kumagai-*san*'s words and relaying questions. After walking through the garden and cemetery full of graceful headstones each with a single number in place of a name. On the way out of the temple one of the students sat down at the piano in the corner and started to play. It was the most haunting, moving melody I'd ever heard. Beethoven would have been proud. Chai wrote the music himself, just for the trip to Japan as a gift to leave behind. I lost it. All the energy I had exerted trying to keep my tears inside me failed. I had to leave and compose myself, embarrassed at the outpouring of emotion.

I had told the American teenagers how proud I was of them, for wanting to make the trip and for wanting to maintain a connection to this city. With every new group of youth that traveled to and from Japan, my faith in the future grew. If the children these students would have someday were anything like their parents, we were all in good hands.

~~~

With more grant money coming in for travel, it was time to take a group of Takata High School students to Crescent City. On their first day abroad, the Japanese students showed up in their school uniforms and were shocked at what greeted them: American high school students had dyed hair and wore makeup and jewelry. Girls wore high heels, boys and girls held hands and hugged openly, a couple kissed before parting ways for different classrooms. Eyes wide, the Takata High School students kept tugging my sleeve or poking my arm, whispering in awe about the next curiosity while keeping their eyes on the unbelievable scenes all around.

"Amya-*san*, Amya-*san*," one boy said, nodding his head toward a boy with a spiked mohawk.
"He's not going to get into trouble for that?"
"No," I said. "There are rules here as well. For example, you can't be violent or not show up for class, but for the most part what you wear and how you look is considered self-expression. It's a right."

"A right?" Another boy listening in asked.
"America is built on freedom," one of the older girls said, proud she knew.
"Isn't that right, Amya-*san*?"
"That's right," I said, surprised but pleased at the impromptu civics lesson.

Del Norte High School held a pep rally. A welcome ceremony, American-style. Student leaders led the American teenagers in a raucous chant confirming for all of the Japanese students how American high schools were nothing like Japanese high schools. The American students cheered every time a Japanese student introduced themselves, leading to furious bouts of blushing and giggles.

Mieko, one of the Japanese girls in attendance, had prepared a traditional Japanese dance for the Del Norte High School students. She had brought along a kimono, which she wore during her performance. With the music, a lot of minor notes again, Mieko started her dance. Her movements were graceful, slow, and deliberate, captivating every student in the gymnasium. I had never heard hundreds of American teenagers so simultaneously silent. When Mieko finished, the roar of cheers and applause and stomping on the bleachers took everyone by surprise. Mieko blushed, then bowed in all four directions.

This silent rapture as the students watched, followed by the absolute explosion of noise banished any lingering doubts I may have had about this program. The cities were twins, the students were sold. This was going to work. Teenagers were going to pave the way. I might nudge them here and there but this was going to work.

The Takata High School students attended classes alongside American students in wheelchairs. They saw that an American public high school had classrooms set up for students their age who had physical challenges that required special education teachers and aides. These students attended the same school even if they couldn't walk or talk, and were not shunted off to a facility somewhere far away, out of sight. They were visible. They were present.

The Japanese students sat in on a class teaching the language and history of the Tolowa, one of the several indigenous Native American tribal nations in the region. This was an eye-opening experience for the students as well as for the Japanese teachers. Northern Japan, specifically northern Honshū, Hokkaido, and Iwate Prefecture certainly, used to be inhabited by the *Ainu*, Japan's first indigenous settlers generations back. The history between the

Ainu and the Japanese who migrated into their lands is complicated and controversial. Seeing the Tolowa language taught as part of the curriculum was tantamount to teaching the *Ainu* language in school—an act and statement that would be unheard of in Japan. For the Takata High School students this was an entirely new perspective, between the inclusion of the students with special needs and the open discussion of the complicated history between indigenous people and white settlers. Del Norte High School was making a point, and the visiting Japanese students understood loud and clear.

Del Norte High School created a Japan Club to host the visitors and a group and to help maintain the burgeoning connection between the schools. The club arranged homestays for the Takata High School students and set up a buddy system. They spent the night in homes of the Del Norte High School students, returning the next morning comparing stories about every new and interesting detail of American life. They played pool. They ate clam chowder. Host parents grilled hot dogs, steak, hamburgers, and corn on the cob that wasn't sweetened with a soy sauce and sugar mixture but instead got slathered with butter and salt. Who knew ice cream was so delicious?

Macaroni and cheese was best piping hot and it brought joy to the Japanese students who didn't realize how hot cheese made a dish so much better. They noted how the salt used on French Fries was different. Mayonnaise was white and not yellow. Root beer wasn't actually beer, and while it tasted like medicine, the students were allowed to drink it.

"How have we not eaten such food before?" one girl asked me. "This makes me want to become a chef." Was this a new dream she now had? A new vocation? This trip was opening her eyes and also giving her a glimpse into a future she'd never imagined.

The novelty of dessert with every dinner, differences in home life, evenings spent chatting and gossiping—the students bombarded me with full reports every morning. No one left anything out. One girl came to me and said, "My host father prayed for me at dinner last night." I looked at her to see if I could read whether this was good, weird, or just unusual. Uncertain, I asked her, "How did that make you feel?"

Her face broke into a huge grin. "I liked it," she said. "It made me feel special."

A group of second-year girls from Del Norte High School cut class one day to join the Takata High School students in the library. The girls took pictures of their new friends, and soon enough arms were extended around shoulders, and more photos were taken—this time mostly group selfies—through giggles and hushed voices. Names and social media accounts and contact information were exchanged.

Furtively, the Japanese students approached their principal Yokota-*sensei* in twos and threes asking, "Did you know they cut class to be here?" At first, he only nodded and grunted in his reply, but as more of his students came to ask if he'd known of this breach in protocol, Yokota-*sensei* became unsure whether he should try to make those girls return to class. Wasn't that his job as principal?

In walked Randy Fugate, the new principal of Del Norte High School, saving Yokota-*sensei* from having to chastise 15-year-old American girls.

"Busted!" yelled one of the girls, quickly shushed by the librarian. Randy came up to me and Yokota-*sensei*. "I told them to get to know their Japanese guests," he said to us. "I didn't tell them they could cut class to do it, but I also didn't tell them they couldn't."
Yokota-*sensei* started laughing and patted Randy on the shoulder. "That's a very American response."

One of the braver Japanese boys asked his principal if he, too, could cut class the next time American teenagers came over for a visit. I interpreted this question for Randy and the American teenagers.

"Absolutely not," Yokota-*sensei* said. His stern and serious expression alone sent Randy and the American students into fits of laughter, despite not speaking the language. The librarian sat at her desk, furious at the noise and glaring at us all.

For everything that was going well between the students, I heard one night after dinner that Yokota-*sensei* had been given an ultimatum from his staff to not sign anything without their consent. The trip was a success for the students, but raised more questions for the administrations of both schools.

"How were we going to keep this up?" Both principals asked each other. I had to interject into this discussion that some day I would no longer be part of this dynamic. There would come a point where I wouldn't work in Japan anymore. This partnership had to be sustainable without my input or grant writing. They understood, but that was going to be the biggest hurdle. Neither community had funding for a project like this, and finances for international travel were nonexistent. That meant any exchange would have to be funded through grants. How long could I keep applying for these grants without the donors eventually turning us down? Who would take over grant writing after I left?

During the next fiscal year Yokota-*sensei* retired. Randy had to meet, get to know, and work with a new principal, Kanno-*sensei*. Randy, too, would not stay principal forever. That meant that whatever commitments the sister school partnership would have, they had to be transferable from one principal to the next. Drafts were written and rewritten, translated and reviewed, and eventually language was agreed upon. On Valentine's Day in 2017, three years after the first trip made by the six students from Del Norte High School, a formal sister school partnership agreement was signed.

~~~

With every exchange, the adults had the same questions. How were the teenagers going to communicate without an interpreter? I laughed every time I heard this.

"Haven't you seen?" I would say. "Teenagers have a remarkable ability to blow past the language barrier." Translation apps were being used as dictionaries, but even more poignant, there was a remarkable embracing of shyness and vulnerability from teenagers on both sides. Something was happening that the adults couldn't comprehend. Teenagers knew they were the same all over. Apps or no apps, they were communicating just fine.

As the adults stood on the sidelines continuing to worry if the kids were really getting along, the students acted as if this new life of theirs was the most natural thing in the world. They had twins and cousins from across the ocean. Laughter and friendship, joy and farewell tears were all part of every visit.

Social media allowed for students to maintain friendships even after their visits had ended. Photos and videos were sent back and forth. The adults' concern was unfounded—the kids were fine–these trips had changed their lives. Students from both high schools had grown bolder and more confident, and returned to their respective communities changed and full of optimism.

Prior to both groups starting the exchange, students had expressed trepida-
tion, concern, and varying degrees of anxiousness. What was the food like?
What would it be like to go to a completely different country? The initial
shock at the sweetness of orange Gatorade and the unfamiliar smell of the
airport turned to gasps over how *ramen* was truly delicious and soy sauce
ice cream was downright incredible. It was possible to have fun in a country
that was far away, strange, and even slightly intimidating. On the first day of
their new experience students were tight-lipped and stern, but by the last
day their faces were wet with farewell tears.

With the students and teachers on both shores communicating, my next
step was to connect the administrators of both cities. Representatives of
both city administrations needed to get together.

I invited Blake Inscore[23] and Chris Howard[24]—the Mayor of Crescent
City and the Chairman of the Del Norte County Board of Supervisors.
After insisting upon my own travel budget and a modest cushion of funds,
Rikuzentakata City Hall staff had written a grant on my behalf. I told Mayor
Inscore and Supervisor Howard I had funds to cover travel for several people. I needed as many people as they could give me to help me sell to people in Rikuzentakata why this relationship needed to be formalized. The
Japanese city officials needed to hear the Americans openly saying, "We've
got your back. Our city understands what your city's been through, and we
want to get to know you. We can help." Here, finally, was a group of people
who could truly empathize and who knew the meaning of resilience. *Kyōkan*
would finally be working without worrying about a mistranslation.

It was important for me that Mayor Inscore and Supervisor Howard include
women in the delegation. The world of politics is still highly resistant against
women in Japan. Here was an opportunity for women to be present at the
table, to show the Japanese that women could play critical roles in local government even if those governments were in a different country. It would
drive home the point that women can do far more than bring tea and make
copies. Hopefully, it would help lay a foundation in Rikuzentakata to have
more women in positions of leadership. Mayor Inscore and Supervisor
Howard and I identified two women who would join the delegation. Adding
Randy Fugate, the high school principal,[25] made the group a five-person delegation. The inclusion of two women was a monumental statement to this
small rural Japanese community.

Heidi Kime was Mayor Pro Tem, in line to be the next mayor of Crescent City. Kymmie Scott[26] was an assistant to the City Manager and the city's liaison to the local office of emergency services, and in charge of day-to-day logistics for their visit. Both women represented positions of authority. The men of Rikuzentakata were initially reluctant to open up as they met with the American delegation, and they were especially unsure how to behave around the two women. They sat with backs straight and expressions rigid, but they slowly warmed up to Kymmie and Heidi over the course of their conversations.

"Here's a photo of my wife who died in the disaster," I saw one city councilman say to Kymmie, offering a photograph. This act of vulnerability caught me off guard, and later on I made sure to tell Kymmie and the others how significant this was. That inner circle of grief was reserved for the trusted few who could truly empathize. It was a compliment to Kymmie and a sign of trust that the man would share such a private memory with her.

By the time their visit concluded a week later, the local Japanese leaders and the American delegation were like family. The Americans dutifully ate every dish placed in front of them, even the "gotcha" foods like fish testicles. Heidi could keep up drinking *sake* along with the middle-aged local politicians, an impressive new experience for the Japanese men in the room. Kymmie made her counterparts remember how easy it was to laugh, as she put at ease in such a way the men from Rikuzentakata collectively felt they had gained a daughter and sister.

I deliberately kept using the word "cousins" and "twins" to describe one party to another, highlighting similarities and commonalities between the histories of the two communities. How profoundly unique our mutual histories were. The boat landed on the Crescent City shores as if to introduce us. As if it knew that the people of Crescent City could relate to the people of Rikuzentakata like nobody else.

Chapter 40

Amya Miller

The detractors to the possibility of becoming sister cities were persistent. "This is not the time," and "We don't have that kind of money in our budgets" and "Fix our potholes first" being the main arguments, residents of Del Norte County took to social media to criticize and ridicule the sister city idea. Although difficult to ignore, in the end ignoring them was the only way to move forward. On one occasion, I personally invited a key detractor to come to Rikuzentakata and see the devastation for himself, offering to pay his way. Me extending the olive branch only made him decline the offer. I was disappointed. Surely, the sight of the aftermath of destruction, the claw marks of the tsunami, once observed, would change his mind. I instead spoke to another detractor who agreed to come in the first man's place. I paid his way. I wanted him to see for himself all that I'd been saying for the past four years in the hope he would convince other detractors. This second detractor returned to Crescent City a convert and a strong proponent of the sister city partnership. The visual had done it.

One of the key messages I repeated during trips back and forth was the absolute power of the visual and the senses. There is no way of describing the panoramic view, the height, scope, depth, width, or smell of the aftermath of destruction. The wind and sun that bakes and dries, the palpable sadness, the grief that hangs over the city, and even the ever-present reminder of death and loss all need to be felt in person. Seeing the experience written online or on paper, as a video taken or a photograph printed, simply did not compare to experiencing it in three dimensions.

This deficiency in presentation was not a reflection on the journalist, videographer, or photographer, but was instead the recognition of the awesomeness of what nature does which can only be seen and felt by being physically present. Nature is absolutely random—senseless and unfair in what it destroys and what it spares. Why was the fifth floor of a building left untouched when every window on the first four floors were blown out? I could tell this story and I could show photos of the building. Standing underneath it and seeing the futon caught on the railing, the telephone hanging down to the next floor with its cord still plugged into the wall, and the lacy curtains fluttering in the wind. These images are powerful and frightening. People needed to see this in person, to experience the cruelty of nature while hearing the stories of bravery and sorrow, not just through me, but in town with the locals.

With all the messiness and grief the disaster had caused, with the turmoil and deep sense of loss I both heard and felt, having spent a better part of eight years traveling to-and-from Rikuzentakata, I wanted to convey an additional message: preparedness and kindness.

Mayor Toba and I had long been preaching the absolute need for reevaluating emergency preparedness manuals and protocol. It was a core part of our talks, and we gave it to every audience along with expressions of gratitude and tales of heroism and intense pain. I had also begun telling the boat story, how a bunch of teenagers had changed the future for two communities—twins across the Pacific—all because they decided to be kind and do something nice for others. The two messages needed to be entwined and to reach a larger audience, one not yet tapped. It needed to reach children.

I needed a book. I decided to collaborate with Professor Lori Dengler, the Geology Professor who had first contacted me about the boat, on a children's book about the two cities. We told the story of the tsunami, the boat, and the subsequent friendship that ensued. We asked Amy Uyeki, a Japanese-American artist from northern California, to join us as illustrator and designer. Soon we had a book ready for publication. *The Extraordinary Voyage of Kamome: A Tsunami Boat Comes Home.*[27] Lori wrote the English and I wrote the Japanese, with Amy providing illustrations for every page.

It was of paramount importance that the book accurately reflect what kindness does to people, that it be a document promoting its significance. This boat's journey had connected two cities and sparked many remarkable acts of kindness and connection between them. Here was proof of what kindness could do. We concluded the book by providing bilingual text to teachers and parents, encouraging them to use the book as a tool to build a dialogue about disaster preparedness. All proceeds from the sales were donated to the sister school exchange.

The time came to share with Mayor Toba my thoughts about reaching the limit of how long I could stay in Japan with next to no pay. My husband had been the sole earner in our family throughout these years. It was time for me to earn what I was worth, and that meant going home. But before that happened, I wanted the sister city partnership made official, and for this, I needed Mayor Toba to travel to Crescent City himself. He needed to observe firsthand what I had been telling him for five years. Mayor Toba agreed and freed up city funds to partially pay for up to twenty residents of Rikuzentakata to accompany him so they too could see the benefits of a sister city arrangement. This trip would be the official beginning of the partnership with the signing of the two cities' agreement. It also signified the end of my involvement.

In April 2018, a delegation of approximately twenty-five people from Rikuzentakata arrived in Crescent City to formally sign the sister city partnership. I stood up and told the several hundred gathered I felt I had been in labor for the last five years, working on this program alone. Connecting the two high schools and then the two cities had been intense. It was painful, but as women who have given birth know, the result was worth it. It was a lonely experience, trying to maneuver through the many obstacles. It was profoundly challenging and frustrating at times, and I lost plenty of sleep over the years, but the five years I spent bringing together the two high schools and two cities was worth it. The pain was worth it. In June of 2018, a similar sized delegation from Crescent City came to Rikuzentakata to sign the document in front of hundreds of residents who had gathered to witness the occasion.

The exchange between the two towns ramped up in 2018 and 2019, first with a delegation of elementary and middle school teachers from Rikuzentakata visiting the various schools in Del Norte County. With the Government of Japan mandating that English be taught in elementary schools, teachers in Japan wanted a firsthand account of effective teaching methods and best practices. Here again, the idea of inclusion was evident. In Del Norte County, teachers from Rikuzentakata saw children with special needs sitting in the same class alongside their friends. There might be an aide or two in the room, but the teacher went on with the lesson as if this was entirely normal. Eyes wide and trying not to show their shock, the Japanese teachers returned to their respective schools full of ideas on how their experiences could be quickly incorporated into their curriculum.

In December 2019, a group of roughly thirty-five city officials, local business owners, and community leaders from Rikuzentakata went to Crescent City on a study mission. With an impressive grant from the U.S. Embassy in Tokyo, they were tasked to learn practical and applicable skills on women's empowerment and leadership, government and healthcare. Along with them, more teachers were sent to learn skills on how to effectively work with children who had experienced trauma.

Not to be outdone, two major businesses in Crescent City—Rumiano Cheese[28] and Seaquake Brewery[29]—stepped up and created a brand unique and specific to the new sister city relationship, a new ale they called *Kamome* and a new cheese also labeled *Kamome*. The next step for Seaquake Brewery was to collaborate with a brewery in Rikuzentakata. An award-winning cheese from the Rumiano family was now going to be made with salt harvested from Hirota Bay in Rikuzentakata. Never mind that no one in Rikuzentakata knew how to harvest salt, they would soon learn. Dozens of bags of white, crisp salt arrived in Crescent City to be used for this new brand of cheese. Proceeds from the sale of the cheese would go toward travel expenses for both high schools.

The sister city relationship came about through such a unique fashion, a remarkable story previously unheard of, bringing with it a richness of newly developed but already deep relationships. It was touted by both governments as a model for how sister city relationships should develop in the future. No one had ever heard of two cities connecting in this way. The relationship broke new ground, and with every new project established in conjunction with their twin and cousin across the Pacific, the bonds and friendships became more meaningful. It was as if this was the way it had always been. It was as if they had known each other their whole lives. I stood back and watched. This was good. This was very, very good.

One boat.

One boat was lost and then found two years later. Early on, after the discovery of *Kamome*, I decided this boat had a life force of its own and a way of making things happen. I didn't understand how, but in the end, I decided I didn't need to understand.

There is no happily ever after in a disaster of this magnitude and scale. At least not yet. There are pockets of happiness, and finding these and cultivating them was the most magical, rewarding, and difficult professional experience I have ever had. I was an accidental volunteer who bumped into an accidental mayor. We waxed and waned between success and failure, elation and utter despair, rejuvenation and intense fatigue. After ten years our bodies were broken but we survived.

Someday, Mayor Toba and I will feel confident enough about the roles we played that we will be ready to fully walk away from our positions. Mayor Toba will step outside his front door and look up at the stars and ask Kumi if he did the right thing. And, someday, I will step outside onto my front porch and look up at the stars and say, "I tried. I really did."

We both believe that day will come.

Epilogue

Futoshi Toba

I have remarried.

I have not made an official announcement yet. It's news I would prefer to share only with those closest to me. At least for now. This makes it sound as if I'm keeping it secret, and the response to that would be "Yes, I am," and "No, I'm not." I'm not embarrassed to be remarried and I'm not the first one in town to remarry.

The reason I have not made it public is because of the way I lost Kumi. If she and I had divorced, an act neither of us would ever have entertained, then while there would have been pity and disappointment among our friends and family, it would have eventually died down. We would both have found new love in time, and that love would have been celebrated. Our lives would have moved on. But that's not what happened.

Kumi and I had no choice in the way we were parted. Finding new love would be seen by some in Rikuzentakata as a betrayal of Kumi. I know it's an unrealistic expectation. How long should I remain a widower? How many years would it take before remarrying would no longer be seen as a betrayal? I wish that hadn't been the expectation, but public perception is powerful. And with the sting of my last election just under the surface everywhere I go and with everyone I meet, a public display of disloyalty to Kumi's memory was something I couldn't afford.

On the other hand, many throughout town have said to me "Mayor, we can't remarry until you do!" Sometimes it was said in jest, though sometimes seriously. Either way I take these comments to heart. I know there's at least some degree of truth in them. I want to be a leader, someone who shows by example, but I also know with leadership comes scrutiny from my constituents. One wrong move and the city swirls with frustration, resentment, and anger.

Public perception notwithstanding, I needed to move on with my life. I met Mariko, fell in love, and asked her to be my wife. She graciously agreed. We live together in the new house I built after the disaster. She loves roses, and I even thought at one point she and I might start a business together growing roses after I complete my tenure as Mayor. The front of our house is lined with terra cotta pots full of rose bushes.

I explained all of this to Amya one night after she asked me point-blank why I hadn't announced my marriage to Mariko publicly. I told her my reasons. It took a while, but after I was done giving my explanation, she sat back and looked at me with a resigned expression.

"This is one of the things I will never understand. You're not allowed to be happy because of the way Kumi died, but people can't move forward until you do? It's a lose-lose situation. No matter what you do, someone will be unhappy with you."

"You're right," I replied. "Maybe this is a local thing, or maybe it's a larger Japanese cultural trait you're unfamiliar with. Either way, it's my reality."

"Reality or not, I want you to be happy," she said, and I was touched by her words. I wanted to be happy too, and I felt someday—hopefully not too far in the future—I would find true peace.

I believe Kumi would want me to be happy as well. I want her to be proud of me, to look down on me and say, "You did everything you could." Until I can hear her voice again, I choose to believe she's cheering me on from the heavens.

A Supplementary Notes

The number of victims and the results of the citizens' survey can be found in the following official announcement by City of Rikuzentakata.

www.city.rikuzentakata.iwate.jp/material/files/group/61/kensyouhoukokusyo.pdf

The titles of the persons mentioned in the main text were their titles at that time, and the information added by NOTES were one as of July 2023.

Names of people appearing in the text (with the exception of politicians, presidents, principals, etc.) are given in pseudonyms.

Notes

1) A magnitude 9 earthquake caused by the rupture of a huge fault line on the seafloor off the coast of Tōhoku.
Two rock masses, the North American Plate and the Pacific Plate, shifted. The rupture of the fault began about 130 km east-southeast of the Oshika Peninsula in Miyagi Prefecture, at a depth of about 24 km. According to the Japan Meteorological Agency, the area of the fault that finally ruptured reached approximately 450 km long and 200 km wide, extending from near the coast of Miyako City, Iwate Prefecture, to near the coast of Ibaraki Prefecture.

2) The Big One (earthquake), an anticipated megathrust earthquake along Western North America or Japan.

3) Operation Tomodachi, or "Friendship", is the name of an American military operation to provide disaster relief, rescue, and reconstruction assistance in response to the Great East Japan Earthquake on March 11, 2011. The operation name was chosen by the Japanese.

4) Hinako Takahashi (Member of the House of Representatives during Dec. 2012 to Oct. 2021. She was appointed Vice Minister of Education, Culture, Sports, Science and Technology in Sept. 2020)

5) The TOMODACHI Initiative is a public-private partnership between the U.S.-Japan Council and the U.S. Embassy in Tokyo, with support from the Government of Japan. Born out of support for Japan's recovery from the Great East Japan Earthquake.

6) Mitsushige Yamanaka (Mayor of the City of Matsuzaka during Feb. 2009 to Sept. 2015)

7) Masuhisa Kobayashi (Deputy Mayor of the City of Matsuzaka during July 2010 to Feb. 2017)

8) Keisuke Hiwatashi (Mayor of the City of Takeo during Apr. 2006 to Dec. 2014)

9) Takashi Kubota (Deputy Mayor of the City of Rikuzentakata during Aug. 2011 to July 2015. Mayor of the City of Kakegawa from Apr. 2021~)

10) Kiyoshi Fuchigami (former city councilman in City of Ōfunato. Mayor of Ōfunato from Dec. 2022~)
11) The building was moved to Marunouchi from 2018.
12) Naoto Kan (94th Prime Minister of Japan from June 2010 to Sept. 2011)
13) Yoshihiko Noda (95th Prime Minister of Japan from Sept. 2011to Dec. 2012)
14) Shinzō Abe (90th,96th, 97th, 98th Prime Minister of Japan from 2006 to 2007 and again from 2012 to 2020) Abe was assassinated on July 8, 2022 while delivering a campaign speech.
15) August 21, 2015 / 6:33 PM / CBS NEWS https://www.cbsnews.com/news/japanese-city-shaves-mountain-to-avoid-future-tsunamis/
16) Today, there is also a local brand called Ippon Matsu Ale. https://www.furusato-tax.jp/product/detail/03210/5553013
17) 2,071,477 yen as of June, 2023.
18) Takashi Kawamura (Mayor of the City of Nagoya from Apr. 2009~)
19) The Qatar Friendship Fund (QFF) was created with a $100 million donation to support the relief efforts for the victims of the 2011 Great East Japan Earthquake in Tōhoku.
20) Nagato Nakazato (Mayor of Rikuzentakata from Feb. 2003 to Feb. 2011)
21) https://www.facebook.com/RikuzentakataCity/?locale=ja_JP (Same face book page mentioned in other chapters)
22) The number of victims is the figure known to the author at the time and has been updated according to the situation.
23) Blake Inscore is now Mayor Pro Tem.
24) Chris Howard is now representative for District 3, DNC BOS.
25) Randy Fugate was the 2nd principal of DNHS after Coleen Parker. He is now principal of Community Day School, Adult Ed, Elk Creek.
26) Kymmie Scott is Administrative Analyst/PIO/City Clerk, City of a Crescent City. Now Senior Emergency Preparedness Specialist with Tidal Basin Government Consulting.
27) Available in Russian, Spanish, French, Swedish, Vietnamese, and Tolowa.
28) Official site: https://rumianocheese.com/pages/kamome-dry-jack
29) Official site: https://seaquakebrewing.com/beer/kamome/